W9-CGT-632

The Politics and Poetics of Transgression

The Politics and Poetics of Transgression

· Peter Stallybrass and Allon White ·

Cornell University Press
Ithaca, New York

© 1986 Peter Stallybrass and Allon White

All rights reserved. Except for brief quotations in a review, this book, or parts thereof, must not be reproduced in any form without permission in writing from the publisher. For information, address Cornell University Press, Sage House, 512 East State Street, Ithaca, New York 14850.

First published 1986 by Cornell University Press.
First published, Cornell Paperbacks, 1986.
Fifth printing 1995.

Library of Congress Cataloging in Publication Data

Stallybrass, Peter.
  The politics and poetics of transgression.
  Bibliography: p.
  Includes index.
  1. Literature and Society. 2. Hierarchies.
  3. Social Psychology. I. White, Allon. II. Title.
PN51.S666 1986 306'.47 85-48241
ISBN 0-8014-1893-3
ISBN 0-8014-9382-x (pbk.)

Printed in the United States of America

⊗ The paper in this book meets the minimum requirements of the American National Standard for Information Sciences—Permanence of Paper for Printed Library Materials, ANSI Z39.48-1984.

For Annie and Jenny

Contents

Acknowledgements

This book was written out of a dialogue not only with each other, but with many other books and other voices. The writings of Mikhail Bakhtin, Norbert Elias, Mary Douglas and Pierre Bourdieu have been a perpetual and special source of inspiration to us.

Sharing a house together led us, first, to fierce and deeply felt intellectual disagreement about domestic filth (about which we still hold principled and completely incompatible views) and thence to a wider discussion of the variety and origins of bourgeois disgust. As each of us attempted, over time, to legitimate his own sphere of domestic negligence in defiance of the bourgeois purity rituals so dear to the other, the net was cast wide for supporting argument and evidence. Mikhail Bakhtin's wonderful book on Rabelais and Carnival, *Rabelais and his World*, with its wealth of information on 'the lower bodily strata' threatened, at one moment, to end the competition unfairly in favour of the first of us to read it. But then the other, countering smartly with Norbert Elias's *History of Manners*, was able to demonstrate indisputable cultural precedence for his curious indifference to the abhorrence in which the middling sort seem to hold aspects of their own bodies. From there it was but a small step to Mary Douglas's *Purity and Danger* and by this time intellectual curiosity about the production of identity and status through a repudiation of the 'low' had roused us to joint authorship.

We owe an enormous debt to all the members of Sussex LTP (Literature/Teaching/Politics) group: Geoff Bennington, Rachel

Bowlby, Margaret Deuchar, Dave Forgacs, Frank Gloversmith, Ann Rosalind Jones, Cora Kaplan, Alison Light, Ulrike Meinhof, Marcia Pointon, William Outhwaite, Alan Sinfield, Brian Street, Joanna Street: Jonathan Dollimore knows more about transgression than most and his generosity, as well as his scepticism about our experiential credentials for writing this book, have been invaluable. We also owe a debt of gratitude to many others at Sussex: to Sussex MEM seminar 1984–5 and Renaissance Graduate students at Sussex, and Paul Brown in particular, for generous and stimulating contributions of information and ideas; to the Anthropology Work-in-Progress Seminar, whose critical observations have, we hope, kept us from the crasser errors of thoughtless ethnocentrism; to Homi Bhabha (likewise), Alun Howkins, Stuart Laing, Linda Merricks and Jacqueline Rose.

In the United States Len Tennenhouse and Nancy Armstrong have been constantly supportive in ways too numerous to mention: to them we owe a deep and lasting debt of friendship. Stephen Greenblatt, Linda Hutcheon, George Levine, Ann Kaplan, Charles Martindale, Sidney Monas, Louis Montrose, Steven Mullaney, Nina Payne, Mary Russo, Frank Wigham and Michael Wilson have all contributed with friendship, advice and encouragement. Both the Five College Renaissance Seminar, Massachusetts, and Fredric Jameson and the Yale Marxist Group stimulated several fresh ideas during our visit in 1982.

Our first readers, Richard Terdiman, John Drakakis and Francis Barker, gave remarkably full, thoughtful and constructive comments on the manuscript and prevented many excesses. We could not have wished for more generous and scrupulous readers.

Thanks to Janice Price of Methuen for her keen interest in our project from its early and uncertain days, and to Bernhard Kendler of Cornell University Press for his swift and positive response to what must have seemed a very wayward and unlikely manuscript. Thanks also to Jane Bamford for her excellence and forbearance in typing and preparing the manuscript and to the University of Sussex for financial assistance. A preliminary version of Chapter 5 appeared in *Semiotica* 54, 1/2 (1985) and we gratefully acknowledge permission to incorporate that material in the present work.

Those who read this book will find it no surprise that academics, apparently the very bearers of the rule of discursive purity and order,

Acknowledgements

are an infinite resource of information about pigs. It was a revelation – and a clear indication that we were on to something – when even the most censorious and combative of our colleagues responded to our work with a wealth of recondite information, clearly of deep personal significance, about the porcine breed. To those of our friends and colleagues who trotted out substantial criticism and help, we are deeply indebted. And to that unknown marksman in the little circus in France whose unerring accuracy with the bow left us mercifully unscathed – if somewhat rueful about participation in the carnivalesque – a very grateful thank you.

The authors and the publishers wish to thank the following copyright holders for permission to reproduce the illustrations appearing in this book: the Günter Böhmer Collection for nos 1 and 7; the Trustees of the British Museum for nos 2 and 4; Macmillan, London and Basingstoke for no. 3; Guildhall Library, City of London for no. 5; the Master and Fellows of Trinity College Cambridge for nos 6a and 6b.

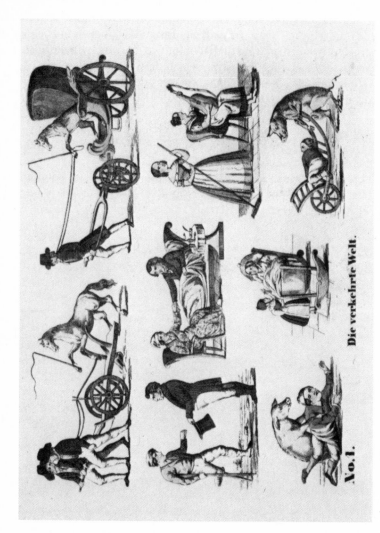

1 'The topsy-turvy world', anonymous coloured lithograph, Nuremburg, c. 1830

Introduction

Amongst the many remarkable things to be found in Ernst Robert Curtius's *European Literature and the Latin Middle Ages* is an account of how the idea of 'the Classic author' was originally derived from ancient taxation categories. In a chapter discussing the idea of model authors and the attendant notion of canon-formation, Curtius explains how tax-bands, a social division of citizens according to property qualifications under the constitutions of Servius, were adopted by Aulus Gellius as a way of designating the prestige and rank of writers. Citizens of the first taxation category, the top rank, came to be known as *'classici'*. This development in the generic terminology of antiquity (Gellius fl. *c.* 123–*c.* 165) subsequently had an enduring influence on the European system of hierarchizing authors and works. It separated out a distinct élite set (the *classici*) from the commonality (the *proletarius*) and used this as a model for literary discriminations. Curtius remarks:

> But it was not until very late, and then only in a single instance, that the name *classicus* appears: in Aulus Gellius (*Noctes Atticae*, XIX, 8, 15) . . . The thing to do is to follow the usage of a model author: 'e cohorte illa dumtaxat antiquiore vel oratorum aliquis vel poetarum, id est classicus adsiduusque aliquis scriptor, non proletarius'; 'some one of the orators or poets, who at least belongs to the older band, that is, a first class tax-paying author, not a proletarian' . . . The *proletarius*, whom Gellius mentions by

way of comparison, belongs to *no* tax class. When Sainte-Beuve, in 1850, discussed the question What is a Classic?, he paraphrased this passage in Gellius: 'un écrivain de valeur et de marque, un écrivain qui compte, qui a du bien au soleil, et qui n'est pas confondu dans la foule des prolétaires.'

(Curtius 1953: 249–50)

And Curtius adds wryly 'What a titbit for a Marxist sociology of literature!'

It was not Curtius's inclination to follow up his own remark and indeed we can detect a certain amused astonishment when he realizes where his investigations have finally led him. From the first it seems that the ranking of types of author was modelled upon social rank according to property classifications and this interrelation was still being actively invoked in the nineteenth century. In recent times we have been inclined to forget this ancient and enduring link between social rank and the organizing of authors and works, including literary genres, although for the major part of European history it was a natural assumption for readers and writers alike. Ian Jack noted that precisely this habit of ranking 'kinds in a hierarchy analogous to that of the state' has led to a contemporary distrust, particularly of Renaissance categories:

> Just as the social hierarchy was traced from the prince through the nobility down to the common people, so the realm of Poetry had its own 'degrees', from Epic, the Prince of all the kinds, down to the lowest species of all, 'from Homer to the *Anthologia*, from Virgil to Martial and Owen's Epigrams . . . that is from the top to the bottom of all poetry'.

(Jack 1942: 4)

It is the contention of the present book that cultural categories of high and low, social and aesthetic, like those mentioned above but also those of the physical body and geographical space, are never entirely separable. The ranking of literary genres or authors in a hierarchy analogous to social classes is a particularly clear example of a much broader and more complex cultural process whereby the human body, psychic forms, geographical space and the social formation are all constructed within interrelating and dependent hierarchies of high and low. This book is an attempt to map some of these interlinked hierarchies on the terrain of literary and cultural history. More particularly it attends both to the formation of these hierarchies and to the processes through which the low troubles the high. The high/low opposition in each of our four symbolic domains – psychic forms, the human body, geographical space and the social order – is a fundamental basis to mechanisms of ordering and sense-making in European cultures. Divisions and discriminations in one domain are continually structured, legitimated and dissolved by reference to the vertical symbolic hierarchy which operates in the other three domains. Cultures 'think themselves' in the most immediate and affective ways through the combined symbolisms of these four hierarchies. Furthermore (and this is where the title of the book comes in) transgressing the rules of hierarchy and order in any one of the domains may have major consequences in the others.

Although there are all sorts of subtle degrees and gradations in a culture it is striking that the extremes of high and low have a special and often powerful symbolic charge. Thus, in the example given above from Curtius, Gellius (as also Cicero and Arnobius) immediately fixes upon the top and bottom, the *classicus* and the *proletarius*, even though the system has five different grades within it. This does not necessarily militate against subtlety since 'above' and 'below' may be inscribed within a minutely discriminatory system of classification, but it does foster a simplifying binaryism of high and low *within which* further classification will be made. In other words the vertical extremities frame all further discursive elaborations. If we can grasp the system of extremes which encode the body, the social order, psychic form and spatial location, we thereby lay bare a major framework of discourse within which any further 'redress of balance' or judicious qualification must take place.

In our study therefore we have focused upon the symbolic extremities of the exalted and the base. We have followed the instruction of Boethius – 'Look to the highest of the heights of heaven' – and we have also plumbed the depths of social classification, the lower bodily stratum, the sewers, the underworld – what one might call the rock bottom of symbolic form. We have tried to see how high discourses, with their lofty style, exalted aims and sublime ends, are structured in relation to the debasements and degradations of low discourse. We have tried to see how each extremity structures the other, depends upon and invades the other in certain historical moments, to carry political charge through aesthetic and moral polarities. Indeed, the oppositions, interpenetrations and transgressions of high and low bear such an enormous weight of cultural organization that one marvels at the sheer labour of transcoding, displacement and partition involved in the elaborate networks of *super-* and *sub-* in our cultural history.

It would be wrong to imply that 'high' and 'low' in this context are equal and symmetrical terms. When we talk of high discourses – literature, philosophy, statecraft, the languages of the Church and the University – and contrast them to the low discourses of a peasantry, the urban poor, subcultures, marginals, the lumpenproletariat, colonized peoples, we already have two 'highs' and two 'lows'. History seen from above and history seen from below are irreducibly different and they consequently impose radically different perspectives on the question of hierarchy.

Indeed they may and often do possess quite different symbolic hierarchies but because the higher discourses are normally associated with the most powerful socio-economic groups existing at the centre of cultural power, it is they which generally gain the authority to designate what is to be taken as high and low in the society. This is what Raymond Williams calls the 'inherent dominative mode' and it has the prestige and the access to power which enables it to create the dominant definitions of superior and inferior. Of course the 'low' (defined as such by the high precisely to confirm itself as 'high') may well see things differently and attempt to impose a counter-view through an inverted hierarchy.

There is a growing body of research devoted to the topic of hierarchy inversion, of 'world upside down' (WUD), and we have much to say about this in the following pages. However the politics of hierarchy inversion as a ritual strategy on the part of subordinate groups is not our principal theme. We have chosen to concentrate rather on the contradictory nature of symbolic hierarchies within the dominant constructions of literature, the body and the social formation.

The primary site of contradiction, the site of conflicting desires and mutually incompatible representation, is undoubtedly the 'low'. Again and again we find a striking ambivalence to the representations of the lower strata (of the body, of literature, of society, of place) in which they are both reviled and desired. Repugnance and fascination are the twin poles of the process in which a *political* imperative to reject and eliminate the debasing 'low' conflicts powerfully and unpredictably with a desire for this Other. Edward Said in his work on *Orientalism* – the myth of the Middle East constructed by Europe to legitimate its own authority – has convincingly shown this operative ambivalence in action. In political terms Orientalism

> . . . depends for its strategy on [a] flexible *positional* superiority, which puts the Westerner in a whole series of possible relationships with the Orient without ever losing him the upper hand.

But at the same time Said notices that

> European culture gained in strength and identity by setting itself off against the Orient as a sort of . . . underground self.
>
> (Said 1979: 3, 7)

'An underground self with the upper hand'. This curious, almost oxymoronic formulation captures a nexus of power and desire which regularly reappears in the ideological construction of the low-Other. It is not only a phenomenon of colonial and neo-colonial representation. We find the same constitutive ambivalence around the slum and the domestic servant in the nineteenth century; around the disposal of 'waste' products in the city (though not in pre-Renaissance rural culture); around the carnival festivity of popular culture; around the symbolically base and abject animals like the pig and the rat. These are the subjects of specific chapters which follow in which we explore the contradictory and unstable representation of low-Others.

A recurrent pattern emerges: the 'top' attempts to reject and eliminate the 'bottom' for reasons of prestige and status, only to discover, not only that it is in some way frequently dependent upon that low-Other (in the classic way that Hegel describes in the master–slave section of the *Phenomenology*), but also that the top *includes* that low symbolically, as a primary eroticized constituent of its own fantasy life. The result is a mobile, conflictual fusion of power, fear and desire in the construction of subjectivity: a psychological dependence upon precisely those Others which are being rigorously opposed and excluded at the social level. It is for this reason that what is *socially* peripheral is so frequently *symbolically* central (like long hair in the 1960s). The low-Other is despised and denied at the level of political organization and social being whilst it is instrumentally constitutive of the shared imaginary repertoires of the dominant culture. This is evidenced by the history of the representation of 'low' entertainment and the carnivalesque, to which we now turn.

FROM CARNIVAL TO TRANSGRESSION

The new historian, the genealogist, will know what to make of this masquerade. He will not be too serious to enjoy it; on the contrary, he will push the masquerade to its limits and prepare the great carnival of time where masks are constantly reappearing. Genealogy is history in the form of a concerted carnival.

(Foucault 1977: 160–1)

In the world of carnival the awareness of the people's immortality is combined with the realisation that established authority and truth are relative.

(Bakhtin 1968: 10)

There is now a large and increasing body of writing which sees carnival not simply as a ritual feature of European culture but as a *mode of understanding*, a positivity, a cultural analytic. How is it that a festive ritual now virtually eliminated from most of the popular culture of Europe has gained such prominence as an epistemological category? Is there a connection between the fact of its elimination as a physical practice and its self-conscious emergence in the artistic and academic discourses of our time? For both Michel Foucault in the passage cited above and for Mikhail Bakhtin in his seminal study *Rabelais and his World*, the Nietzscheian study of history leads to the ideal of carnival. Everywhere in literary and cultural studies today we see carnival emerging as a model, as an ideal and as an analytic category in a way that, at first sight, seems puzzling.

Undoubtedly it was the translation of Mikhail Bakhtin's monumental study of Rabelais and the carnivalesque which initially catalysed the interest of Western scholars (albeit slowly – the book was only translated into English in 1968) around the notion of carnival, marking it out as a site of special interest for the analysis of literature and symbolic practices. Since the 1970s there has been an increasing number of literary and historical studies devoted to the topic. In 1978 Krystyna Pomorska could write with every justification that 'Mikhail Bakhtin is today one of the most popular, if not the most popular, figures in the domain of humanistic studies' (Pomorska 1978: 379). More recently Tony Bennett averred that Bakhtin's study of Rabelais should hold an exemplary place in materialist cultural criticism (Bennett 1979: 90–2). This is surely correct: *Rabelais and his World* is ostensibly a scholarly study of Rabelais's popular sources in carnivalesque folk-culture which shows how indebted Rabelais is to the popular, non-literary, 'low' folk humour of the French Renaissance. His intention in the study was self-consciously iconoclastic.

> No dogma, no authoritarianism, no narrow-minded seriousness can coexist with Rabelaisian images; these images are opposed to all that is finished and polished, to all pomposity, to every ready-made solution in the sphere of thought and world outlook.
>
> (Bakhtin 1968: 3)

Naturally this reading of Rabelais has not gone unchallenged by conventionally learned scholars (Screech 1979: 1–14, 479; also 1984: 11–13, but in this latter article, 'Homage to Rabelais', Screech is much closer in spirit to Bakhtin than in the earlier book). But although Bakhtin is deeply concerned to elucidate the sources of Rabelais's work, the main importance of his study is its broad development of the 'carnivalesque' into a potent, populist, critical inversion of *all* official words and hierarchies in a way that has implications far beyond the specific realm of Rabelais studies. Carnival, for Bakhtin, is both a populist utopian vision of the world seen from below and a festive critique, through the inversion of hierarchy, of the 'high' culture:

> As opposed to the official feast, one might say that carnival celebrates temporary liberation from the prevailing truth of the established order; it marks the suspension of all hierarchical rank, privileges, norms and prohibitions. Carnival was the true feast of time, the feast of becoming, change and renewal. It was hostile to all that was immortalized and complete.
>
> (Bakhtin 1968: 109)

Carnival in its widest, most general sense embraced ritual spectacles such as fairs, popular feasts and wakes, processions and competitions (Burke 1978: 178–204), comic shows, mummery and dancing, open-air amusement with costumes and masks, giants, dwarfs, monsters, trained animals and so forth; it included comic verbal compositions (oral and written) such as parodies, travesties and vulgar farce; and it included various genres of 'Billingsgate', by which Bakhtin designated curses, oaths, slang, humour, popular tricks and jokes, scatalogical forms, in fact all the 'low' and 'dirty' sorts of folk humour. Carnival is presented by Bakhtin as a world of topsy-turvy, of heteroglot exuberance, of ceaseless overrunning and excess where all is mixed, hybrid, ritually degraded and defiled.

If there is a principle to this hotch-potch it resides in the spirit of carnivalesque laughter itself, to which Bakhtin ascribes great importance:

> Let us say a few initial words about the complex nature of carnivalesque laughter. It is, first of all, a festive laughter. Therefore it is not an individual reaction to some isolated 'comic' event. Carnival laughter is the laughter of all the people. Second, it is universal in scope; it is directed at all and everyone, including the carnival's participants. The entire world is seen in its droll aspect, in its gay relativity. Third, this laughter is ambivalent: it is gay, triumphant, and at the same time mocking, deriding. It asserts and denies, it buries and revives. Such is the laughter of the carnival.
>
> (Bakhtin 1968: 11–12)

Carnival laughter, then, has a vulgar, 'earthy' quality to it. With its oaths and profanities, its abusive language and its mocking words it was profoundly ambivalent. Whilst it humiliated and mortified it also revived and renewed. For Bakhtin ritual defilements went along with reinvigoration such that 'it was precisely this ambivalent abuse which determined the genre of speech in carnival intercourse' (Bakhtin 1968: 16). The 'coarse' and familiar speech of the fair and the marketplace provided a complex vital repertoire of speech patterns excluded from official discourse which could be used for parody, subversive humour and inversion. 'Laughter degrades and materialises' (Bakhtin 1968: 20). Fundamental to the corporeal, collective nature of carnival laughter is what Bakhtin terms 'grotesque realism'. Grotesque realism uses the material body–flesh conceptualized as corpulent excess – to represent cosmic, social, topographical and linguistic elements of the world. Thus already in Bakhtin there is the germinal notion of *transcodings* and *displacements* effected between the high/low image of the physical body and other social domains. Grotesque realism images the human body as multiple, bulging, over- or under-sized, protuberant and incomplete. The openings and orifices of this carnival body are emphasized, not its closure and finish. It is an image of impure corporeal bulk with its orifices (mouth, flared nostrils, anus) yawning wide and its lower regions (belly, legs, feet, buttocks and genitals) given priority over its upper regions (head, 'spirit', reason).

Bakhtin is self-consciously utopian and lyrical about carnival and grotesque realism. 'The leading themes of these images of bodily life are fertility, growth and a brimming-over abundance. Manifestations of this life refer not to the isolated biological individual, not to the private, egoistic, "economic man", but to the collective ancestral body of all the people' (Bakhtin 1968: 19). To complete the image of grotesque realism one must add that it is always in process, it is always *becoming*, it is a mobile and hybrid creature, disproportionate, exorbitant, outgrowing all limits, obscenely decentred and off-balance, a figural and symbolic resource for parodic exaggeration and inversion. All these grotesque qualities have a positive force in Bakhtin. It was only after the Renaissance, according to Bakhtin, that the principles of grotesque realism were subjected to a monologic reading. Stigmatized as the vulgar practices of a superstitious and crude populace, the carnivalesque was prettified, incorporated into commercial or civic display or regarded as a purely negative phenomenon. Bakhtin's optimistic populism is at its most insistent (and problematic) in those passages where he emphasizes the positivity of the grotesque bodily element.

The grotesque body was traditionally presented, Bakhtin argues,

> not in a private, egotistic form, severed from the other spheres of life, but as something universal, representing all the people. As such it is opposed to the severance from the material and bodily roots of the world; it makes no pretense to renunciation of the earthy, or independence of the earthy and body. We repeat: the body and bodily life have here a cosmic and at the same time an all-people's character; this is not the body and its physiology in the modern sense of these words, because it is not individualised. The

material bodily principle is contained not in the biological individual, not in the bourgeois ego, but in the people, a people who
are continually growing and renewed. This is why all that is bodily
becomes grandiose, exaggerated, immeasurable.

(Bakhtin 1968: 19)

It is difficult to disentangle the generous but willed idealism from the
descriptively accurate in passages like these. Bakhtin constantly
shifts between prescriptive and descriptive categories in his work. In
this passage the cosmic populism, which seems to us rather wishful
and finally unusable as an analytic tool, assorts with an acute
perception about the historically variable nature of the body-image.
In this latter respect recent thinking has largely confirmed Bakhtin's
insistence on the relation between body-image, social context and
collective identity. 'The whole concept of body-image boundaries
has implicit in it the idea of the structuring of one's relations with
others' (Fisher and Cleveland 1958: 206), and in the 1972 edition of
the *International Encyclopaedia of the Social Sciences* Fisher writes:

> The investigation of body-image phenomena has become a vigor-
> ous enterprise ... Speaking broadly, one may say there is an
> emphatic need to ascertain the principal axes underlying the
> organization of the body image. . . There is also a need to examine
> the relationships between body attitudes and socialization modes
> in different cultures. There is evidence in the anthropological
> literature that body attitudes may differ radically in relation to
> cultural context.
>
> (Fisher 1972: 116)

It is a major premise of Bakhtin's work that this is so. Moreover,
body-images 'speak' social relations and values with particular force.

In Bakhtin's schema grotesque realism in pre-capitalist Europe
fulfilled three functions at once: it provided an image-ideal of and for
popular community as an heterogeneous and boundless totality; it
provided an imaginary repertoire of festive and comic elements
which stood over against the serious and oppressive languages of the
official culture; and it provided a thoroughly materialist metaphysics
whereby the grotesque 'bodied forth' the cosmos, the social formation and language itself. Even linguistic rules are played up by what
Bakhtin calls a *grammatica jocosa* whereby grammatical order is
transgressed to reveal erotic and obscene or merely materially satis-

fying counter-meaning. Punning is one of the forms taken by the *grammatica jocosa*, and recently it has been argued, in Bakhtinian style, that the pun

> violates and so unveils the structure of prevailing (pre-vailing) convention; and it provokes laughter. Samuel Beckett's punning pronouncement 'In the beginning was the Pun' sets pun against official Word and at the same time, as puns often do, sets free a chain of other puns. So, too, carnival sets itself up in a punning relationship with official culture and enables a plural, unfixed, comic view of the world.
>
> (Arthur 1982: 1)

Arthur is one of the many contemporary critics who has been profoundly influenced by Bakhtin's work, and even from the cursory outline which we have provided here it is possible to see some of the suggestive force of his project. Certainly the enthusiastic adoption of the 'carnivalesque' as formulated by Bakhtin has resulted in articles and monographs on specific works, authors and periods far removed from Rabelais and the Renaissance. Film critic Robert Stamm writes:

> The notion of the carnivalesque, as elaborated by literary theorists like Mikhail Bakhtin and social anthropologists like Roberto da Matta is a potentially indispensable instrument for the analysis not only of literary and filmic texts but also of cultural politics in general.
>
> (Stamm 1982: 47)

However it is striking that the most successful of these attempts to apply Bakhtin *tout court* focus upon cultures which still have a strong repertoire of carnivalesque practices, such as Latin America, or upon literatures produced in a colonial or neo-colonial context where the political difference between the dominant and subordinate culture is particularly charged. Régine Robin's study of Soviet Yiddish literature (Robin 1983) is of this sort and gains some of its strength from the extent to which Bakhtin's own work was already, in its original form, a cryptic anti-Stalinist allegory. *Rabelais and his World* pits against that 'official, formalistic and logical authoritarianism whose unspoken name is Stalinism the explosive politics of the body, the erotic, the licentious and semiotic' (Eagleton 1981: 144). Robin's work on Soviet Yiddish nicely applies Bakhtin's use of the polyphonic 'multi-voicedness' of Yiddish (arguably in itself already a 'carnivalesque' language), the language of the oppressed Jewish minority. The rightness of this is underwritten by Bakhtin's indirect championing of the humorous resistance of the 'folk' through the darkest period of Stalinist terror.

For similar reasons Bakhtin has been used almost unchanged and unchallenged to provide readings of Latin American culture (Stamm 1982; Vilar de Kerkhoff 1983; Hill 1972; Malcuzynski 1983) and of minority culture in Canada (Godard 1983; Thurston 1983). Eisenstein may well have drawn upon Bakhtin's ideas in the final scenes of his film *Que viva México* in which macabre mockery of the Catholic ministers is effected through the use of carnival effigies (Ivanov 1976). Todorov's recent work on the colonization of the Americas (Todorov 1985) owes much to his recent critical interest in Bakhtin (Todorov 1984), and for some years now the appropriateness of Bakhtin to a study of James Joyce has been recognized. Joyce's 'carnivalization' of 'The King's English', his interest in and use of grotesque realism (Parrinder 1984: 16; Lodge 1982), suggested to Pomorska in the early 1960s that *Finnegans Wake* was the exemplary carnivalesque modernist work and recently Sidney Monas (1983) has gone some way to substantiating this view. In 1976 Ivanov wrote:

> One cannot help seeing the profound likeness between novelistic regularities discovered by Bakhtin and the structure of such twentieth century works as Joyce's *Ulysses* whose period of creation coincided with Bakhtin's youth: the intertwining and dialogic opposition of different speech genres; their conflict within the novel; the parodic and travestied features of the genre of the novel – all qualities which are at their fullest in *Ulysses* whose very structure is parodic, a travesty of the structure of Homer's *Odyssey*.
>
> (Ivanov 1976: 27)

The poetry of Shelley (Sales 1983), the plays of Samuel Beckett (Van Buuren 1983) and the writing of Jean-Claude Germain (Short 1983) have all been examined in recent criticism within a Bakhtinian frame and with a straightforward and unproblematical enthusiasm for his conceptual schema.

Others, however, have been more critical. Whilst almost every reader of Bakhtin admires his comprehensive and engaged generosity, his combination of festive populism and deep learning, and whilst few would deny the immediate appeal and the vitality of the notion of carnival, various writers have been sceptical of Bakhtin's overall project.

Terry Eagleton thinks that the weakness of Bakhtin's positive embrace of carnival is transparent:

> Indeed carnival is so vivaciously celebrated that the necessary political criticism is almost too obvious to make. Carnival, after all, is a *licensed* affair in every sense, a permissible rupture of hegemony, a contained popular blow-off as disturbing and relatively ineffectual as a revolutionary work of art. As Shakespeare's Olivia remarks, there is no slander in an allowed fool.
>
> (Eagleton 1981: 148)

Most politically thoughtful commentators wonder, like Eagleton, whether the 'licensed release' of carnival is not simply a form of social control of the low by the high and therefore serves the interests of that very official culture which it apparently opposes. The classic formulation of this is in Max Gluckman's now somewhat dated *Order and Rebellion in Tribal Africa* (1963) and *Custom and Conflict* (1965), in which he asserted that while these 'rites of reversal obviously include a protest against the established order . . . they are intended to preserve and strengthen the established order' (Gluckman 1965: 109). Roger Sales amplifies both on this process of containment and its ambivalence:

> There were two reasons why the fizzy, dizzy carnival spirit did not necessarily undermine authority. First of all, it was licensed or sanctioned by the authorities themselves. They removed the stopper to stop the bottle being smashed altogether. The release of emotions and grievances made them easier to police in the long term. Second, although the world might appear to be turned upside down during the carnival season, the fact that Kings and Queens were chosen and crowned actually reaffirmed the *status quo*. Carnival was, however, Janus-faced. Falstaff is both the merry old mimic of Eastcheap and the old corruptible who tries to undermine the authority, or rule, of the Lord Chief Justice. The carnival spirit, in early-nineteenth century England as well as in sixteenth century France, could therefore be a vehicle for social protest and the method for disciplining that protest.
>
> (Sales 1983: 169)

As Georges Balandier puts it succinctly in *Political Anthropology*: 'The supreme ruse of power is to allow itself to be contested *ritually* in order to consolidate itself more effectively.'

It actually makes little sense to fight out the issue of whether or not carnivals are *intrinsically* radical or conservative, for to do so automatically involves the false essentializing of carnivalesque transgression (White 1982: 60). The most that can be said in the abstract is that for long periods carnival may be a stable and cyclical ritual with no noticeable politically transformative effects but that, given the presence of sharpened political antagonism, it may often act as *catalyst* and *site of actual and symbolic struggle*.[1]

It is in fact striking how frequently violent social clashes apparently 'coincided' with carnival. Le Roy Ladurie's *Carnival in Romans* (1981) has popularized one such incident when the 1580 festival at Romans in eastern France was turned into armed conflict and massacre. Other social historians have documented similar occurrences (Davis 1975; Burke 1978; Thompson 1972). However to call it a 'coincidence' of social revolt and carnival is deeply misleading, for as Peter Burke has pointed out, it was only in the late eighteenth and early nineteenth centuries – and then only in certain areas – that one can reasonably talk of popular politics *dissociated* from the carnivalesque at all. John Brewer has described English politics in the eighteenth century as 'essentially a calendrical market', by which he designates a deliberate commingling of holiday and political events (in this case organized by the Hanoverians for conservative motives):

> Far too little attention had [sic] been paid to the emergence during the eighteenth century of a Hanoverian political calendar, designed to inculcate loyal values in the populace, and to emphasize and encourage the growth of a national political consensus. Nearly every English market town celebrated the dates which were considered the important political landmarks of the nation. They can be found in most almanacs of the period, barely distinguishable from the time-honoured dates of May Day, Plough Monday, Twelfth Night, Shrove Tuesday and the like... In the early eighteenth century, these dates, together with the occasion of the Pretender's birthday, were occasions of conflict. The year of the Jacobite Rebellion, 1715, was especially contentious, with Hanoverian Mug House clubs fighting it out in the streets with

Jacobite apprentices and artisans. On October 30, frequenters of a Jacobite alehouse on Ludgate Hill were beaten up by members of the Loyal Society who were celebrating the birthday of the Prince of Wales, the future George II. A Jacobite attempt to burn William III in effigy on November 4 was thwarted by the same Whig clubmen who the next day tried to cremate effigies of the Pretender and his supporters. On 17 November further clashes ensued and two Jacobites were shot dead.

(Brewer *et al.* 1983: 247)

Again this should act as a warning against the current tendency to essentialize carnival *and* politics. On the one hand carnival was a specific calendrical ritual: carnival proper, for instance, occurred around February each year, ineluctably followed by Lenten fasting and abstinence bound tightly to laws, structures and institutions which had briefly been denied during its reign. On the other hand carnival also refers to a mobile set of symbolic practices, images and discourses which were employed throughout social revolts and conflicts before the nineteenth century.

Recent work in the social history of carnival reveals its political dimensions to be more complex than either Bakhtin or his detractors might suspect. Bob Scribner has shown convincingly the importance of popular carnival practices in German Reformation struggles against Catholicism, particularly in the propagandistic application of ritual defilement to the Papacy; Martine Boiteux has shown the lengths to which the ecclesiastical powers were prepared to go in Rome in 1634 in order to 'upstage' the regular, popular carnival with a patrician counter-festival designed, says Boiteux, to 'repress, control and mutilate' the carnival of the common people. Whilst Simon Schama emphasizes the 'benign license' of Dutch seventeenth-century carnival and its avoidance of Calvinist bourgeois strictures, David Kunzle has emphasized the directly political use of Dutch carnival forms in the War of the Netherlands (Scribner 1978; Boiteux 1977; Schama 1979; Kunzle 1978).

In recent social histories of England there has been a considerable debate over the interrelationship between popular culture and class conflict (Yeo and Yeo 1981; Bushaway 1982; Walvin 1978; Cunningham 1980; Thompson 1972; Malcolmson 1973; Stedman Jones 1983). Most of these studies unearth evidence of a long battle (with occasional truces) waged by the State, ecclesiastical and bourgeois authorities against popular custom. It is a battle that goes back well beyond the Renaissance but which, from the Renaissance on, produced local festivities as sites of resistance to the extension of power by the propertied and the State. Bushaway remarks:

> Custom and ceremony became a battleground in the struggle between the labouring poor and the increasingly wealthy landowners and proprietors over the defence of popular rights and the protection of a normative view of the structure of the community held by the labouring poor.
>
> (Bushaway 1982: 21–2)

This seems an altogether more accurate way of conceiving the relationship. Carnivals, fairs, popular games and festivals were very swiftly 'politicized' by the very attempts made on the part of local authorities to eliminate them. The dialectic of antagonism frequently *turned* rituals into resistance at the moment of intervention by the higher powers, even when no overt oppositional element had been present before. All these issues in their historical complexity are discussed at greater length in the chapters which follow. In introducing them here we are only underscoring the banal but often ignored truth that the politics of carnival cannot be resolved outside of a close historical examination of particular conjunctures: there is no a priori revolutionary vector to carnival and transgression.

In his research on the carnivalesque Bakhtin had substantially anticipated by some thirty years main lines of development in symbolic anthropology. In his exploration of the *relational* nature of festivity, its structural inversion of, and ambivalent dependence upon, 'official culture', Bakhtin set out a model of culture in which a high/low binarism had a fundamental place. Bakhtin's use of carnival centres the concept upon its 'doubleness . . . there is no unofficial expression without a prior official one or its possibility. Hence, in Bakhtin's analysis of carnival, the official and unofficial are locked together' (Wilson 1983: 320). Symbolic polarities of high and low, official and popular, grotesque and classical are mutually constructed and deformed in carnival. Two of the best general synopses of Bakhtin's work correctly perceive this to be the most significant aspect of *Rabelais and his World*. Ivanov (1976) links Bakhtin's discovery of the importance of binary oppositions with the work of Lévi-Strauss:

the books by Bakhtin and Lévi-Strauss have much in common in their treatment of the functioning of oppositions in the ritual or the carnival which can be traced back historically to ritual performance. For Lévi-Strauss the chief purpose of the ritual and the myth is the discovery of an intermediate link between the members of a binary opposition: a process known as *mediation*. The structural analysis of the ambivalence inherent in the 'marketplace word' and its corresponding imagery led Bakhtin to the conclusion (made independently from and prior to structural mythology) that the 'carnival image strives to embrace and unite in itself both terminal points of the process of becoming or both members of the antithesis: birth–death, youth–age, top–bottom, face–lower bodily stratum, praise–abuse' [Bakhtin 1968: 238]. From this standpoint, Bakhtin scrutinized various forms of inverted relations between top and bottom 'a reversal of the hierarchy of top and bottom' [Bakhtin 1968: 81] which takes place during carnival.

(Ivanov 1976: 35)

The convergence of Bakhtin's thinking and that of current symbolic anthropology is highly significant. Where Ivanov points to the kinship Bakhtin shares with Lévi-Strauss and Edmund Leach (particularly Leach's essay on carnival, 'Time and false noses', 1961), Masao Yamaguchi suggests that Bakhtin's work significantly parallels that of Victor Turner, Barbara Babcock and Mary Douglas in their shared interest in cultural negations and symbolic inversions (Yamaguchi 1983). We may note, for instance, the similarity of Bakhtin's concept of carnivalesque high/low inversion to the concepts developed in *The Reversible World*, a collection of essays on anthropology and literature edited by Barbara Babcock. Although apparently unaware of Bakhtin's study she assembles a range of writing on 'symbolic inversion and cultural negation' which puts carnival into a much wider perspective. She writes:

'Symbolic inversion' may be broadly defined as any act of expressive behaviour which inverts, contradicts, abrogates, or in some fashion presents an alternative to commonly held cultural codes, values and norms be they linguistic, literary or artistic, religious, social and political.

(Babcock 1978: 14)

This is what we refer to in this book as 'transgression' (though there is another, more complex use of the term which arises in connection with extremist practices of modern art and philosophy; these designate not just the infraction of binary structures, but movement into an absolutely negative space *beyond the structure of significance itself*). For the moment it is enough to suggest that, in our view, the current widespread adoption of the idea of carnival as an *analytic* category can only be fruitful if it is displaced into the broader concept of symbolic inversion and transgression.

This is not to deny the usefulness of the carnivalesque as a sort of 'modelling', at once utopian and counter-hegemonic, whereby it is viewed, in Roberto da Matta's words, as a *privileged locus* of inversion. In his attempt to go beyond Bakhtin's nostalgic and over-optimistic view of carnival, Matta acknowledges the degree to which festivity is licensed release, but he also praises its deep modelling of a different, pleasurable and communal ideal 'of the people', even if that ideal cannot immediately be acted upon. Victor Turner has similarly argued with respect to role reversal that carnival is 'a moment when those being moved in accordance to a cultural script were liberated from normative demands, where they were . . . betwixt and between successive lodgements in jural political systems'. Carnival in this view has been defended as having a persistent *demystifying* potential (Jones 1983; Arthur 1982; Stamm 1982; Davis 1975). Even Terry Eagleton wants to salvage Bakhtin's carnivalesque by seeing it as a utopian modelling yoked to a glimpse through the ideological constructs of dominance, a 'kind of fiction', a

> temporary retextualizing of the social formation that exposes its 'fictive' foundations.
>
> (Eagleton 1981: 149)

In this perspective the carnivalesque becomes a resource of actions, images and roles which may be invoked both to model and legitimate desire and to 'degrade all that is spiritual and abstract'. 'The cheerful vulgarity of the powerless is used as a weapon against the pretence and hypocrisy of the powerful' (Stamm 1982: 47). In a most engaging description of this utopian/critical role of carnival Stamm continues:

> On the positive side, carnival suggests the joyful affirmation of becoming. It is ecstatic collectivity, the superseding of the indi-

viduating principle in what Nietzsche called 'the glowing life of Dionysian revellers' . . . On the negative, critical side, the carnivalesque suggests a demystificatory instrument for everything in the social formation which renders such collectivity difficult of access: class hierarchy, political manipulation, sexual repression, dogmatism and paranoia. Carnival in this sense implies an attitude of creative disrespect, a radical opposition to the illegitimately powerful, to the morose and monological.

(Stamm 1982: 55)

Refreshingly iconoclastic, this nevertheless resolves none of the problems raised so far concerning the politics of carnival: its nostalgia; its uncritical populism (carnival often violently abuses and demonizes *weaker*, not stronger, social groups – women, ethnic and religious minorities, those who 'don't belong' – in a process of *displaced abjection*); its failure to do away with the official dominant culture, its licensed complicity.

In fact those writers and critics who remain purely within the celebratory terms of Bakhtin's formulation are unable to resolve these key dilemmas. It is only by completely shifting the grounds of the debate, by transforming the 'problematic' of carnival, that these issues can be solved. It is precisely such an intervention in the current surge of Bakhtin-inspired studies which we have attempted in this book. The remainder of our introduction endeavours to sketch out a kind of political and aesthetic analysis building upon the work of Bakhtin but attempting to avoid the limitations here identified in his work. We have chosen therefore to consider carnival as one instance of a generalized economy of transgression and of the recoding of high/low relations across the whole social structure. The symbolic categories of grotesque realism which Bakhtin located can be rediscovered as a governing dynamic of the body, the household, the city, the nation-state – indeed a vast range of interconnected domains.

Marcel Détienne puts a similar notion most persuasively in *Dionysos Slain*:

A system of thought . . . is founded on a series of acts of partition whose ambiguity, here as elsewhere, is to open up the terrain of their possible transgression at the very moment when they mark off a limit. To discover the complete horizon of a society's symbolic values, it is also necessary to map out its transgressions, its deviants

(Détienne 1979: ix)

By tracking the 'grotesque body' and the 'low-Other' through different symbolic domains of bourgeois society since the Renaissance we can attain an unusual perspective upon its inner dynamics, the inner complicity of disgust and desire which fuels its crises of value. For the classificatory body of a culture is always double, always structured in relation to its negation, its inverse. 'All symbolic inversions define a culture's lineaments at the same time as they question the usefulness and the absoluteness of its ordering' (Babcock 1978: 29). Indeed by attending to the low and the marginal we vindicate, on the terrain of European literary and cultural history, the more general anthropological assertion that the process of symbolic inversion,

> far from being a residual category of experience, is its very opposite. What is socially peripheral is often symbolically central, and if we ignore or minimize inversion and other forms of cultural negation, we often fail to understand the dynamics of symbolic processes generally.

(Babcock 1978: 32)

This is a scrupulously accurate and indispensable formulation. The carnival, the circus, the gypsy, the lumpenproletariat, play a symbolic role in bourgeois culture out of all proportion to their actual social importance. The dominant features of the psycho-symbolic domain cannot be mapped one-to-one onto the social formation. Thus 'work', for example, which occupied such a central place in individual and collective life, is notoriously 'underrepresented' in artistic forms (Barrell 1980) but this should not be ascribed to some wilful act of ideological avoidance. Although work is 'actually central' in the production and reproduction of the whole social ensemble there is no reason, beyond an irrationally vulgar Marxist one, to suppose that capitalism should be totally different from other societies in locating its most powerful *symbolic* repertoires at borders, margins and edges, rather than at the accepted centres, of the social body. Thus a writer such as Arnold Bennett, committed to a realist and sympathetically accurate account of commercial working life in the industrial Midlands, reaches out to the circus, the Burslem

Introduction

Wakes, a hot-air balloon ascent and a public execution for significant climaxes in the dramatic narrative of *The Old Wives' Tale*. The complex of utilitarianism, industry and calculating parsimony which were fundamental to the English bourgeoisie by the nineteenth century drew its imaginative sustenance from precisely those groups, practices and activities which it was earnestly and relentlessly working to marginalize and destroy. In chapters 3, 4 and 5, we explore the contradictory constructions of bourgeois desire to which this led in the nineteenth century – a construction of subjectivity through totally ambivalent internalizations of the city slum, the domestic servant and the carnivalesque.

At various points throughout this book we have turned to Bakhtin's vocabulary of 'classical' and 'grotesque' in our exploration of high/low symbolism. In Bakhtin the 'classical body' denotes the inherent *form* of the high official culture and suggests that the shape and plasticity of the human body is indissociable from the shape and plasticity of discursive material and social norm in a collectivity. 'No absolute borderline can be drawn between body and meaning in the sphere of culture' (Ivanov 1976: 3). Because he is at pains to hold onto the mediating role played by the body in cultural designation, Bakhtin is undeniably ambiguous in his use of the terms 'classical body' and 'grotesque body', yet the imprecision seems not unjustifiable. Clearly, as often as they are able, 'high' languages attempt to legitimate their authority by appealing to values inherent in the classical body. Bakhtin was struck by the compelling difference between the human body as represented in popular festivity and the body as represented in classical statuary in the Renaissance. He noticed how the two forms of iconography 'embodied' utterly contrary registers of being. To begin with, the classical statue was always mounted on a plinth which meant that it was elevated, static and monumental. In the one simple fact of the plinth or pedestal the classical body signalled a whole different somatic conception from that of the grotesque body which was usually multiple (Bosch, Bruegel), teeming, always already part of a throng. By contrast, the classical statue is the radiant centre of a transcendant individualism, 'put on a pedestal', raised above the viewer and the commonality and anticipating passive admiration from below. We *gaze up* at the figure and wonder. We are placed by it as spectators to an instant–frozen yet apparently universal – of epic or tragic time. The presence of the statue is a problematic presence in that it immediately retroflects us to the heroic past, it is a *memento classici* for which we are the eternal latecomers, and for whom meditative imitation is the appropriate contrition. The classical statue has no openings or orifices whereas grotesque costume and masks emphasize the gaping mouth, the protuberant belly and buttocks, the feet and the genitals. In this way the grotesque body stands in opposition to the bourgeois individualist conception of the body, which finds *its* image and legitimation in the classical. The grotesque body is emphasized as a mobile, split, multiple self, a subject of pleasure in processes of exchange; and it is never closed off from either its social or ecosystemic context. The classical body on the other hand keeps its distance. In a sense it is disembodied, for it appears indifferent to a body which is 'beautiful', but which is taken for granted.

Vasari's codification of Vitruvian categories, the famous list of *regola, ordine, misura, disegno* and *maniera* is an interesting example of some of the governing principles of the classical body. Taking formal values from a purified mythologized canon of Ancient Greek and Roman authors – the 'classic' with which this introduction began – the classical body was far more than an aesthetic standard or model. It structured, from the inside as it were, the characteristically 'high' discourses of philosophy, statecraft, theology and law, as well as literature, as they emerged from the Renaissance. In the classical discursive body were encoded those regulated systems which were closed, homogeneous, monumental, centred and symmetrical. It began to make 'parsimony' of explanation and 'economy' of utterance the measure of rationality, thus institutionalizing Lenten rule as a normative epistemological standard. Gradually these protocols of the classical body came to mark out the identity of progressive rationalism itself. These are the terms of Foucault's 'regimen' and Weber's 'rationalization', the strong forms of functional purity which, certainly by the eighteenth century in England, led to the great age of 'institutionalizing' – asylums, hospitals, schools, barracks, prisons, insurance and finance houses – which, as Foucault has suggested, embody and assure the maintenance of classical bourgeois reason. Furthermore Foucault's concentration upon the contained outsiders-who-make-the-insiders-insiders (the mad, the criminal, the sick, the unruly, the sexually transgressive) reveals just how far these outsiders are constructed by the dominant culture in terms of the grotesque body. The 'grotesque' here designates the marginal, the low and the outside from the perspective of a classical body situated as high, inside and central by virtue of its very exclusions.

The grotesque body, as Bakhtin makes clear, has *its* discursive norms too: impurity (both in the sense of dirt and mixed categories), heterogeneity, masking, protuberant distension, disproportion, exorbitancy, clamour, decentred or eccentric arrangements, a focus upon gaps, orifices and symbolic filth (what Mary Douglas calls 'matter out of place'), physical needs and pleasures of the 'lower bodily stratum', materiality and parody. The opposition between classical and grotesque in this sense is invoked as automatically and unconsciously by Charcot in his description of the female hysteric as it is by the police spokesperson in a description of pickets or Auberon Waugh in his description of the women encamped at Greenham Common ('smelling of fish paste and bad oysters'). The grotesque physical body is invoked both defensively and offensively because it is not simply a powerful image but fundamentally constitutive of the categorical sets through which we live and make sense of the world.

The encampment of women protesters positioned on common land outside the entrance to the Cruise Missile Base near Newbury focuses many of these issues, and so powerfully, that it provides an exemplary instance. Malise Ruthven writes:

> all the women arouse a degree of hostility far in excess of any inconvenience they may cause to soldiers, policemen or residents living near the base. Shopkeepers and publicans refuse to serve them; hooligans unexpectedly join forces with the establishment and actualize the verbal insults by smearing the benders [home-made tents] with excrement and pig's blood . . . This spontaneous and voluntary association of females, without formal leadership or hierarchy, seems to threaten the soldiers, the local gentry, the bourgeoisie of Newbury and even its hooligans far more than the missiles, although the latter would be a prime target in the event of nuclear war.
>
> (Ruthven 1984: 1048)

'What is socially peripheral may be symbolically central'. The women at Greenham Common in their precarious and vulnerable condition by the roadside entrance to a vast military installation, 'On the perimeter' as Caroline Blackwood describes it, occupy a very powerful *symbolic* domain *despite and because of* their actual social marginalization. They constitute what Edmund Leach calls an 'intermediate and taboo-loaded category' and their association with excrement and pig's blood by a hostile local populace strongly attests to the fear and loathing which they have excited. They were accused, amongst other things, of having smeared the local town of Newbury with excrement. On one occasion, some soldiers as they were leaving the Base in a military coach ritually bared their backsides to the women 'in a gesture that had clearly been rehearsed with parade-ground precision' (Ruthven 1984: 1048). So many of the themes of this book intersect here, where transgressions of gender, territorial boundaries, sexual preference, family and group norms are trans-coded into the 'grotesque body' terms of excrement, pigs and arses. We would argue that this is ascribable neither to a residual super-stitious primitivism on the part of the good people of Newbury nor to trivial or accidental alignments. The women of Greenham Common are drawing (in some cases self-consciously) upon historical and political resources of mythopoetic transgression and conjuring from their antagonists not dissimilar reservoirs of material symbolism. They outrage the military establishment and the politicians by flagrantly maintaining their 'low' hovels at the very door of the mighty military estate; they outrage the local ratepayers (RAGE – Ratepayers Against Greenham Encampment) by transgressing the neat boundaries of private and public property as the Levellers and the Diggers did before them, occupying common land in the name of the people. They outrage local youths by breaking the norms of women's dependence upon men and by their independant sexual stance and are visited, in consequence, with a 'charivari' – a scapegoating carnivalesque ritual, usually carried out by young men against those whom they feel have broken the customs of courtship and sexual duty in the locality (Le Goff and Schmitt 1981; Desplatt 1982): charivari was a rowdy form of crowd behaviour often used against 'unruly women', and here it is an overt reminder of patriarchal dominance.

The women live 'on the wire', 'on the perimeter', neither fully outside nor fully inside, and they have triggered powerful associative chains which connect the international issue of nuclear missiles with pigs' blood and excremental vandalism: the cosmic with the local, the topographic with the sexual. Arguably a special (in every sense) and privileged case, the Greenham Common women nevertheless reveal how the grotesque body may become a primary, highly-charged intersection and mediation of social and political forces, a sort of intensifier and displacer in the making of identity. The exorbitant contrast between the closed, monumental, classical body of the multi-million dollar American Military Complex and the open, muddy, exposed huddle of higgledy-piggledy polythene tents is a scandal to hegemonic dignity which it can scarcely sustain. It is indeed wonderful that so little can make so great a difference.

This book aims to give a number of exploratory testings from early modern and modern Europe (particularly England), by mapping domains of transgression where place, body, group identity and subjectivity interconnect. Points of antagonism, overlap and intersection between the high and the low, the classical and its 'Other', provide some of the richest and most powerful symbolic dissonances in the culture. In mapping some of these spaces we illuminate the discursive sites where social classification and psychological processes are generated as conflictual complexes. It is precisely here where ideology and fantasy conjoin. The topography of realms which, *by virtue* of exclusions at the geographical, class, or somatic level, traces lines of desire and phobic contours which are produced and reproduced through one another. There is a secular magic to these displacements, and its law is the law of exclusion.

Thus the logic of identity-formation involves distinctive associations and switching between location, class and the body, and these are not imposed *upon* subject-identity from the outside, they are the core terms of an exchange network, an economy of signs, in which individuals, writers and authors are sometimes but perplexed agencies. A fundamental rule seems to be that what is excluded at the overt level of identity-formation is productive of new objects of desire. As new classificatory sets emerge with new forms of production and new social relations, so the carnivalesque and transgressive anti-structure of the emergent classical body will also change, marking out new sites of symbolic and metaphorical intensity in the ideological field. In class society where social conflict is always present these sites do not necessarily coincide with the 'objective' conflict boundaries of antagonistic classes but will nevertheless function to the advantage of one social group rather than another. In Chapter 3 for example we note how certain middle-class fantasies about the lumpenproletariat in the nineteenth century effaced the centrality of issues around the proletariat. On the other hand transgressive symbolic domains and the fetishism which attaches to them are never merely diversionary. There is no simple fit between the imaginary repertoire of transgressive desire and economic and political contradictions in the social formation, and yet the two are always deeply connected.

It is perhaps worth recapitulating the points we have made so far. By focusing upon the 'taboo-laden' overlap between high and low discourse which produces the grotesque, we have tried to effect a transposition of the Bakhtinian conception of the carnivalesque into a framework which makes it analytically powerful in the study of ideological repertoires and cultural practices. If we treat the carnivalesque as an instance of a wider phenomenon of transgression we move beyond Bakhtin's troublesome *folkloric* approach to a political anthropology of *binary extremism* in class society. This transposition not only moves us beyond the rather unproductive debate over whether carnivals are politically progressive or conservative, it reveals that the underlying structural features of carnival operate far beyond the strict confines of popular festivity and are intrinsic to the dialectics of social classification as such. The 'carnivalesque' mediates between a classical/classificatory body and its negations, its Others, what it excludes to create its identity as such. In this process discourses about the body have a privileged role, for transcodings between different levels and sectors of social and psychic reality are effected through the intensifying grid of the body. It is no accident, then, that transgressions and the attempt to control them obsessively return to somatic symbols, for these are ultimate elements of social classification itself.

NOTE

1 Kateryna Arthur: 'The question I shall be addressing throughout my exploration of carnivalesque activity is: how can carnival be simultaneously revolutionary and law-abiding?' (Arthur 1982: 4). Terry Eagleton: 'Carnival laughter is incorporating as well as liberating, the lifting of inhibitions politically enervating as well as disruptive. Indeed from one viewpoint carnival may figure as a prime example of that mutual complicity of law and liberation, power and desire, that has become the dominant theme of contemporary post-marxist pessimism.' (Eagleton 1981: 149).

I

The Fair,
the Pig,
Authorship

How does one 'think' a marketplace? At once a bounded enclosure and a site of open commerce, it is both the imagined centre of an urban community and its structural interconnection with the network of goods, commodities, markets, sites of commerce and places of production which sustain it. A marketplace is the epitome of local identity (often indeed it is what defined a place as more significant than surrounding communities) and the unsettling of that identity by the trade and traffic of goods from elsewhere. At the market centre of the polis we discover a commingling of categories usually kept separate and opposed: centre and periphery, inside and outside, stranger and local, commerce and festivity, high and low. In the marketplace pure and simple categories of thought find themselves perplexed and one-sided. Only hybrid notions are appropriate to such a hybrid place.

It sometimes seems that the commonplace is what is most radically unthinkable. The market square – that epitome of the 'common place' – so definite and comforting in its phenomenological presence at the heart of the community, is only ever an *intersection*, a crossing of ways. If it exists at all it is as a conjuncture of distribution entirely dependent upon remote processes of production and consumption, networks of communication, lines of economic force. As much a process of commercial convergence as an open space, the marketplace gives the illusion of independent identity, of being a self-sustaining totality, and this illusion is one of separateness and enclosure. Thinking the marketplace is thus somewhat like thinking the body: adequate conception founders upon the problematic familiarity, the enfolding intimacy, of its domain. The tangibility of its boundaries implies a local closure and stability, even a unique sense of belonging, which obscure its structural dependence upon a 'beyond' through which this 'familiar' and 'local' feeling is itself produced. Thus in the marketplace 'inside' and 'outside' (and hence identity itself) are persistently mystified. It is a place where limit, centre and boundary are confirmed and yet also put in jeopardy.

In his work on 'The language of the marketplace in Rabelais', Bakhtin emphasized only one side of this complex doubleness which constitutes the marketplace. By dwelling upon the 'collective gaiety of the people' (Bakhtin 1968: 146) as it is expressed in the popular festivals held in the market square, Bakhtin focused exclusively upon a single aspect of the market space – its special status at fair-time as a popular domain created outside, and beyond, the official sites of authority. In the fair, he argues, one could experience 'a certain extraterritoriality' from 'official order and official ideology' (154):

> Abuses, curses, profanities, and improprieties are the unofficial elements of speech . . . Such speech forms, liberated from norms, hierarchies, and prohibitions of established idiom, become themselves a peculiar argot and create a special collectivity, a group of people initiated in familiar intercourse, who are frank and free in expressing themselves verbally. The marketplace crowd was such a collectivity, especially the festive, carnivalesque crowd at the fair.
>
> (Bakhtin 1968: 187–8)

Above all for Bakhtin the fair finds its place in the open, extraterritorial space of the marketplace, 'outside' of the official local hierarchy and its languages and 'within' the popular festive body: it is the grotesque body at home with itself, evading the spatial constraints of the public building (the Church, the Law-Court) and the private house. Partly because he associated it with the utopian, the 'no-place' of collective hopes and desires, Bakhtin simplified the paradoxical, contradictory space of the market and the fair as a place-beyond-place, a pure outside.

But the fair, like the marketplace, is neither pure nor outside. The fair is at the crossroads, situated at the intersection of economic and

2 'The Fair on St George's Day', etching attributed to Jan or Lucas van Duetecum, after Pieter Bruegel
the Elder, Dutch, second half of the sixteenth century
(Reproduced by courtesy of the Trustees of the British Museum)

cultural forces, goods and travellers, commodities and commerce. It is a gravely over-simplifying abstraction therefore to conceptualize the fair purely as the site of communal celebration. In developing this concept, Bakhtin succumbs to that separation of the festive and the commercial which is distinctive of capitalist rationality as it emerged in the Renaissance. As the bourgeoisie laboured to produce the economic as a separate domain, partitioned off from its intimate and manifold interconnectedness with the festive calendar, so they laboured *conceptually* to re-form the fair as *either* a rational, commercial, trading event *or* as a popular pleasure-ground. As the latter, the fair had from classical times been continually subject to regulation and suppression on both political and moral grounds. But although the bourgeois classes were frequently frightened by the threat of political subversion and moral licence, they were perhaps more scandalized by the deep conceptual confusion entailed by the fair's inmixing of work and pleasure, trade and play.

In so far as the fair was *purely* a site of pleasure, it could be envisaged as a discrete entity: local, festive, communal, unconnected to the 'real' world. In so far as it was *purely* a commercial event it could be envisaged as a practical agency in the progress of capital, an instrument of modernization and a means of connecting up local and communal 'markets' to the world market. This separation of popular pleasure from the emergent economic domain has to a large extent been unconsciously internalized by modern scholarship in its disciplinary divisions. From the perspective of cultural studies, folklore and social history, the fair has been predominantly thought of in terms of popular revelry and political subversion. From the perspective of economic history, on the other hand, fairs have been seen above all as the sites of commercial distribution whose rise and fall depended upon national and international market forces. This conceptual separation was not without its material effects, as magistrates increasingly attempted to distinguish between the fair which was economically useful and the pleasure fair.

It became increasingly difficult, with the development of the 'economic' as a separate conceptual sphere in the unfolding of bourgeois thought, to countenance the muddling together of work and pleasure/leisure as they regularly occurred in the fair. The fair had to be split into two opposed parts: in so far as it could be thought of as low, dirty, extraterritorial, it could be demonized (and in time, idealized) as the locus of vagabond desires. In so far as it was economically useful, it could be seen as part of what Norbert Elias has called 'the civilizing process', relating villages to county town, provinces to the capital, peripheries to the centre, binding in tributary areas of production and consumption to a network of national and urban values. However, such oppositional splitting into incompatibles required much conceptual (and material) labour. The fair as a site of hybridization epistemologically undermined the separation of the economic from 'play' and the clean from the dirty. As a result the emergent middle classes *worried away at it*, particularly striving to separate and consolidate the binaries which the fair so mischievously seemed to intermix and confuse.

Such an attempt to clean up the fair's hybridization was a paradoxical, even contradictory ideological project, for the labour of conceptual separation was itself subject to the seductive power of the hybrid. As these boundaries were constructed they were haunted by the play *between* the oppositions which had been formulated. Indeed, as we shall see, the fair reflected for the bourgeoisie its own uneasy oscillation between high and low, business and pleasure, and consequently retained a potent imaginative charge in the culture of those who increasingly defined themselves as above its gaudy pleasures.

CONCEPTUALIZING THE FAIR

The Magistrates decree that 'Fair is foul',
And put a stop to profitable sport;
They exorcise the Lion's shilling howl,
And cut the Irish Giant's income short . . .

Take warning then, ye fair, from this fair's fall.
One Act – the Vagrant Act – hath been its ruin.
Listen, oh listen, to Law's *Serious Call*,
For fun and pleasure lead but to undoing.
(*Elegy on the Death of Bow Fair*,
after its suppression in 1822)

We now have evidence over a long historical period of the

discursive construction of the fair as the antithesis of order, civility and decorum. The medieval homilist listed the fair amongst a catalogue of iniquities: there shall be no 'jangeling, rowning [chattering], no cry, no din in church or churchyard . . . no striving, no fighting, no merchandize, no markets, no fairs . . . no dances, no worldly songs, no interludes, no castings of the stone, steracles [performances], no playing at the ball, nor idle japes and plays' (Clark 1983: 27). Ned Ward was similarly censorious when he visited St James's Fair in the early eighteenth century and observed 'a parcel of scandalous boozing kens where soldiers and their trulls were skipping and dancing' (Clark 1983: 200). Daniel Defoe commented that the October Fair at Charlton was 'infamous for the yearly collected rabble of mad-people'; the 'mob', he claimed, were given to 'all kinds of liberties, and the women are especially impudent that day; as if it were a day that justify'd the giving themselves a loose to all manner of indecency and immodesty . . .' (Defoe 1962: I, 97). In 1711, a petition by London citizens claimed that at Bartholomew Fair a 'lewd and ravenous Crew . . . become an open and daring Enemy to good Government, are able to make a stand against Authority, and are evidently an Overmatch to inferior Officers' (Morley 1859: 380). And in the early nineteenth century, R. C. Dillon published *A Sermon on the Evils of Fairs in General and of Bartholomew Fair in Particular*, where he argued that at fairs 'the disobedient and rebellious subjects of God countenance and strengthen one another in the ways of sin' (Malcolmson 1973: 103).

Attacks on the fair have, indeed, been one of the main historical written sources of our knowledge of the fair – an occasional event which in itself left few permanent traces. But the nature of this evidence, always hostile and aiming at suppression, has meant that the fair has been studied from the perspective of its demise. Thus the history of the fair has been written as the story of a long decline. And the suppression of the fair has been thought of in two opposing, but mutually reinforcing, ways: either as the necessary triumph of the civilizing process or as the brutal stamping out of popular culture by the Church and the bureaucratic, centralizing State. The first position is represented by Robert Chambers in his *Book of Days* (1863–4). Despite some nostalgia for what had been lost, Chambers's perspective on fairs tended to endorse that of the magistrates. Of Greenwich Fair he wrote: 'for some years past, this has been a bygone glory, for magistrates found that the enjoyments of the festival involved much disorder and impropriety' (Chambers 1863–4: I, 643). And of Bartholomew Fair, which had been prohibited in 1855, he wrote: 'Originally established for trading purposes, it had long survived its claim to tolerance, and as London increased, had become a great public nuisance, with the scenes of riot and obstruction in the very heart of the city' (Chambers 1863–4: II, 263). Chambers, in other words, saw the fair as the necessary, if sometimes unfortunate, casualty of the development of the city and trade. On the other hand recent social historians like Robert Malcolmson have seen the suppression of the fairs as part of the hegemonic struggle waged by the state against 'traditional' popular recreation. For Chambers the nature of a 'public nuisance' is self-evident; for Malcolmson, the label is itself an instrument of social control.

Certainly, Malcolmson's perspective marks a significant advance over Chambers. Malcolmson, following his mentor E. P. Thompson, sees popular culture as a site of struggle. Fairs do not simply die; they are stamped out. On 28 July, 1664, the *Newes* announced that the 'Fair at St James's is put by, as considered to tend rather to the advantage of looseness and irregularity, than to the substantial promoting of any good, common and beneficial to the people'. In 1697 the Lord Mayor called for 'the suppression of vicious practices in Bartholomew Fair, as obscene, lascivious, and scandalous plays, comedies and farces, unlawful games and interludes, drunkenness, etc., strictly charging all constables and other officers to use their utmost diligence in prosecuting the same'. In 1708, the May Fair at Westminster was suppressed as a 'vile and riotous assembly' (Morley 1859: 242, 336, 386). In 1781–2, standing orders prohibited twenty-four fairs; in the 1780s and 1790s, more orders attacked 'pretended fairs not warranted by law'; in 1803 the Society for the Suppression of Vice argued that it would 'be expedient to suppress all Fairs whatever, unless when they are really wanted for the purpose of useful traffic'; in 1817, St Bartholomew's Fair, suspected of being a breeding ground of sedition, was attacked by four regiments of horse; in 1871, an Act of Parliament allowed local and central government to abolish fairs deemed 'unnecessary . . . the cause of grievous immorality, and . . . very injurious to the inhabitants of the towns in which such fairs are held', and from 1871–8 the Act was used to close down more than 150 fairs (Malcolmson 1973: 149–50; Yeo and Yeo 1981: 138–9). Similarly in France, the grand Council of Rhône refused all applications for new Fairs in 1859 on the grounds that they were excuses for idleness and dissipation and usually ended in disorder and debauchery (Weber 1979: 411fn.).

In fact, in suppressing fairs magistrates usually invoked the key distinction between a fair which was economically useful and a 'mere' pleasure fair. An 1875 petition against two annual fairs in Sawbridgeworth clearly shows this: 'whilst these fairs are of the smallest conceivable worth in a commercial point of view, indefensibly and indisputably they are the prolific seed plots and occasions of the most hideous forms of moral and social evil – drunkenness – whoredom – robbery – idleness – neglect of work . . .' (Malcolmson 1973: 151).

Idleness, dissipation, disorder, debauchery: these are the demonized terms for the topology which Bakhtin celebrated, from the perspective of the low, as the grotesque. But in taking over and inverting the binary terms by which the bourgeoisie structured the social formation, Malcolmson, like Bakhtin, tends to repeat the division of work from pleasure. The fair is located on one side of a series of oppositions as 'popular', celebratory, grotesque, and its history becomes one of a transformation from 'licence' (i.e. excess) to 'licensed' (i.e. authorized), with the concomitant suppression of the 'unlicensed' fairs.

There are two major problems with this view. Firstly, it tends towards a misleading historical chronology in which the 'traditional' fair undergoes a steady process of decay. In fact, whilst some fairs were suppressed in the nineteenth century, there was also a massive explosion of new fairs. This was perhaps most dramatic in France. In Puy-de-Dôme in 1903, for instance, there were said to be 172 annual fairs, of which forty-four were 'timeless' and of which twenty-one dated from before 1850. But from 1851 to 1870 there were fourteen new fairs created, thirty-nine from 1871 to 1880, twenty-one from 1881 to 1890, and 33 from 1897 to 1903 (Weber 1979: 408). In England too, fairs, far from being 'relics of a barbarous age', proved highly adaptable to industrialization, as Hugh Cunningham has shown (Cunningham 1980). The railway made excursions to quite distant fairs possible; Croydon and Barnet fairs flourished as a result of the day-trippers from London and in 1850, 900 people travelled to St Giles's Oxford from Banbury alone, while excursions were later organized from Cardiff, Gloucester, London and Birmingham (Cunningham 1980: 159). In the third quarter of the nineteenth century new levels of investment and organization made the expansion of fairs possible. And whilst many small fairs were suppressed, the authorities tended to look favourably on the larger circuses, music halls, sports meetings and fairgrounds: 'leisure for the mass of people was now judged to be legitimate' (Cunningham 1980: 174, 184).

But there is a second, more serious objection to seeing the fair as necessarily opposed to 'official order and ideology' (Bakhtin 1968: 154). For the fair itself played a crucial part in the formation and transformation of local socio-economic relations and the State. This is clearest in the case of the large city fairs. The fortunes of Leipzig depended upon its fairs: buildings were knocked down and squares were rebuilt to make more space for them. In seventeenth-century Frankfurt-am-Main, the fair drew foreign merchants from Italy, the Swiss cantons and Holland, some of whom settled there permanently, thus changing the composition of the city. The Leipzig riot of 1593 against the Calvinists has been interpreted as an attack upon the similar settlement of Dutch merchants there (Braudel 1982: 83–4). And Natalie Davis has argued for the interconnection between the fair and the settlement of foreigners in Lyons upon which the prosperity of that city depended in the sixteenth century. In the mid-sixteenth century, 19 per cent of the adult males of Lyons came from outside the kingdom of France, and the 'Messieurs des nations' (the foreign merchants who controlled the money-markets at the four annual fairs) had their own political institutions and organized their own lavish festivals, mummings and games (Davis 1981: 43–5).

It is surely mistaken then, to see the fair simply as the popular festival of rural life. Indeed it was great trading centres like Holland and Venice which were most famous for their fairs. In the seventeenth century, the *kermis* at the Hague lasted for two weeks:

Soothsayers and clairvoyants would usurp the prophetic roles of the preacher; actors would, literally, make a mummery of historical heroes and contemporary pretensions, quacks and alchemists would take the place of the physicians, and pedlars and hawkers that of guildsmen. Its stables were dwellings for those who had no fixed abode, no claims on 'Burgerschap' (residential citizenship): gypsies, transient musicians and tumblers; exotics of doubtful origin; freed slaves with hair-raising tales of Turkish barbarity; and the ultimate parody of the 'normal' — freaks, midgets and giants'.

(Schama 1979: 119)

Indeed fairs were as much an agent of transformation as of 'popular tradition', since they brought together the exotic and the familiar, the villager and the townsman, the professional performer and the bourgeois observer. Fairs actually promoted a conjuncture of discourses and objects favourable to innovation. The market square was a crossroads, and if it was the focus of 'community' it was also the point of intersection of different cultures. The variety of commodities, buyers and spectators was necessarily linked to the variety of economic and political connections between villages, regions and nation-states. At Sturbridge Fair in Cambridge, the greatest of all the English Fairs and the model for John Bunyan's Vanity Fair in *Pilgrim's Progress*, the Cambridge student bought and sold books culled from the breadth of Europe: it was at this great fair in 1661 that Newton purchased his first book on astronomy (Addison 1953: 42). At Sturbridge Daniel Defoe noted clothiers from Halifax, Leeds, Wakefield and Huddersfield; a dealer in 'Norwich Stuffs only'; 'Western Goods' from Exeter, Taunton and Bristol; hops from Chelmsford, Canterbury, Maidstone, Farnham and London. And Defoe went on to observe 'the prodigious Resort of the Trading people of all parts of England to this fair' (Walford 1883: 133–9). At its height Sturbridge Fair would witness one of the most cosmopolitan and intensely heterogeneous gatherings of Christendom:

The Venetian and Genoese merchant came with his precious stock of Eastern produce, his Italian silks and velvets, his store of delicate glass. The Flemish weaver was present with his linens of Liege and Ghent. The Spaniard came with his stock of iron, the Norwegian with his tar and pitch. The Gascon vine-grower was ready to trade in the produce of his vineyard; and, more rarely, the richer growths of Spain, and still more rarely, the vintages of Greece were also supplied. The Hanse towns sent furs and amber, and probably were the channels by which the precious stones of the East were supplied through the markets of Moscow and Novgorod.

(Roger 1866: I, 141)

Of course, small rural fairs might be primarily marts for the hiring of labour on Lady Day or the exchange of purely local produce, but even the smallest fair juxtaposed both people and objects which were normally kept separate and thus provided a taste of life beyond the narrow horizons of the town or village. Part of the transgressive excitement of the fair for the subordinate classes was *not* its 'otherness' to official discourse, but rather the disruption of provincial habits and local tradition by the introduction of a certain cosmopolitanism, arousing desires and excitements for exotic and strange commodities. The fair 'turned the world inside out' in its mercantilist aspect just as much, if not more, than it 'turned the world upside down' in its popular rituals.

Whilst this process might well present itself to the bourgeois bystander as the elevation or corruption of the rustic, to the villager it may well have been a more complex process – a form of defamiliarization in which the romantic–commercial novelty of foreign commodities confronted and relativized local custom. Nostalgia for the 'truly' local and communal was undoubtedly more prevalent amongst the élite than amongst those who, at the fair, had a rare opportunity to admire and try on the customs of the world.

There is a saying in Tarn-et-Garonne about Monbequi, a poor south-western village: 'At Monbequi they are not civilized. They have neither fair nor market' (Weber 1979: 408). The fair then, was, from the perspective of *below*, as much about the relativizing of cultures and the intersection of languages and objects as about the self-representation of *communitas*. To see the fair as simply the festive voice of the community is to adopt a nostalgic perspective which mystifies the conditions which determined the fair's existence. Moreover such a perspective tends towards an uncritical acceptance of popular festivity as 'traditional'. But, as Eric Wolf has cogently argued, the dividing up of societies into 'traditional', 'transitional' and 'modern' has 'blocked effective understanding of relationships among them': to define societies as autonomous and bounded structures discourages 'analysis of intersocietal or intergroup interchanges, including internal social strife, colonialism, imperialism, and societal dependency' (Wolf 1982: 13).

Against the populist element in Bakhtin, we must emphasize the fair as a point of economic and cultural intersection, of hybridization, to use his own term, not just as the potential space of popular and local subversion. If, indeed, the fair could be the site of opposition to official ideologies, it was also the means by which emergent mercantile interests could stimulate new desires. Languages, images, symbols and objects met and clashed at the fair and it was their *interconnection* which made for their significance. One could even mount the precise contrary argument to Bakhtin: that the fair, far from being the privileged site of popular symbolic opposition to hierarchies, was in fact a kind of educative spectacle, a relay for the diffusion of the cosmopolitan values of the 'centre' (particularly the capital and the new urban centres of production) throughout the provinces and the lower orders.

Thus, for example, eighteenth-century industrial innovators consciously used the fair circuits to stimulate new tastes and fashions amongst the general populace. A print of the Pot Fair, Cambridge, in 1777, shows the latest neo-classical Wedgewood sauce-boats and soup tureens being sold on open stalls. And the female pot-seller is wearing currently fashionable dress: mobcap, high-heeled shoes, buckles and bows (McKendrick *et al.* 1982: 59). If permanent shops were increasingly to take their place as 'a continuous fair', as a late-eighteenth-century Russian traveller in England put it, the commercial revolution still penetrated the countryside through itinerant pedlars. Matthew Boulton, remembered now mainly for his role in the invention of the steam engine, was also a toymaker and toyseller who analysed the means by which commercial manufacture could reach new markets. In 1794 he wrote to Chippendall:

We think it of more consequence to supply the people than the Nobility only; and though you speak contemptuously of Hawkers, Pedlars and those who supply Petty Shops, yet we must own that we think they will do more towards supporting a great manufactory than all the Lords in the Nation.

(McKendrick *et al.* 1982: 77)

Certainly the fair as a nexus of commodity exchange was eventually superseded by shops, but it was only after it had served its function as a principle mediator between the new manufacturers and 'the dark corners of the land'. At the same time, the fair mediated between the individual consumer and the major European trade routes. In a ballad called 'The Pedlar opening of his Packe' (c. 1620), the pedlar asks his prospective customers to 'come and see my packet' and 'view the Fayre'. In his 'Fayre' there is soap from Turkey, bone lace from Flanders, needles from Spain, looking-glasses from Venice and medicines for the teeth and gums from 'Western Iles' (Rollins 1922: 116–20). Where Bakhtin emphasized the dirt of the fair and the lower bodily stratum, the pedlar displays soap, mirrors and items of dental care, commodities of beautification (particularly for women) of a cosmetic nature. Consumption here is not the drunken excess of physical indulgence but rather the subtle intimation of lack in the very display of cosmetic repair. The body of the rural woman, reflected in 'looking-glasses from Venice', witnesses a triangulation of desire and body-image through 'worldly' goods. These commodities measure the body by another standard, they reveal its provincialism at the very moment of provoking, and appearing to satisfy, narcissistic desires. The pedlar's pack, like Belinda's dressing table in *The Rape of the Lock*, critically 'speaks' the woman's body through the display of fashionable commodities. If the fair displayed the grotesque body, it also displayed the 'fair'.

Like the commodities which were sold at it, the fair was structured by the juxtaposition of the domestic and the bizarre, the local and the exotic. Of course, the juxtaposition was not always a success. Kilvert recalls Wombwell's Menagerie travelling away from Brecon Fair: 'the elephant, a very small one, and three camels or dromadaries came shuffling and splashing along the muddy road in heavy rain looking cold and miserable and shivering as if they were wet through' (Walvin 1978: 115). But Thomas Frost recalls how in his childhood he could 'never sufficiently admire' Wombwell's or Atkin's shows when they visited Croydon Fair, with their bands blaring from noon to night and their 'elephants and giraffes, lions and tigers, zebras, boa constrictors, and whatever else was most wonderful in brute creation' (Cunningham 1980: 35). The fair was indeed radically hybrid. At Sturbridge Fair, for instance, as Charles Caracioli noted in the eighteenth century, there were 'Coffee-houses, Taverns, Eating

Houses, Music Shops, Buildings for the exhibition of Drolls, Puppet Shows, Legerdemain, Mountebanks, Wild Beasts, Monsters, Giants, Rope Dancers, Etc.' And an Essex doctor commented on the fair at Prittlewell in 1826: 'The fair is a very decent one. An exhibition on our right of a Giant, Giantess, an Albiness, a native of Baffins Bay and a Dwarf – very respectable. We had a learned Pig and Punch on our left and in front some Theatrical Exhibition. All in very good order' (Malcolmson 1973: 20–1). In fact the doctor's account is troubled by his fear of the subversions to which such juxtapositions might lead. If a world of learned pigs could be 'very decent', 'very respectable' with '[all] in very good order', the emphatic 'verys' testify by antithesis to the strain to which decency, respectability and order were put by the spectacle.

Yet the exoticism of the Albiness and the native of Baffins Bay is hardly in itself 'subversive'. Indeed, most important of all in countering nostalgic, populist interpretations of the fair is the recognition that it was a crucial point of intersection between the imperialist spoils of the nation-state and the European citizen.

In *The Tempest*, Trinculo reacts to his first sight of Caliban by observing that he would be marketable in England: 'Not a holiday fool there but would give a piece of silver . . . When they will not give a doit to relieve a lame beggar, they will lay out ten to see a dead Indian' (II.ii. 29–33). And in the last act of the play, Antonio, the usurping Duke of Milan, notes that Caliban is 'a plain fish, and no doubt marketable' (V.i. 266). Increasingly from the sixteenth century, the fair's 'monsters' (Siamese twins, a calf with a pig's head) were supplemented by a display of the exotic – i.e. the marketable wonders of the colonized world. A midget from the West Indies was shown at the May Fair in 1704, at Leeds in 1706, and at a booth in Lincoln's Inn Fields some time after 1708, when the May Fair had been suppressed. A portrait emphasized his 'bizarre and regal appearance', whilst a handbill played upon his exoticism and remote origin (Taylor 1957: 64–5). At the Highworth Fair in the 1870s, among the exhibitions of beasts, birds, waxworks, model machinery and cotton spinning, 'a great Zulu and several negroes performed the war dance' (Walvin 1978: 116). In Conan Doyle's *The Sign of Four*, Jonathan Small exhibits his 'savage' follower, Tonga, 'at fairs and other such places as "the black cannibal". He would eat raw meat and dance the war dance' (quoted in Farrell 1984: 36). In such acts as these, the 'Other' is reduced to a frightening or comic spectacle set over against the antithetical 'normality' of the spectator.

And then there were the animals: '[A] little Marmoset from the East Indies . . . is now brought to that perfection, that no Creature of his Kind ever perform'd the like; he Exercises by Word of Command, he dances the Cheshire Rounds he also dances with 2 Naked Swords, and performs several other Pretty Fancies'; 'a little Black Hairy Pigmey (presumably a monkey), bred in the Deserts of Arabia, a Natural Ruff of Hair about his Face, two Foot high, walks upright, drinks a Glass of Ale or Wine, and does several other things to admiration'; a 'Manteger . . . lately brought from the East Indies, is astonishing not only for its teeth and colour but because 'twould drink out of a Cup as Man does with his lips and not lap with his Tongue'; a 'Noble Creature, which much resembles a Wild Hairy man . . . pulls off his Hat, and pays his respects to the Company, and smoaks a Pipe of Tobacco as well as any Christian' (Taylor 1957: 31, 59–60, 63).

It might seem from these examples as if the fair was simply a museum in which the spoils from colonized cultures went on display (cf. Mullaney 1983), but when we look closely at the acts and the little performances which these creatures are taught to do, we can see that they play with the thresholds of culture in an interesting fashion. The marmoset dances Cheshire rounds; the 'pigmey' walks upright and drinks wine; the manteger drinks with his lips 'like a Man'; the creature looking like a wild man politely removes his hat to the crowd. In each case the manners taught imitate European forms of culture or politeness and amusingly transgress, as well as reaffirm, the boundaries between high and low, human and animal, domestic and savage, polite and vulgar. We might say that these token transgressions model the double process of colonialism. The Other must be transformed into the Same, the savage must be civilized (like the wild creature who smokes a pipe 'as well as any Christian'); but at the same time, the Other's mimicry of the polite is treated as absurd, the cause of derisive laughter, thus consolidating the sense that the civilized is always-already given, the essential and unchanging possession which distinguishes the European citizen from the West Indian and the Zulu as well as from the marmoset and manteger.

Is the spectacle of the fair, then, no more than the display of the grotesque body for the edification of a national public and the confirmation of its imperial superiority? This inversion of Bakhtin is certainly *one* possibility. But the observer at the fair is also a potential participant and so the *relation* between observer and observed is never fixed. Indeed (and this is a point to which we return in the next chapter), the plebeian fair-goers were themselves part of the spectacle for the bourgeois observer. At the fair the subordinate classes became the object of a gaze constituting itself as respectable and superior by substituting observation for participation ('The pure gaze implies a break with the ordinary attitude towards the world, which, given the conditions in which it is performed, is also a social separation': Bourdieu 1984: 4). Yet this positioning of the subordinate classes as the object of the respectable gaze created the possibility of identification and even a sort of alliance between the 'official' objects of display (the exotics from the colonies, the dwarf, the pig) and the 'disobedient and rebellious subjects' who, the respectable claimed, used the fairs as 'excuses for idleness and dissipation'. For the 'disobedient' subject as much as the dwarf or the pig was one of the socially inferior groups whose low status was displayed and celebrated at the fair. If, contrary to Bakhtin's view, there were critical divisions between spectator and spectacle, those divisions were constantly renegotiated and unstable, providing opportunity for symbolic acts of a self-consciously political kind.

It is not surprising, then, that bourgeois commentators felt uneasy, even as they delighted in 'a dance in imitation of a Footpad's Robbery', or a popular performance of *The Beggar's Opera* or *Robin Hood*. The enthusiastic familiarity shown by the crowd for the outlaw and the villain could easily carry a boisterous defiance or rowdy hostility to 'gentlemen' standing amongst them in the audience, as indeed was the case with the Merry Andrew whose first jest was 'a singular Instance of his Cleanliness, by blowing his Nose upon the People'. The liberties of the fair could always be articulated *politically* against the propertied and the State. In 1755, Bartholomew Fair hid boys who had escaped from Bridewell, and the following year a crowd from Smithfield 'mobbed the gates of Bridewell, and knocked down officers of the place' (Morley 1859: 450). And in the early nineteenth century radical politics and the fatness of fairground consumption came together in the cry of 'Walk into Wilkes's parlour', the cause of 'Liberty' being inscribed in the sausage-rooms which were named after the radical Wilkes (Morley 1859: 477). This political connection had lasted over half a century, from the time when

> The Southwark inns which staged the theatrical performances during the Southwark and Bartholomew fairs could readily switch their resources and expertise to more overt political activity. Indeed this is exactly what happened on 1 May 1769 in Lime Kiln Dock in Bristol, and on Whit Monday of the same year at St George's Fields, where traditional May and Whitsuntide activities were transformed into Wilkite fairs and festivities.
>
> (Brewer, in McKendrick *et al.* 1982: 242)

– there was never a guarantee that the 'low' spectator would not find his or her own radical identity in the 'low' spectacle of the fair.

We may return here to Bakhtin's central insight: that play, in the fair, is symbolic action which is rarely *mere* play: it articulates cultural and political meanings, and any simple elision of 'real' politics with the 'serious' consigns the subordinate classes to contesting state and class power within a problematic which has positioned them as ignorant, vulgar, uninitiated – as low. In fact 'low' knowledge frequently foregrounds not only the actual conditions of production but also the conditions of bodily pleasure. To define the grotesque, then, as a process of hybridization is not to neutralize its role as a kind of contestation. Rather it is to acknowledge that the grotesque tends to operate as a critique of a dominant ideology which has already set the terms, designating what is high and low. It is indeed one of the most powerful ruses of the dominant to pretend that critique can only exist in the language of 'reason', 'pure knowledge' and 'seriousness'. Against this ruse Bakhtin rightly emphasized the logic of the *grotesque*, of excess, of the lower bodily stratum, of the fair. This logic could unsettle 'given' social positions and interrogate the rules of inclusion, exclusion and domination which structured the social ensemble. In the fair, the place of high and low, inside and outside, was never a simple given: the languages of decorum and enormity 'peered into each other's faces' (Bakhtin 1968: 465).

THINKING WITH PIGS

In the previous section, we argued that Bakhtin shifts, sometimes unwittingly, between two different models of the grotesque and of the fair. In the first model, the grotesque is simply the opposite of the classical – it is the Other to the set of values and forms which make up the classical. In the second model, the grotesque is formed through a process of hybridization or inmixing of binary opposites, particularly of high and low, such that there is a heterodox merging of elements usually perceived as incompatible, and this latter version of the grotesque unsettles any fixed binaryism. It is this latter notion, we have argued, which is more adequate to thinking the complexity of high–low relations on the site of the fair.

•

Amongst the menagerie of fairground creatures, it was undoubtedly the pig which occupied a focal symbolic place at the fair (and in the carnival), and in this section we will attempt to sketch out a social semiotics of the pig in its relation to 'low' discourses, the body and the fair.

Fairs in which pigs were the sole or principal commodity were extremely rare in England and in Europe generally, largely because unlike sheep, horses and cattle, pigs cannot be driven over long distances and so were usually disposed of at small, weekly markets (or indeed, raised and slaughtered by cottagers themselves at home). The Haywards Heath Dolphin Fair in Sussex was remarked upon as very unusual for being a pig fair (Addison 1953: 154). On the other hand the symbolic importance of the pig at the fair and its long association with the festive scene have tempted commentators to view the pig and its 'low' significance as a fixed, transhistorical notion going back to 'time out of mind'.

From early records of Greek and Latin slang, where χοῖρος and *porcus* or *porcellus* were used to describe the female genitalia, through to modern uses of 'pig' to mock the police, the fascist and the male chauvinist, pigs seem to have borne the brunt of our rage, fear, affection and desire for the 'low'. Bakhtin's major advance in 'thinking pigs' was to recognize that the pig, like the fair itself, had in the past been *celebrated* as well as reviled. It was precisely the ambivalence of the pig, at the intersection of a number of important cultural and symbolic thresholds, which had traditionally made it a useful animal to think with. This ambivalence was certainly registered in classical usage. In Attic Comedy the description of the female genitalia as pig is often an aggressive form of degradation or violence – prostitutes were called χοιϱοπωλαι (pig merchants), and in *The Archanians*, χοιϱοι are pierced by meat-roasting spits; but also, according to Varro, *porcus* was above all 'a nursery word used by women, especially nurses, of the pudenda of little girls' (Henderson 1975: 72).

Certainly, a frequent cause of disgust was the pig's specific habits: its ability to digest its own and human faeces as well as other 'garbage'; its resistance to full domestication; its need to protect its tender skin from sunburn by wallowing in mud ('if deprived of mud, it has no choice but to control its hyperthermia by rolling in its own dung, and will even create a wallow by repeatedly urinating on a chosen spot in its pen' (Harrison 1982: 57). But the pig could also be praised as well as abused for its appetites. 'The utilitie and profit of them will easily wipe away [their] offence', wrote Gervase Markham in his *Cheape and Good Husbandry*:

> for to speake truely of the Swine, he is the Husbandmans best scavenger, and the Huswifes most wholesome sink.
>
> (Markham 1614: 87)

Pig-loathing is in no sense a cultural given. Indeed, the Tsembaga of New Guinea treat pigs as members of the family: piglets are led on leads to the gardens under cultivation; they are 'petted, talked to, and fed choice morsels'; until they are nearly a year old they live in the woman's house; and 'the climax of pig love is the incorporation of the pig as flesh into the flesh of the human host and of the pig as spirit into the spirit of the ancestors' (Rappaport 1968: 58; Harris 1978: 39).

But if the pig is not the fixed and universal object of human abuse, might it not be possible to sketch out a theory of its *ambivalence*?

This is what Edmund Leach attempts in 'Anthropological aspects of language: animal categories and verbal abuse', which remains one of the finest essays on the use of animals as social categories of thought. Leach emphasizes that taboos on animals are culturally specific. Many cultures eat dogs, for example, but in England

> Man and dogs are 'companions'; the dog is 'the friend of man'. On the other hand man and food are antithetical categories. Man is not food so dog cannot be food either.
>
> (Leach 1964: 32)

Leach believes that it is possible to construct cultural grids which will define *structurally* the fixed interrelations between animals, topography and human kinship in a given social system. Leach believes there is a direct connection between the grid of animal categories, the grid of spatial organization and the grid of kinship nomination. Taken together, these three grids 'discriminate areas of social space in terms of "distance from Ego (self)"', in the following manner:

(a)	Self	Sister	Cousin	Neighbour	Stranger	(KINSHIP)
(b)	Self	House	Farm	Field	Far	(TOPOGRAPHY)
(c)	Self	Pet	Livestock	'Game'	Wild Animal	(ANIMALS)

Leach argues that these three sets, or grids, are homologous: 'in other words, the way we employ the words in set (c), a set of animals, allows us to make statements about the human relationships which belong to set (a)' (1964: 36–7). Symbolically, one's siblings, one's house and one's pets are transformations of one another. At the same time, the end terms of each of the three sets, (a), (b), and (c), are supposedly stabilized by their opposition to each other: that is to say, the self is set over against the stranger, the far (forest), and the wild animal. Between the two ends of each set there is an area of ambiguity where the laws of incest and the boundaries of ownership become less clear. In the case of animals, Leach argues, ambiguity particularly attaches to pets and to game, and he sets up the following table:

p	both p and $\bar{p}$	$\bar{p}$
man	man–animal	not man
(not animal)	('pets')	(animal)
TAME	GAME	WILD
(friendly)	(friendly/hostile)	(hostile)

In Leach's view, the pig is a particularly striking example of the intermediate category: both 'man' and animal, friendly and hostile, the pig transgresses major oppositions and co-ordinates in the cultural grid. Indeed Leach's homologous sets would suggest that we can locate the ambivalence of the pig in its contradictory position within European agricultural practices. Not only did the pink pigmentation and apparent nakedness of the pig disturbingly resemble the flesh of European babies (thereby transgressing the man–animal opposition), but pigs were usually kept in peculiarly close proximity to the house and fed from the household's leftovers. In other words, pigs were *almost*, but not quite, members of the household and they *almost*, but not quite, followed the dietary regimes of humans.

Whereas animals which ate grass or berries could be thought of as part of a different habitat and different food system, the pig overlapped with, and confusingly debased, human habitat and diet alike. Its mode of life was not different from, but alarmingly imbricated with, the forms of life which betokened civility. It is precisely 'creatures of the threshold' which become the object of fear and fascination. Mixing faeces and food, human and animal, human skin and animal hide, the household and the farmyard and the field, the pig also lived to die – unlike sheep, cows and chickens, the pig was useful only to eat and, proverbially, only became valuable when dead. In 1564, Bullein wrote of 'covetous usurers, which be like fat unclean swine, which do never good until they come to the dish', and in 1621 William Mason argued that until the usurer 'come unto the earth, hee minds nothing but earthly things, like a Swine he never doeth good till his death' (Wilson 1983: 94). Moreover, the pig's death was particularly brutal. An Elizabethan manual recommends 'after he is brawned for your turn, thrust a knife into one of his flanks, and let him run with it till he die; [or] gently bait him with muzzled dogs' (Thomas 1983: 94). The pig then resembled a baby, lived in overlapping proximity to humans, ate similar food to its owners and yet, at the same time, it was perceived as a greedy scavenger fit only to be devoured.

Certainly then, Leach's essay helps us to understand some aspect of the multiple ambivalences of the pig in Europe and provides good reasons for its role as the low grotesque, a hybrid creature whose 'open-mouthed squeal' became such a powerful figure for the festive and sinister imaginary. Furthermore, Leach's essay confirms Bakhtin's occasional use of the grotesque of hybridization, the intense interfusion of incompatibles which was such anathema to classical reason, with its predilection for a rhetoric of clean antithesis.

However, Leach anchors his three grids, or sets (kinship, topography and animals) to a 'self' which, as the first term in all three sets, is implicitly located at the centre of an *agricultural* milieu. The topographical grid fans out from the self to 'house . . . farm . . . field . . . far'. If this 'self' is not a farmer or rural inhabitant, the topographical order of the grid is disturbed. Indeed, if the 'self' is an urban-dweller the 'farm' becomes 'far' and the sequence is actually inverted. Consequently the homology of space, kinship and animals will no longer hold when the 'self' changes place. Just as Bakhtin tended to elide the pig with its festive location at the fair, so Leach anchors the ambivalence of the pig in a topography mapped from the fixed perspective of the rural subject. He assumes a privileged site of discourse and meaning-making (the house, the rural self/ego) located in the agricultural domain. Consequently Leach's model does not help us to understand *changes* in the pig's semiotic function in early modern Europe as it was positioned and recoded from the perspective of *different* domains of discourse.

There can be no simple correlation between the pig and the threshold areas of the farmyard, for instance. Indeed, increasingly from the sixteenth century pigs were present and highly visible *in the city*. They wandered through the streets, sometimes biting and even killing small children: in 1608 the young Sir Hugh Cholmley was attacked by a sow. A Jacobean starchmaker kept 200 pigs in his London backyard, and as late as 1851 there were three pigs to every one person in the slums of North Kensington (Thomas 1983: 95; Dyos and Reeder 1973: 372). Did the pig's significance remain the same in town and country alike?

Fraser Harrison, in his fine book *Strange Land*, has argued persuasively to the contrary. In the country the pig had, in medieval times, been incorporated into the 'liturgy' of the *cochonnailles*, when friends and neighbours came together after the killing of the family pig between December and March. In the late nineteenth century in the countryside Flora Thompson could still describe the pig as 'an important member of the family' and its killing as 'a time to rejoice' (Goody 1982: 134; Harrison 1982: 63). But Harrison argues that as pigs were herded into the cities their symbolic ambivalence was slowly lost as they became more clearly objects of hatred, fear and abuse. If this was partly because the pig's dung was now a filthy nuisance on the city street rather than a useful source of manure and refertilization, it was also because the pig now stood 'as a sign of the gross immiseration of its fellow slum-dwellers' (Harrison 1982: 61). At the same time the pig was appropriated by the city underworld to describe the 'filth' from above, a particularly urban 'world upside down' political strategy which removed any trace of affectionate ambivalence from its symbolism. In the early nineteenth century the police (and especially the 'feared plainclothes man') were first called 'pigs' or 'grunters'. Harrison's view of the debased transformation of the pig's significance provides a striking analogy to Bakhtin's view of the historical transformation in attitudes to the grotesque, from praise—abuse to pure abuse. In this view we could say that the pig was symbolically shifted from the ambivalent low of the fair to the unambivalent low of the slum. We return to this shift in Chapter 3 below.

Harrison rightly emphasizes historical transformations and the difference which a change of domain makes to the creation of cultural grids, particularly the change from a rural to an urban milieu. In fact however, the semiotics of the pig is even more complex than Harrison allows, since he uses an over-simplified before/after model: first the pig is richly ambivalent, then it is merely demonized. Against such a model we would suggest that the pig, like the fair, is a site of competing, conflicting and contradictory definitions. It is not that pigs go to town and lose their rural ambivalence. It is rather that, in different domains of discourse, 'pigs' are constructed according to different grids or sets which, in the social ensemble taken as a whole, are often brought into conflict with each other. Since they articulate the symbolic and metaphorical resources of different classes and groups whose anchorage points occupy distinct and different sites and locations, they co-exist in an uneven and often incompatible way. Definitions could be produced in the slum as well as on the farm, but also in the Church, at the fair, in the theatre, or the study. Each domain structured its own complex and contradictory discursive practices. This is not to abandon the whole issue to a random relativism of arbitrary definitions in some free-for-all, since all *sites* of discursive practice are themselves ranked and valued. Certain sites of discourse belonging to dominant groups have privileged power to define and hierarchize all the other sites of discourse, and therefore have the power to proscribe or endorse the value of their utterances. Other sites, placed by the above into subordinate positions, may re-order, or subvert, this privileged ranking in a contestatory manner. Leach's model seems correct for the site of discourse which has the farm as its focal point. What it does not take into account is the relative location of that site of discourse in the competing ensemble of such meaning-producing sites in any given period.

The Church was another domain which produced and maintained its own significance for the pig – to think the pig an 'abomination' was certainly no innovation of the nineteenth century. Its uncleanness had been defined by Judaic dietary laws and its associations with sin were inscribed in Christian parable. The prodigal son was redeemed from his miserable life in the pig-sty. And nowhere is the demonization of the pig more literally enacted than in the story of Christ casting out the demons:

> And [Jesus] asked him, 'What is thy name?' And he answered, saying, 'My name is Legion: for we are many'. And he besought him much that he would not send them away out of the country. Now there was there nigh unto the mountains a great herd of swine feeding. And all the devils besought him, saying, 'Send us into the swine, that we may enter into them'. And forthwith Jesus gave them leave. And the unclean spirits went out, and entered into the swine: and the herd ran violently down a steep place into the sea (they were about two thousand,) and were choked in the sea.
>
> (St Mark 5: 9–13)

The 'unclean' spirits are *literally* displaced from man to pig which, in its turn, becomes the demonized extraterritorial, literally driven off into space from the edge of a cliff to become the pure outside.

With later Christian sermons, treatises and iconography, the pig became an emblem of greed, drunkenness and lechery. Alexander Barclay's version of *The Ship Of Fools* (1509) denounces 'immoderate vyleness' as characteristic of the pig:

> The swynes lyvynge we all ought to eschewe
> In worde and dede we ought to avoyde excesse.
>
> (1509: 265)

The woodcut which accompanies his chapter on 'foles abhomynable in fowle wordes of rybawdry', depicts a fool with a jester's cap leading a sow by the ear, 'His bestely lyfe of this vyle beste to lere':

> The hogge promotyd out of the myre and dust
> Vyle and ungoodly of body and usage
> Promotyth and admyttyth men after his lust
> The vylest settynge most hye upon his stage
> And some are so past shame in theyr langage
> So fowle and lothly, that they moste comenly
> Have all theyr wordes in viciouse rybawdry.
>
> (1509: 53–5)

If the 'ungodly' beast was associated with the corruption of language in this Christian attack on Folly, it was also associated with alcoholic derangement. A woodcut by Edward Schoen, depicting the 'Four Properties of Wine' (c. 1528), shows a group of drunkards vomiting whilst two pigs eat up the vomit, and a print after Bruegel shows a crowd pushing a drunken peasant into a pig-sty (Geisberg 1974: III, 1122; Hollstein 1954: III, 288). After the Reformation the pig became more specifically related to heresy or the corruption of 'pure' doctrine. A Bavarian print of 1569 entitled 'the origin and character of the swine who call themselves Jesuits', portrays Pope Paul IV as a disgusting old sow. The accompanying poem describes how the sow copulated with a dog, giving birth to Jesuit swine who were later taught by Pig, professor of Epicurean philosophy, to 'live in filthy luxury'. One of the final scenes in the print threatens the Jesuits with the fate of the Gadarene swine, which are shown leaping to their death in the sea (Kunzle 1973: 32). And in a German print of 1545 the Pope, with steaming excrement in his hand, rides on a sow (Scribner 1981: 83). The didactic moralism of these woodcuts and prints draws palpably on the carnivalesque tradition, but largely in order to turn it against itself, or to demonize a specific religious enemy. The prints harness the festive symbolism of the carnival pig to a discourse of sin and evil, seeking to arouse a moral panic around some ideological enemy.

If, within Christian discourse, the pig was usually emblematic of definable sin, from the seventeenth century it became increasingly associated by the bourgeoisie with offences against good manners. The pig was demonized less for its supposed evils than for its rustic boorishness from which polite citizens must dissociate themselves. In

Fielding's *Joseph Andrews*, the association of the mean-spirited Parson Trulliber with pigs probably implies less about his lack of Christian charity than about his rural ignorance and his gross physical appearance:

> The hogs fell chiefly to his care, which he carefully waited on at home, and attended to Fairs; on which occasion he was liable to many Jokes, his own Size being with much Ale rendered little inferior to that of the Beasts he sold.

> (Fielding 1742: 145)

Parson Adams, on the other hand, despite falling in the mire of the pig-sty, resolutely defends his loss of dignity with the cry 'nihil habeo cum Porcis' (Fielding 1742: 147). To have nothing in common with pigs – was not that the aim of every educated bourgeois subject – to get as far away from the smell of the pigsty as possible? Lewis Carroll's Alice may be occasionally nonplussed by the trans-mutations of Wonderland, but she knows where to draw the line, especially when it is between people and pigs: '"that's not at all a proper way of expressing yourself"', she tells the Duchess's baby as it grunts at her. '"If you're going to turn into a pig, my dear", said Alice seriously, "I'll have nothing more to do with you. Mind now"' (Carroll 1937: 70).

In *Great Expectations*, Pip, aspiring to leave behind his lowly village origins, arrives in London only to be confronted by what he had sought to escape:

> So I came into Smithfield; and the shameful place, being all asmear with filth and fat and blood and foam, seemed to stick to me. So, I rubbed it off with all possible speed by turning into a street where I saw the great black dome of Saint Paul's bulging at me from behind a grim stone building which a bystander said was Newgate prison.

> (Dickens 1861: 189)

Turning from the filth of the market (that 'shameful place') which sticks to him, Pip encounters only the grim institutions of Church and State, the instruments of correction and punishment with which his own life has become so entangled. With such 'reminders', it is scarcely surprising that the vagrant desires of the adult and the child should turn again to the pig, the fair and the market.

In the fair and the carnival, we would expect to find a quite different orientation toward the pig: in 'Carne-levare' the pig was celebrated; the pleasures of food were represented in the sausage and the rites of inversion were emblematized in the pig's bladder of the fool (the origin, incidentally, of our party balloons). Yet there is no sense in which the carnival and the fair can be taken as simply the antithetical sites to the Church and the State. Even in the carnival the pig was the locus of conflicting meanings. If the pig was duly celebrated, it could also become the symbolic analogy of scapegoated groups and demonized 'Others'. Like the pigs in the Venice carnival, which were chased across Piazza San Marco and stoned, in Rome Jews were forced into a race at carnival time and stoned by the onlookers (Burke 1978: 200). This similarity between the fate of Jews in Rome and the fate of pigs in Venice during carnival time points up a frequent association whereby the pig became a focus of what we call *displaced abjection*, the process whereby 'low' social groups turn their figurative and actual power, *not* against those in authority, but against those who are even 'lower' (women, Jews, animals, particularly cats and pigs).

It is not difficult to see why, in the case of Jews, the carnival 'celebration' centred on devouring pig could incorporate rituals of racist violence. Cultures, as both Lévi-Strauss and Mary Douglas have pointed out, are frequently identified and stigmatized through culinary habits which infract the taboos and culinary habits of the identifying group (the English mockery of the French as 'frogs'). The Jews, usually a 'low' and marginal group within European cultures, had been defined in popular Christian mythology as the *antithesis* of the pig: 'And the swine, though he divideth the hoof, and be clovenfooted, yet he cheweth not the cud; he is unclean to you. Of their flesh shall ye not eat, and their carcass shall ye not touch; they are unclean to you' (Leviticus 11: 7–8). By eliding the Jew with the pig the carnival crowd were producing a grotesque hybridization of terms expressly antithetical to each other according to the dietary rules of their victims who, at carnival time, would be self-excluded from the great pig-feast. This offensive transgression through 'grotesque realism', though in formal accordance with the symbolic procedures identified by Bakhtin, simply reaffirmed the existing dominance of Christian laws: it was far from challenging the dominant.

The conjunction of Jew and pig is particularly prominent in popular German anti-semitic prints. A late-fifteenth-century print from Nuremberg entitled 'The Jewish Sow', depicts a pig surrounded by Jews. Whilst one rabbi is saying 'We Jews should observe what we do with the sow', another is saying 'We must not forget that we are not allowed to eat pork, we are therefore yellow [skinned] and our breath stinks'. At the back of the sow, one Jew sucks its tail whilst another says 'Suck, dear brother Hartz, and I will blow up her arse' (Kunzle 1973: 24). A Frankfurt print of 1600, 'The Jewish Bathing House', shows an old Jew riding backwards on a sow, whilst one man sucks her teats and another eats her excrement. The caption asserts, 'you suck the milk, and gobble up the filth you find so delicious' (Kunzle 1973: 180). All these prints adapt carnivalesque rituals and symbolism to anti-semitic purposes. The 'Fête aux Cendres' (Ash Wednesday) was often symbolized by a figure blowing bellows into the arse, either of a fellow reveller, or an animal (there is an unusual carved *armoire* which depicts this in the Château de Montal at St Céré); riding backwards on a lowly animal, a 'skimmington ride', was also a carnivalesque form of ritual humiliation sometimes used in charivaris.

Hatred against the Jews at carnival time was further motivated by their potential association with the forces of Lenten abstinence, the traditional enemy of carnival. Feasting came before fasting, shroving before shriving, carnival before Lent. In all these pairings it was the second of each which was the officially dominant one, dictated as it was by the institutional power of the Church. There is good evidence, from studies of late medieval and early Renaissance songs about the traditional battle of carnival and Lent in France, that it was comparatively late (around the end of the fifteenth century) before the songs and rhymes celebrating the struggle took on any sort of convivial and celebratory tone: from the 'Bataille de Caresme et de Charnage' of the late thirteenth century, through Eustache Deschamps' 'Contre le Carême', there is conspicuous lack of good cheer, the tone being one of resignation to the hardship of 'jours maigres' (Chevalier 1982: 193–9). The carnival never took place very far from the steps of the church, and to the degree that the temporary rule of carnival was a cyclical event 'timetabled' by ecclesiastical time and the Church calendar, the latter always re-established itself and shadowed the former (the phonological resemblance between 'feast' and 'fast', 'shroving' and 'shriving', is revealing).

Thomas Platter, for instance, witnessed a confrontation between two processions as carnival drew to its close at Avignon in 1596. The first procession (which included transvestites and people in motley costume dressed as sailors, Italians, Spaniards and Alsatians) broke into houses and danced to the noisy clashing of cymbals; the second procession (whose participants were dressed as apostles, evangelists and saints) walked in an orderly manner around the churches. When the carnival crowd met the religious procession, 'they ceded the middle of the road to it'. 'Indeed', wrote Platter, 'they could do no less, for, I was assured, it was to obtain God's pardon for their folly that this procession was instituted' (Platter 1963: 76–8). But if Lent's triumphant defeat of carnival could not be stopped, the subordinate and vulnerable Jew *could* be derided and defeated, and the carnival crowd could displace the anger of its defeat by Lent onto the Lenten Jew, seen as pig-hating, parsimonious, anti-festive. In this way Jews became 'pigs' as easy substitutes for the Lenten Church, the 'outside' of carnival.

The Jew then was at times made an enforced symbolic focus to the jeering violence of carnival. Viewed as Lenten and closed, the Jew could be seen within early capitalism as a *calculating* enemy of carnival, a repressive bearer of cold rationality and profiteering individualism which ran counter to the communal spirit of free expenditure and careless exuberance characteristic of the festival. Hence Shylock's admonition to his daughter in *The Merchant of Venice*

> What, are there masques? Hear you me Jessica:
> Lock up my doors, and when you hear the drum
> And the vile squealing of the wry-necked fife,
> Clamber not you up to the casements then,
> Nor thrust your head into the public street
> To gaze on Christian fools with varnish'd faces;
> But stop my house's ears, I mean my casements;
> Let not the sound of shallow foppery enter
> My sober house. By Jacob's staff I swear
> I have no mind of feasting forth to-night
>
> (II.v. 28–37)

Just as the orifices of the house (the doors and windows) are locked up, so the orifices of the body are sealed off against the music and feasting outside. The sober house mirrors the sober head, contrasting with the 'varnish'd masks' outside in the protean revelry of the street. Yet interestingly, the sober and calculating Shylock is envisaged in the play as the cannibalistic butcher. In the common prints of the world turned upside down which circulated throughout the fairs and markets of early modern Europe, the pig is often shown as slitting the butcher's throat (Böhmer 1985: 58, 62, 64). Similarly, in *The Merchant of Venice*, the conventional victim threatens to become the butcher who will kill his oppressor. Shylock, then, would transform the Christian into the pig and, as Arabella tells Jude in Hardy's *Jude the Obscure*, pig's meat 'must be well bled and to do that he must die slow . . . Every good butcher keeps 'un bleeding long.' But, of course, Shylock's inversion of religious dominance is itself inverted: Christian carnival finally triumphs at the expense of the 'monstrous' Jew.

Even in carnival, then, as in official discourse, the pig could be the symbolic instrument, and even the victim, of demonization. However, alongside demonization in the carnival and the fair (as later, in the circus), there were two other fundamentally important symbolic processes at work: inversion (the world turned upside down), and hybridization. These two strategies are related, but not synonymous. The precise mobilization of any of these three symbolic processes (demonization, inversion, hybridization), or indeed their combination, cannot be predicted for any specific historical location, since they foreground diverse ways of manipulating cultural classifications and particularly the relationship between social strata of 'high' and 'low'.

Inversion addresses the social classification of values, distinctions and judgements which underpin practical reason and systematically inverts the relations of subject and object, agent and instrument, husband and wife, old and young, animal and human, master and slave. Although it re-orders the terms of a binary pair, it cannot alter the terms themselves. It is commonly found in popular woodcuts and prints and its most frequent representation is 'the world turned upside down' (*die verkehrte Welt; le monde renversé; il mondo alla rovescia*) which we mentioned above. In these woodcuts and prints, relations of power and dominance are reversed and the pig butchers the butcher; the ass whips its laden master; the mice chase the cat; the deer and the rabbit pursue the huntsman; the servant rides on a horse followed by the king on foot; the general is inspected by the private; the woman stands with a gun in her arms whilst the husband sits spinning; the wife holds her husband down and beats him, the daughter feeds her mother, the son rocks his father in the cradle (Kunzle 1978; Böhmer 1985).

A set of forty-eight playing cards made in Germany about 1535 from designs by Peter Flötner depicts, in the land of Cockayne, many such popular inversions. One of the suits is of acorns (pig feed) and on one of these cards two pigs are holding a cradle in their mouths and rocking a pile of excrement; on another they are roasting a pile of excrement on a spit and on another they are devouring it. The playing cards depict that important aspect of the inverted festive world which celebrated filth and excrement – here in a mocking appropriation of the activities of nursing and the preparation of food (Geisberg 1974: III, 817–20).

The play which inverted the hierarchy that elevated human above animal could always be mobilized more or less politically, more or less self-consciously, as a direct message about social inequality. The peasant carnival 'kingdoms' (carnival groups, each with its own totemic symbol and commanding fierce allegiance) of Romans in 1580, for instance, represented their own subordination through the choice of the animals after which they were named (the hare, the sheep, the capon [a castrated fowl]). But as they danced through the streets in that particularly fateful year when the carnival was to turn to rebellion and bloodshed, they proclaimed 'that the rich of their town had grown rich at the expense of the poor people' (Le Roy Ladurie 1981: 174). Similarly one peasant leader of the German Peasants' War of 1525 described himself as 'a beast that usually feeds on roots and wild herbs, but when driven by hunger, sometimes consumes priests, bishops, and fat citizens' (Kunzle 1978: 63). Inversion, so dominant a feature of carnival and fairground acts, could be mobilized then as a way of remodelling social relations. Yet for all its political potential, inversion, at least in most forms, shares with demonization the acceptance of the existing binary categories of high and low, although where demonization depended upon strategies of exclusion, inversion celebrated excluded elements and the lower terms of a diacritical pairing.

Hybridization, a second and more complex form of the grotesque than the simply excluded 'outside' or 'low' to a given grid, produces new combinations and strange instabilities in a given semiotic system. It therefore generates the possibility of shifting *the very terms of the system itself*, by erasing and interrogating the relationships which constitute it. In practice we often find hybridization, inversion and demonization mixed up together. In 1833, for instance, 'Toby the Real Learned Pig' was presented at Bartholomew Fair as the 'Unrivalled Chinese Swinish Philosopher' (a designation which in itself combines racial demonization, inversion of high and low (philosophy/bestiality)and hybridization (Toby performed various 'learned' tasks)). Indeed, Toby's learning was prodigious:

He will spell, read, and cast accounts, tell the points of the sun's rising and setting, discover the four grand divisions of the Earth, kneel at command, perform blindfold with twenty handkerchiefs over his eyes, tell the hour to a minute by a watch, tell a card, and the age of any party. He is in colour the most beautiful of his race, in symmetry the most perfect, in temper the most docile. And when asked a question he will give an immediate answer.

(Morley 1859: 480)

Paul Bouissac describes a modern circus act which gives a more detailed example of how the pig could function within the grotesque aesthetic, though still operating through forms of hybridization and inversion. In the act, the 'August' (a clown who is normally tramp-like, 'ill shaven, ill combed, ill behaved . . . inarticulate' (Bouissac 1976: 164)), puts on 'grotesque' female clothes with huge artificial bosoms and enters carrying a 'baby' in a blanket. The 'baby' starts screaming and a vast bottle of milk is brought in with a rubber pipe connected to it, through which the infant rapidly sucks all the milk. When the baby cries again, August picks it up and the audience suddenly discovers that the baby is actually a piglet:

Sometimes the act is expanded in the following manner: . . . either because [the piglet] keeps shrieking or because the August wants to engage in some other temporary action, he trusts his charge to a 'spectator' or circus hand. Then the piglet abundantly 'urinates' on its new guardian and is carried away, still dripping . . .

(Bouissac 1982: 11)

Paul Bouissac treats this act in terms of 'the profanation of the sacred': the mother is transformed into the grotesque August, the baby into a piglet, the child's cries become squeals and grunts. The act, Bouissac notes, depends upon foregrounding similarities which are culturally suppressed. We have already seen how often aspects of the human world are coded through perceived homologies with the pigs' world, particularly those qualities which are denied or negated as being supposedly antithetical to the civilized world (dirt, greed, indiscriminate appetite). These qualities, of course, are frequently found in babies, and the circus act, by forcing the audience to acknowledge the interchangeability of pig and baby (for a time the audience could not tell the difference), transgresses the human/animal distinction in such a way as to allow the audience to enjoy what it had always 'known' but found it difficult to acknowledge except in moments of frustration: that there is no clear separation of the human from the animal, that the squealing, urinating baby is, in the language of praise-and-abuse, a little pig (the vicious attitude displayed to 'the Baby' by Punch, who tosses it out of the window when it cries, perhaps has an analogous function). Indeed, even the diet of pigs bears an interesting resemblance to the diet of children. In North-West England, the word 'kets' which to adults means 'garbage', has been redefined by children to refer to their most valued consumables, which, unlike adult meals, can be eaten at any time of the day (James 1982). The circus act transgresses and interrogates the norms of adult civility by forcing the audience to acknowledge what it has repressed in order to become what it is.

FAIRS, THEATRES, AUTHORS

When Bakhtin came to consider the connection between the fair and 'textualization', its informing representation in (literary, theatrical and other) written texts, he also moved uneasily between two distinct models. In the first, he assumed that the carnival, the fair and the literary texts of the Renaissance which he termed 'carnivalesque' were actually *homologous* – different versions or embodiments of a common folk humour and folk culture. Bakhtin tended to move indifferently across a number of diverse domains of symbolic action and discourse, bringing together rituals (aristocratic pageants and triumphal entries as well as comic shows of the marketplace); comic verbal compositions (Latin as well as vernacular texts); the 'various genres of Billingsgate' (curses, oaths, slang epithets, crude and practical jokes); and also literary texts such as *Gargantua* and *Pantagruel*.

This collapse of the fair into the literary text and vice versa is understandable given Bakhtin's struggle to free Rabelais from a literary history which read the past only in terms of its 'official framework' (Bakhtin 1968: 132). Against such diverse literary historians as Abel Lefranc and Lucien Lefebvre, Bakhtin emphasized the formation of the Rabelaisian text in the context of popular cultural activities and languages which leave few traces and are generally ignored. To read Rabelais exclusively through the high literary codes of the dominant classes was, Bakhtin argued, to condemn oneself to at most a half-truth, since even the dominant codes could only be fully understood in relation to their active negotiation with low discourses.

In his second model however, Bakhtin avoids a misleading elision of 'real' fairs and written literary texts, by emphasizing the 'dialogic' interrelation of different discourses, showing how Rabelais brings the 'high' languages of classical learning, medicine, theology and the Court into a relativizing dialogue with the low languages of the fair and the marketplace. Here, by revealing the centrality of carnival-esque tropes and structures in Rabelais, Bakhtin at least avoided the problem of the *difference* between popular festive rituals and the literary appropriation of such rituals, by treating the former as *thematic repertoires* available for use in the written text. There were certain tactical gains to be made through this strategy, not least the cutting of conventional disciplinary boundaries such as to re-open the literary to a political dialogue with the non-literary, thereby refusing to accept the ideologically motivated closure of literary studies.

Even in this second model however, Bakhtin never sufficiently clarified the key issue of *distinct discursive domains*, and the connection which these domains – each with its own languages and symbolic practices – had with each other. It is not sufficient to think of the relationship between, say, a book of fiction and a rural market fair as either an homology or as one of thematic reflection. The question of the actual formation of separate domains, such as authorship and popular festivity, cannot be taken for granted. It is not the case that discursive material is transmitted intact between existing, fully-formed discursive spaces which act as donors or hosts. *Whole domains* are constructed in interconnection with each other. The symbolic domain of 'authorship' as it emerged in the late sixteenth century was produced *over against* the popular, as embodied in the festive scene of the fair and the carnival and as embodied in the popular drama. As we shall see in detail below, in a consideration of Ben Jonson's *Bartholomew Fair*, there can be no question of understanding that play either as an homology of the 'real' Bartholomew Fair, or as a mere thematic pillaging of popular custom by an aloof and appropriative high culture. Sites and domains of discourse, like the theatre or the author's study or the marketplace, are *themselves* hierarchized and ranked, emerging out of an historical complex of competing domains and languages each carrying different values and kinds of power. Writing about a fair, as we shall see, could be as much an act of dissociation from, as a sign of engagement with, its festive space.

Bouissac commented upon the 'profanation of the sacred' through inversion and hybridization: if this was foregrounded in the fair and the circus, was it not also central to the emergence of the secular theatre in early modern England? Its enemies certainly thought so. If Zeal-of-the-Land Busy in *Bartholomew Fair* proclaimed that it was 'prophane, as being the page of pride and the waiting woman of vanity', so, in a more serious vein, did Grindal, then Bishop of London, request the Privy Council to close the theatres in 1564 since 'goddes worde by [the actors'] impure mouthes is prophaned, and turned into scoffes'.

Whilst the godly railed at the theatre for its idolatry and its impiety, the State, even as it patronized the actors, feared their potential for sedition and subversion. Kett's Rebellion of 1549 followed the assembly of a large crowd at Wymondham, Norfolk, to see a 'plaie'. Immediately after the rebellion there was a proclamation banning all plays 'in the English tongue' since 'most contain matter tendying to sedicion and contempnying of sundry good orders and lawes'. In 1597, Elizabeth I ordered all theatres to be closed because of the 'verie great disorders' which the 'lewd matters' of plays encouraged, and because the theatres were the 'resorte and confluence of bad people'. Not only were the theatres, like the fairs, thought of by the authorities as irreligious and seditious, but, it was claimed, in 'being spectacles of pleasure, too commonly expressing lascivious mirth and levity', they encouraged 'great wasting both of time and thrift' (Wickham 1963: 67, 77, 95; 1972: 10). In 1764, John Wesley wrote to the Mayor and Corporation of Bristol objecting to the proposed new theatre in the city:

> Most of the present stage entertainments sap the foundations of all religion, as they naturally tend to efface all traces of piety and seriousness out of the minds of men; but . . . they are peculiarly hurtful to a trading city, giving a wrong turn to youth especially, gay, trifling, and directly opposite to the spirit of industry and close application to business.
>
> (Quoted in Wickham 1963: 23)

The theatre's 'games' and plays' (until the end of the sixteenth century the words were interchangeable) were perceived by many of the 'better sort' as pagan entertainments indistinguishable from fairs, where the godly would only find 'sinfull, heathenish, lewde, ungodly Spectacles, and most pernicious Corruptions' (quoted in Wickham 1963: 95).

Well into the eighteenth century, as we shall explore further in the next chapter, there were intimate connections between the fair and the theatre. Indeed the shows of the fair included many theatrical 'shows', and nowhere is the complex interconnection of theatre, fair and authorship more evidenced than in Ben Jonson's *Bartholomew Fair*.

Both Smithfield and Jonson's play, initially at least, seem to conform to the tradition of the world upside down, in which authority may be easily challenged, excessive feasting and drinking threaten order and decorum and where a multiplicity of languages (in Jonson's play, Irish, Welsh, North Country, West Country dialects, Latin, Biblical prophecy and Billingsgate obscenity) clash and commingle. Edmund Wilson was not, perhaps, entirely mistaken in viewing the play as a 'pig-wallow' (Wilson 1948: 216–17): the problem, rather, was that he failed to understand the significance of the pig.

The pig is the centre of Jonson's text, as it was also the centre of the Smithfield fair, and in this play we can see the intertextual dialogue between almost all of the various symbolic views and strategies which we have explored so far. Ideological combat is enjoined around the pig which becomes the site of competing definitions and desires. Ursula's pig-booth probably occupied a dominant position at stage left, which had been traditionally the location of Hellmouth. Above her booth hangs 'the Pig's head with a large writing under it' (III.ii. 51), and it is to the pig's head that nearly all the play's characters are drawn to eat, drink, conceal stolen goods, urinate, and quarrel. Indeed, it is Win-the-Fight Littlewit's supposed desire for pig which sets the plot in motion. And as Win's husband tells her, once she has 'begun with pig' she may 'long for anything' (III.vi. 8–9) – including hobby-horses, drums, rattles, the bull with five legs and the great hog.

In *Bartholomew Fair*, the simplest manipulation of the pig's symbolism is as an emblem of moral corruption within Christian discourse. Dame Purecraft (her name suggesting the slide between the purity of her craft and the craftiness of her purity) asks her daughter Win, 'What polluted one was it that named first the unclean beast, pig, to you child?', and she detects in the 'fleshly motion of pig', with its 'carnal provocations', the workings of 'the Wicked Tempter' (I.vi. 8–17). The proverbial filth of the pig is here but a synecdoche for sexual desire, the longings of the flesh. Similarly, Justice Overdo finds in 'punk and pig' alike 'the fatness of the fair' (II.v. 41; II.ii. 112), and he censors that fatness in Ursula, 'the sow of enormity'.

This rhetorical equation between pig, sexuality and greedy incontinence invoked by Overdo and Dame Purecraft does not hold for the Puritan, Zeal-of-the-Land Busy. Indeed, rather surprisingly, the pig (not without satirical irony) is a relative good in Busy's cosmology: 'Now pig, it is meat, and a meat that is nourishing, and may be longed for, and so consequently eaten' (I.vi. 46–9). Busy's words telescope logical connection to make the shortest link between appetite and satisfaction. For Busy, abomination is to be found not in the real meat but in the *symbolization* of the meat. To transform a pig into a Bartholomew pig is, he claims, the sin of idolatry (and this makes eating it rather problematical). But the fact that the pig is always-already situated in various symbolic systems (one might say, following contemporary critical fashion, that no pig is innocent) gives Busy a way out of his dilemma. Since pork is taboo within Judaism, he will mark the difference of the godly from the Jews 'by publicly eating of swine's flesh' (I.vi. 88–9). He will thereby liberate a very nourishing meat from its contamination by idolatrous symbolic structures. At one level then, Busy repeats the manoeuvre of *Christian* carnival which we saw above, demonizing the 'Lenten Jew'. But Busy is a hypocritical Puritan and makes a pig of himself in his sophistical defence of his own appetites – and he is elided not only with the pig but with the Jew whom he uses and scorns for he is called 'Rabbi Busy'.

The absurdity of Busy lies not only in the theological niceties which enable him to satisfy his greed but also in his futile attempts to separate out the literal from the symbolic. His journey to the fair takes on something of the quality of the Catholic pilgrimages which he would anathematize. As the pilgrim travelled to the place of holy relics, so Busy travels to Ursula's tent, where the prophane sacrament of pig awaits him. As the true believer zealously pursues the good, so, a stage direction tells us, Busy 'scents after [pig] like a hound' (III.ii. 63). Indeed, pig becomes Busy's supreme good: as he tells Knockem, 'Only pig was not comprehended in my admonition' (III.vi. 26). And like the god who kept Herbert in a 'repining restlessness', the pig awakens in Busy a desire which can never be sated: 'more pig? there is no more', he declares. '. . . Is there?' It is Busy who fantasizes the 'lubberland' or Land of Cockaigne which Littlewit dismissively conjures up as a place where the pig will 'run off o' the spit into our mouths' (III.ii. 69).

At the fair, the pig which the 'pure' have demonized and excluded returns as that which is voraciously desired and devoured. The ambivalence of the pig is organized above all around Ursula, the pig-woman. She is belly, womb, gaping mouth, udder, the source and object of praise and abuse. Above all, like the giant hog displayed at the fair, she is *excessive*. Like the pigs which she roasts, her element is grease: she is a 'walking sow of tallow' (II.v. 70–1), 'a whole shire of butter' (II.v. 89), and her language is 'greasier than her pigs' (II.v. 121). As she walks she lards the ground: 'I am all fire and fat . . . I do water the ground in knots as I go, like a great garden-pot; you may follow me by the S's I make' (II.ii. 51–2). But the sweat which pours from her is only one of the many ways in which she transgresses the 'closed, smooth and impenetrable surface of the classical body' (Bakhtin 1968: 317). She is the celebrant of the open orifice: her pores are open as is her mouth when she roars out for a 'bottle of ale to quench me' or for her pipe to suck or when she spits forth a mouth-filling oath. Bakhtin comments as follows on the mouth, the belly, the anus and the genitals which dominate the grotesque image of the body:

> All these convexities and orifices have a common characteristic; it is within them that the confines between bodies and between the body and the world are overcome: there is an interchange and an interorientation. This is why the main events in the life of the grotesque body, the acts of the bodily drama, take place in this sphere. Eating, drinking, defecating and other elimination (sweating, blowing the nose, sneezing) as well as copulation, pregnancy, dismemberment, swallowing up of another body – all of these acts are performed on the confines of the outer world . . .
>
> (Bakhtin 1968: 317)

In Ursula the overcoming of the confines between bodies, and between the body and the world, is dramatized. She is, indeed, the *go-between*, not only in her role as bawd and as the mediator between the fairgoers and food, but also in the symbolic functioning of her bodily processes which move continuously between the inner and the outer. At the same time, the boundaries of the body, gender and status are destabilized. Whilst in the learned pig, human intelligence is ascribed to the animal, in Ursula's discourse, animals and humans are interchangeable. Her tapster Mooncalf is a 'stote', a 'vermin', a 'thin, lean, polecat', a 'weasel', whilst Quarlous is a 'hedgebird', a 'dog's-head', a 'treandle-tail' [mongrel].

Not only does Ursula's own body undergo a series of metamorphoses but she is also the agent of the transformation of others. Around her tent, food, drink, sex, urine and even property in the form of Edgeworth's stolen goods, constantly circulate. In her tent, Win-the-Fight is transformed into a punk, and Mistress Overdo into a vomiting drunk. From outside her booth, the religious censor, Busy, the educational censor, Wasp, and the state censor, Overdo, are taken away to be put in the stocks. As in *Measure for Measure*,

> Liberty plucks justice by the nose;
> The baby beats the nurse, and quite athwart
> Goes all decorum.
>
> (I.iii. 29–31)

But whereas in *Measure for Measure*, the disguised Duke returns to restore that lost decorum, in *Bartholomew Fair* the disguised Justice is silenced and ends up by inviting the whole fair (cutpurse, bawds and all) to further feasting at his house (on the disguised ruler in early Jacobean drama, see the fine essay by Tennenhouse, 'Representing power: *Measure for Measure* in its time': 1982). Ursula, the 'sow of Smithfield' (IV.v. 71), the 'mother o' the pigs' (II.v. 68), moves out from the fair to enter and transform the space of official law and order, uncontainable within any one of the discursive confines applied to her, comprehensible here as the confounder of the closed, hierarchical and strictly individuated classical body.

SMITHFIELD AND AUTHORSHIP: BEN JONSON

In the last chapter of *Rabelais and his World*, Bakhtin argues that 'the literary and linguistic consciousness of the Renaissance' was formed 'at a complex intersection of languages, dialects, idioms and jargons':

> The primitive and naive coexistence of languages and dialects had come to an end; the new consciousness was born not in a perfected and fixed linguistic system but at the intersection of many languages and at the point of their most intense interorientation and struggle. Languages are philosophies – not abstract but concrete, social philosophies, penetrated by a system of values inseparable from living practices and class struggle. This is why every object, every concept, every point of view, as well as every intonation found their place at this intersection of linguistic philosophies and was drawn into an intense ideological struggle.
>
> (Bakhtin 1968: 470–1)

This dialogic emphasis on what Bakhtin called *heteroglossia* is a more powerful and useful model of cultural formation than his earlier model of popular symbolism simply 'emerging' out of the literary text. The dialogic model inscribes the discourse of the fair within the wider, contestatory arena of the social formation. No one was more conscious of that arena of 'intense ideological struggle' than Jonson. Indeed, Jonson's specific intervention in that struggle contributed significantly to the construction of the domain of 'authorship' in the period. And the notion of 'authorship' to which Jonson dedicated his poetic career was in every way in contradiction to Saturnalia, the grotesque, even to the theatre itself.

There is no easy sense in which Jonson's work can be considered as an extension of the fair or as an immediate 'copy' of popular symbolic practices. On the contrary: all of Jonson's critical comments are resolutely directed against the popular audience and the 'hacks' whom he saw as serving it. If Jonson's early life had been spent 'as an apprentice brick-layer, then as a soldier in Flanders, and finally (and most significantly) as a common player and play patcher' (Helgerson 1983: 145), his career as laureate poet was spent in scourging players, play-patchers and 'groundlings'. In the 1607 preface to *Volpone*, he attacks the 'licence' of those mere playwrights who debase 'stage-poetry'; in the 1612 preface to *The Alchemist*, he derided those plays in which 'the concupiscence of dances and of antics so reigneth'. By contrast he proclaimed his own writing to be 'quick comedy refined' or 'a legitimate poem' or 'one such as other plays should be'. Again and again, Jonson defines the true position of the playwright as that of the poet, and the poet as that of the classical, isolated judge standing in opposition to the vulgar throng. In this, of course, he was not alone. Few 'serious' poets prided themselves on their plays. Drayton, for instance, 'who had a hand in some two dozen plays, kept all but one from publication and even that one appeared anonymously' (Helgerson 1983: 146).

But whilst even such 'elevated' forms of writing as George Chapman's translation of Homer were dismissed by their authors as 'the droppings of an idle humour; far unworthy the serious expense of an exact gentleman's time', Jonson strove to tell the world, as Suckling put it, that 'plainly he deserved the bays, / For his were called *Works*, where others were but plays' (quoted in Helgerson 1983: 21, 37). But the problem remained: who did 'the author' (itself a problematic concept) write *for*? Who were to be his judges? With extraordinary vituperative energy, Jonson proceeded to answer these questions by a series of negations. *Bartholomew Fair* itself provides an illuminating example of Jonson at work. The title page of the 1631 edition contains the following quote from Horace's epistles: 'If Democritus were still in the land of the living, he would laugh himself silly, for he would pay far more attention to the audience than to the plays, since the audience offers the more interesting spectacle. But as for the authors of the plays – he would conclude that they were telling their tales to a deaf donkey' (trans. Hibbard, see Jonson 1977: 2). The title page is followed by a prologue 'To the King's Majesty', in which the 'place', the 'men' and the 'language' of the play are mockingly excused as appropriate to a fair.

And then, mediating between the reading-text and the perform-ance-text, we are presented with 'The Induction on the Stage', in which Jonson dramatizes the relationship between the author and the fair and between the author and the text. As Jonson demons-trates, the question of whom he writes for (which kind of audience?), what he writes, and how it is to be judged are intimately connected. The Induction opens with the Stage-keeper, whose function is to sweep the stage and to gather up 'the broken apples' (Jonson 1977: *Ind.*: 50) for the bears who alternated with the actors as the attraction of the Hope Theatre. The Stage-keeper appeals to 'the understanding gentlemen o' the ground' (*Ind.*: 47) – i.e. to the groundlings who stood under the stage – against 'these master-poets' who 'will ha' their own absurd courses' and 'will be informed of nothing' (*Ind.*: 25–26). Jonson's play, he claims, 'is like to be a very conceited scurvy one':

> When it comes to the Fair once, you were e'en as good go to Virginia for anything there is of Smithfield. He has not hit the humours, he does not know 'em; he has not conversed with the Bartholomew-birds.
>
> (*Ind.*: 9–12)

The Stage-keeper's first accusation, then, is that Jonson is simply ignorant of Smithfield. But from attacking Jonson for failing to represent the sights of the fair, he moves to a second accusation: that Jonson has failed in the very methods of his representation. 'In Master Tarlton's time' – in other words, in the age of the improvising clown – things were done better. And the radical break between Tarlton's theatre and Jonson's can be accounted for by the shift from improvisation to 'master-poets' who stand above and detached from their audiences and thus are as incapable of representing the fair on stage as they are of understanding it at Smithfield.

The 'free' conversation of the Stage-keeper with his 'familiars', though, is ended by the entrance of the Book-holder and the

Scrivener. As Jonathan Haynes writes in his fine essay on *Bartholomew Fair*:

> The opposition between the popular and coterie theatres is perfectly expressed in this moment: groundlings vs. gentlemen; the Stage-keeper with his memories of an improvisational theatre vs. the Book-holder and Scrivener, men of the master-poet's written text.

(Haynes 1984: 659)

In contrast to the Stage-keeper's familiarity, the Scrivener proceeds to read out a legal contract which will define the obligations of author and audience alike. In fact, this contract is a mock-version of the critical positions which Jonson had ferociously argued in his previous work. As before, these positions are defined negatively. In the contract, the author attacks those who admire old plays like *The Spanish Tragedy* and *Titus Andronicus*, for although that betrays 'a virtuous and staid ignorance' it is still 'a confirmed error' (*Ind.*: 106–71); he attacks contemporary playwrights, like Shakespeare, for their Calibans, their drolleries, their 'concupiscence of dances and of antics' (*Ind.*: 122–7); he attacks informers who would read his plays as political allegories (*Ind.*: 130–40); he attacks those who confuse the author's morality with the scurrility and profanity of his characters (*Ind.*: 143–7).

But above all, the contract attempts to define the nature of Jonson's 'public' (see Salingar 1979: 151–2). On the one hand, the 'Articles of Agreement' insist that the audience is composed of free, rational individuals and that 'every man here exercise his own judgement, and not censure by contagion, or upon trust' (*Ind.*: 94–5). On the other hand, the articles emphasize the division of the audience into separate classes. The patricians, who are themselves divided into 'the curious and envious' and 'the favouring and judicious', are set against the plebeians with their '*grounded* judgments and understandings' (*Ind.*: 72–3). (It is worth noting how the contract punningly conflates rational judgement and the physical positions of the plebeians who 'stood under' on the 'ground', but the conflation is intended only to act as a reminder of the abyss between the author and the vulgar. In the Latin tag on the title page of his *Workes* (1616), Jonson proudly announced that he did not write for the crowd but for the readership of a select few.) But if the audience is divided into patrician and plebeian on an imaginary scale of 'wit', it is also divided more crudely between those who can afford to pay for the expensive seats and those who cannot. And Jonson is mockingly prepared to let each spectator buy his or her right to proclaim judgement: 'it shall be lawful for any man to judge his six penn'orth, his twelve penn'orth, so to his eighteen pence, two shillings, half a crown to the value of his place' (*Ind*.: 84–5). The juxtaposition of judgement and money is curious, though, a reminder that the author, for all his contempt, is a bought man, dependent for his success upon the applause of conflicting social groups. And even as the author attempts to situate his audience, he himself is positioned in multiple and contradictory ways.

Moreover, the very notion of contract which the Induction proposes is subverted in the play which follows. The contract of marriage between Grace Wellborn and the simpleton Bartholomew Cokes is stolen by Edgworth; Justive Overdo's contract to Grace, whom he bought from the Court of Wards, is rewritten by Quarlous in his own favour; Busy makes himself 'feofee in trust to deceased brethren' (V.ii. 65–6) so as to cozen their heirs. In *Bartholomew Fair*, to insist upon contract is to be mad or a fool. It is the lunatic Trouble-All who makes repeated demands to see the fairgoers' licences: 'Have you a warrant?' (IV.i. 98); 'Whither go you? Where's your warrant?' (IV.ii. 2); 'There must be a warrant had, believe it' (IV.iii. 69). And Justice Overdo's attempts to track down the unwarranted, unlicensed doings of the fair lead only to a cudgelling and the stocks. Similarly, Busy's insistence on the godly contract which prohibits 'Fairs and May-games, Wakes and Whitsun-ales' (IV.vi. 81–2) as well as 'stage-players, rhymers, and morris-dancers' (V.v. 9–10) lands him in the stocks.

In the fair, 'judgement' belongs not to the enforcers of contract but to the cutpurse, the bawd, the ballad-singer and the hobby-horse seller. And in the judgements of the fair, it is the language of the grotesque body which triumphs over the languages of the Scriptures and of the classics. No Latin tags come to Justice Overdo's aid as he is confronted by his drunk wife vomiting, and no Biblical wisdom helps Busy when the puppet Dionysius pulls up his/her skirt to ridicule 'all fundamentalist distinctions between male and female, righteous and unrighteous, saved and damned' (Barish 1972: 29). It is as if in silencing the censors (Overdo, Busy, Wasp), Jonson is silencing the classical satiric voice of the 'master-poet', a voice for which he, above all contemporary writers, was responsible. Indeed, even in the Induction where Book-holder and Scrivener assert the authority of the author's text over the actor's performance, Jonson seems aware that here, for once, he may have produced a play which is in keeping with the grotesque, saturnalian traditions of the Elizabethan theatre. Although the 'rascal' Stage-keeper is dismissed, the Book-holder tells us that the play is written for his understanding and to 'the scale' of the plebeian audience. It is, the Induction rightly claims, a play as 'full of noise as sport' (79), suited to the Hope, sometimes theatre, sometimes bear-pit, a place 'as dirty as Smithfield, and as stinking every whit' (154).

But this returns us to the contradictions out of which Jonson's 'authorship' was formed. To the extent that *Bartholomew Fair* was a *popular* play, Jonson could scarcely claim it as his own. For within a classical aesthetic, the text was 'contaminated' both by its subject-matter and by its relation to the 'dirt' of the theatre and the theatrical marketplace. This second form of 'contamination' is also imagined by Shakespeare when he is writing in the more 'elevated' form of the sonnet, a form inscribed within a network of aristocratic traditions and patronage:

> O for my sake do you wish fortune chide
> The guilty goddess of my harmful deeds,
> That did not better for my life provide
> Than public means which public manners breeds.
> Thence comes it that my name receives a brand,
> And almost thence my nature is subdued
> To what it works in, like the dyer's hand.
>
> (*Sonnet 111*)

Jonson wrote obsessively about the contaminating influence of 'public means' and 'public manners', and resented more than Shakespeare the 'brand' which dubbed him a mere playwright. But in *Bartholomew Fair*, Jonson was 'subdued' not only by the Hope audience but also, from the perspective of a classical aesthetic, by his own choice of subject-matter. One consequence of this choice was the kind of arduous labour which Dryden, for instance, undertook to separate Jonson from his material. In Dryden's view, *Bartholomew Fair* is the 'lowest kind of comedy', but then Jonson 'does so raise his matter . . . as to render it delightful'. Jonson has made 'an excellent lazar of the fair' and 'the copy is of price, though the original be vile' (Dryden 1966: 74–5). But however much the author may be praised for his act of 'elevation', a classical aesthetic remains deeply suspicious of saturnalian comedy: however brilliant, it is 'the lowest kind', however excellent, it is a 'lazar', a beggar with some loathsome disease all too liable to be contagious. Perhaps it was *Bartholomew Fair* which Dryden had in mind when he published *A Parallel of Poetry and Painting* in 1695. There again he approaches comedy as 'a representation of human life in inferior persons, and low subject', comparable to 'the painting of clowns' or 'the representation of a Dutch kermis'. And again, Dryden returns to the image of a diseased beggar: comedy is 'a Lazar in comparison to a Venus'. But here, Dryden goes on to imagine an even lower form of art: farce or 'the grotesque'. The grotesque is 'a very monster in a Bartholomew Fair, for the mob to gaze at for their two-pence'. And laughter itself is now conceptualized as lazar-like:

> Laughter is indeed the propriety of a man, but just enough to distinguish him from his elder brother with four legs. 'Tis a kind of bastard pleasure too, taken in at the eyes of the vulgar gazers, and at the ears of the beastly audience.
>
> (Dryden 1926: 132–3)

What justification can there be, then, for the grotesque or even for comedy? Dryden's answer is that plays serve a *political* function. He concludes his discussion of the grotesque by quoting Davenant's preface to *Gondibert*:

> 'Tis the wisdom of a government to permit plays [he might have added – farces] as 'tis the prudence of a carter to put bells upon his horses, to make them carry their burthens cheerfully.
>
> (Dryden 1926: 133)

We have moved a long way from Jonson's concept of the true dramatist as the corrector of ignorance and vice: for Davenant *all* plays, and for Dryden comedies in particular, are legitimate only as placebos, suitable to dampen the dangerous political propensities of 'the vulgar gazers' and 'the beastly audience'. From this perspective, plays, fairs and festivals were interchangeable as safety valves: as Sir Henry Wotton commented on the Venetian carnival in 1622, public festivals were necessary because 'the restrained passions [are] indeed the most dangerous' (Wotton 1907: 265). This was a position which was most vigorously argued after the Civil War. The Duke of Newcastle, for instance, wrote to Charles II that

> ther Shoulde be playes to Goe upp and downe the Counterye . . .
> The devirtismentes will amuse the peoples thaughtes, and keepe them In harmless action which will free your Majestie from faction and Rebellion.
>
> (Strong 1903: 227)

And Newcastle makes it clear that he thinks of plays as only an extension of morris dances, cakes and ales, and May, Christmas and Shrovetide festivities, all of which are conducive to the good order of 'merrye Englande'. Jonson was not unfamiliar with these arguments: James I supported popular festivity, publishing his *Book of Sports* in 1618, and Jonson himself submitted a poem to *Annalia Dubrensia*, a collection which proclaimed the Cotswold Games as 'harmless [i.e. depoliticized] Olimpicke exercises', in opposition to the 'standings, lectures, exercises' of the Puritans (Whitfield 1962: 23). *Bartholomew Fair* itself could be read as a 'harmless action' dedicated to the suppression of 'faction and Rebellion'.

But to do so, of course, would be to conflate festival, fair and theatre as public arenas. And it was precisely against this conflation that Jonson's elevated concept of authorship was directed. One strategy which Jonson adopted was to elide the position of the poet with that of the monarch. As Don Wayne argues, in Jonson

> The place of the author is finally privileged in opposition to that of the theatre audience by an identification of his own judgement with the 'power to judge' of the king. In this way, the place of the king, the highest earthly place, functions as more than just that of another audience of the play; it is the place of final authority.
>
> (Wayne, 1982: 118)

Associated with his royal patron, Jonson could adopt a position above groundlings and learned critics alike. Helgerson notes that '*Solus Rex aut poeta non quotannis nascitur*' was 'one of Jonson's favourite Latin tags' (Helgerson 1983: 50). Jonson believed that ideally there should be a 'consociation of offices' between the monarch and the scholar, in which power was exchanged for learning and learning for power (Jonson 1925–52: 565).

But the relation of poet to prince was not an equitable 'consociation' as Jonson knew to his cost. In 1597, he was arrested for his part in *The Isle of Dogs*; in 1603, 'he was called before the Council for his *Sejanus* and accused both of popery and treason by [Northampton]'; in 1605, he was imprisoned for his part in *Eastward Ho*, and it was reported that he would have his nose and ears cut off (Dutton 1983: 6–8). Thus, the epilogue of *Bartholomew Fair* can be read both as an invocation of his royal patron against '[the] envy of a few' and as an ironic acknowledgement that the play, despite having 'the Master of the *Revels*' hand for it' (V.v. 15), could still be adjudged, as Busy says of all plays, 'scurrility' and a production of 'the Master of *Rebels*' (V.v. 16–17). In its address to the king the epilogue turns upon the relation of the licensed to the licentious:

> Your Majesty hath seen the play, and you
>> Can best allow it from your ear and view.
> You know the scope of writers, and what store
>> Of leave is given them, if they take not more,
> And turn it into license. You can tell
>> If we have used that leave you gave us well;
> Or whether we to rage or license break,
>> Or be profane, or make profane men speak.
> This is your power to judge, great sir

Even if the play did gratify the 'ear and view' of a king, the writer's claim to 'authority' was by no means assured. As Jonson's act of negation antithetically witnesses, the poet's success with the court opened him up to the charges of 'servile flatterie' and of 'smelling parasite' (Jonson 1925–52: VIII, 41, 48).

Certainly, Jonson wanted to believe in the alliance between prince and poet whilst rarely showing enthusiasm for his role as a writer in the popular theatre. Against both of these positions however he tried to define a new role in which authority was invested in authorship itself. Hence Jonson's troubled, problematic relationship to both the high and the low symbolic positions of the social hierarchy. We see him trying to stabilize and dignify an emergent place for authorship at a distance both from the aristocracy and the plebeians, and yet this authorial investiture – for that is what it aspired to be – was only locatable, 'groundable', through its symbolic relation to existing hierarchies, existing languages, symbols and practices of high and low. The insertion of professional authorship *between* these was a fraught negotiation of a 'middle' space and a complex contestation of traditional dichotomies. Authorship in this sense required a two-handed fending off of royal and popular patronage alike, since both entangled the poet in symbolic arrangements, rituals and deferences which no longer quite answered his *professional* needs.

The 'contagion of the low' is felt much more pressingly by Jonson, at least when he was writing for the theatre. The 'authorship' of his plays, indeed, was an act performed *on* and *against* the theatrical script, so as to efface its real conditions of production. The *Workes* which Jonson published in 1616 were the result of a labour whereby his plays appeared as literary texts, miraculously freed from the contagion of the marketplace. Stephen Orgel has reminded us of the *collaborative* process through which plays of the period were formed:

> The company commissioned the play, usually stipulated the subject, often provided the plot, often parcelled it out, scene by scene, to several playwrights. The text thus produced was a working model, which the company then revised as seemed appropriate. The author had little or no say in these revisions: the text belonged to the company, and the authority represented by the text – I am talking now about the *performing* text – is that of the company, the owners, not that of the playwright, the author.
>
> (Orgel 1981: 3)

Orgel then brilliantly demonstrates how Jonson transformed *Sejanus* from theatrical script to literary text:

> The play was first written in collaboration with another playwright; that was the version the actors performed. But in preparing the play for publication, Jonson *took control* of the text: he replaced his collaborator's scenes with ones of his own, and added a good deal of new material, largely historical documentation . . . Jonson here has succeeded in suppressing the theatrical production, and has replaced it with an independent, printed text, which he consistently refers to, moreover, not as a play but as a poem.
>
> (Orgel 1981: 4)

The literary text, though, was haunted by these 'suppressions'. The more it strove to be 'independent', the more the author needed to deny the patron, the audience, the collaborators, even the readers upon whom he was dependent. In fact the author remained, like the dyer's hand, subdued to the elements he worked in, but these appear as negated or denied elements, taking on a new and different form under the sign of their negation. This process is analogous to that described by Freud in his essay 'On negation': the content of the repressed image does indeed make its way into consciousness, but on the condition that it is denied, devalued and negated. 'Negation is a way of taking cognizance of what is repressed; indeed, it is already a lifting of repression, though not, of course, an acceptance of what is repressed' (Freud 1925: 437–8). Negation was Jonson's way of taking cognizance, even as he rejected, the hybridization of his medium and his audience. The theatre was, as Dekker observed in *The Gull's Hornbook*, a 'Royal Exchange', and the poet's muses were 'Merchants'. And in the theatre, 'your stinkard has the self-same liberty to be there in his tobacco fumes which your sweet courtier hath, and . . . your carman and tinker claim as strong a voice in their suffrage, and sit to give judgement on the play's life and death, as well as the proudest *Momus* among the tribe of Critic' (Dekker 1967: 98). It was from the theatre that Jonson's plays had to be removed so that they could become 'literature' within a classical canon.

For all the deliberate conservatism of this strategy, we should recognize that Jonson was demanding a status which, as Don Wayne has argued, 'was unacknowledged in the traditional social and cultural system from which England was then emerging' (1982: 129). Jonson was attempting to dissociate the professional writer from the clamour of the marketplace and to install his works in the studies of the gentry and the libraries of the universities. In this, he succeeded. When Sir Thomas Bodley wrote to Thomas James in 1612 about the establishment of his library, he classed plays as 'idle bookes, and riffe raffes': even if 'some little profit might be reaped . . . out of some of our playbookes, the benefit therof will nothing countervaile, the harm that the scandal will bring into the Librairie, when it shalbe given out, that we stuffe it full of baggage bookes' (quoted in Holland 1979: 115). In publishing his plays as part of his folio *Workes*, Jonson removes them from the ranks of play-quartos which could be catalogued along with 'the *Academy of Complements, Venus undress'd, Westminster Drollery* and . . . a Bundle of *Bawdy* Songs in Manuscript' (quoted in Holland 1979: 115). His plays were to become fitting companions to the works of Horace and Virgil on the library shelves.

As 'master-poet', then, Jonson constituted his identity in opposition to the theatre and the fair. Through the imaginary separation of the scholar's study and library from the theatrical marketplace, Jonson simultaneously mapped out the divisions between the 'civilized' and the grotesque body, between the stunted quarto and the handsome folio, between the 'author' and the hack, between 'pure' literature and social hybridization. In the image of the fair, the author could rewrite the social and economic relations which determined his own existence; in the fair he could stigmatize the voices which competed against his own and reveal just how 'dirty' were the hands which sullied his 'pure' wares.

But disgust bears the impress of desire, and Jonson found in the huckster, the cony-catcher and the pick-pocket an image of his own precarious and importuning craft. Proclaiming so loudly how all the other plays were mere cozenings, did not Jonson pursue the perennial techniques of the mountebank who decried the deceptions and the false wares of others the more easily to practise his own deceptions and pass off his own productions as the 'real thing'?

In separating self from the popular festive scene, authorship after Jonson gradually developed in accordance with the ideal of the individual which was emerging within bourgeois culture – the individual, that is, as 'the proprietor of his own person and capacities, for which he owes nothing to society' (quoted in Fish 1984: 26). Authorship became a visionary embodiment of this ideal to the degree that it represented itself as transcendent to the 'common' place of the market. In so far as the author still inhabited the fair, it was increasingly either as an aloof spectator or as spectacle and freak. As the latter, he appears most poignantly in the work of Kafka, himself both hunger-artist and most resourceful of conmen.

In 'A Fasting Showman', Kafka wrote of a hunger-artist who draws large crowds to the cage in which he fasts and where he lives at first in 'visible glory, honoured by the world' (Kafka 1949: 243). But as the years pass, the crowds dwindle; a fasting showman is not, after all, much of a spectacle. The hunger-artist is reduced to performing at a side-show in the circus and the crowds hurry on past him to see the animals. Finally, he stages a fast unto death, after which he is replaced by a young panther whose 'noble body' is 'furnished almost to bursting point with all that is needed' and whose freedom 'seemed to lurk in its jaws' (Kafka 1949: 250). But before the hunger-artist dies, the overseer asks him why he has spent his life trapped within the cage of his own wasting body. 'Because I couldn't find any food that I liked', he replies (Kafka 1949: 249).

Like the hunger-artist, Jonson presented withdrawal as a spectacle. Authorship, as he made it, was a series of leave-takings – from other writers, from theatrical audiences, from actors, even from patrons. In his poetry, as Stanley Fish says, Jonson emphasized 'the notion of the "gathered self" which is always to itself "the same" (Epigram 98), a self which presents such a closed face to the world that it is invulnerable to invasion and remains always "untouch'd"' (Fish 1984: 39). Yet within his writings Jonson also projected a self quite antithetical to this, the man 'of prodigious wast', 'laden with bellie', who knew 'the fury of men's gullets' (Jonson 1925–52: I, 179, 226–30). This was the Jonson who concluded *Every Man Out of his Humour* with the 'violently impatient' Macilente (whose name means 'lean' or 'meagre') turning from his 'envious apoplexy' with the help of the audience's applause to become 'as fat as Sir John Falstaff'. If, as master-poet, Jonson could find no food that he liked, as a dramatist in the popular theatre he knew the appetites, if not of the panther, at least of the pig.

Yet *Bartholomew Fair*, his 'pig-wallow', was, for whatever reason, excluded from the 1616 *Workes*. Although we know that Jonson worked on producing a copy of the play for the 1631 Folio, the play was printed, but never distributed, in Jonson's lifetime. Not attaining the status of 'literature', it remained until 1640 simply a play that had been performed in the popular theatre. And that seems appropriate, for with its enormities, abominations and its intimacy with 'low' forms, it would certainly have compromised the haughty individuation of the classical to which Jonson so avidly aspired. Dryden was right to see *Bartholomew Fair* as 'the lowest kind of comedy'. Inheriting (in part from Jonson) a classical aesthetic by then deeply committed to separation from the repertoires of the fair and marketplace, Dryden could conceptualize the 'low' only negatively.

After the Restoration, the 'logic' of excess, of the lower bodily stratum, of the fair, even of popular theatre itself, was re-inscribed as the 'bastard pleasure' of 'vulgar gazers' and 'beastly audiences'.

3   'Don't grunt', said Alice; 'that's not at all a proper way of expressing yourself'. Illustration by John Tenniel to Lewis Carroll's *Alice's Adventures in Wonderland*, 1865

2

The Grotesque Body and the Smithfield Muse: Authorship in the Eighteenth Century

'Every place is a different language'

Susan Sontag

Patterns of discourse are regulated through the forms of corporate assembly in which they are produced. Alehouse, coffee-house, church, law court, library, drawing room of a country mansion: each place of assembly is a different site of intercourse requiring different manners and morals. Discursive space is never completely independent of social place and the formation of new kinds of speech can be traced through the emergence of new public sites of discourse and the transformation of old ones. Each 'site of assembly' constitutes a nucleus of material and cultural conditions which regulate what may and may not be said, who may speak, how people may communicate and what importance must be given to what is said. An utterance is legitimated or disregarded according to its place of production and so, in large part, the history of political struggle has been the history of the attempts made to control significant sites of assembly and spaces of discourse.

In this chapter we examine some significant sites of assembly and spaces of discourse which from the Restoration to the end of the eighteenth century formed a topographical network within which aesthetic, moral and political judgements in the public domain were produced. After the Restoration the traditional élites of court, city and country remapped and realigned their inherited symbolic realms, negotiating their ideological struggles within a distinctive network of places and sites of exchange. In recent critical discussion some attention has been given to the formation, in the late seven-

4 'Southwark Fair', etching and engraving by William Hogarth, January 1733/4
(Reproduced by courtesy of the Trustees of the British Museum)

teenth and early eighteenth centuries, of what has come to be called the 'public sphere' of opinion in England, through which emerging bourgeois and urban professional classes (whose prescient pioneer Ben Jonson had shown himself to be) expressed and consolidated their views. Such a sphere undoubtedly did emerge around this time, though it was neither as homogeneous nor as free-floating as it is sometimes represented (see Parrinder 1985). There is a curious temptation even on the part of materialist historians, after a cursory nod in the direction of the coffee-house, to 'dematerialize' this discursive realm, to represent it in terms of class ideas and ideals sundered from the matrix of places, times and habits which informed them. In fact it is of considerable importance to understand that this 'public sphere' was rooted in new kinds of social space and institution – the coffee-house, the clubroom, 'Grub Street', the assembly rooms of the spas and resorts, the salon, the pleasure gardens of Vauxhall and Ranelagh and the tea gardens such as those popular resorts of Chelsea, Hampstead, Marylebone and Bagnigge Wells. Discussing this sphere of polite, informed critical opinion Terry Eagleton writes:

> in the seventeenth and eighteenth centuries the European bourgeoisie begins to carve out for itself a distinctive discursive space, one of rational judgement and enlightened critique rather than of the brutal ukases of an authoritarian politics. Poised between the state and civil society, this bourgeois 'public sphere' as Jürgen Habermas has termed it, comprises a realm of social institutions – clubs, journals, coffeehouses, periodicals – in which private individuals assemble for the free, equal exchange of reasonable discourse, thus welding themselves into a relatively cohesive body whose deliberations may assume the form of a powerful political force.
>
> (Eagleton 1984: 9)

Having established this important connection between discourse and topographical network Eagleton does not follow up the implications which it has for analysis and, like the initial work of Habermas (1962) and of Negt and Kluge (1972) on the formation of the bourgeois public sphere, he only gestures to the network of discursive sites and institutions within which eighteenth-century notions of the 'public', the 'author' and 'constituencies' were emerging. It is only when such related concepts as critical judgement, taste, authorship and writing are reconnected to their 'planes of emergence' as Foucault has called them, the social points at which such ideas surface, that they can be fully understood. In part it is that task of reconnection, bringing topography, body symbolism, social stratification and authorship together upon their significant planes of emergence, which we have attempted here.

Peter Hohendahl has related the rise and expansion of literary criticism as both institution and profession, to the creation of the public sphere:

> Seen historically, the modern concept of literary criticism is closely tied to the rise of the liberal, bourgeois, public sphere in the early eighteenth century. Literature served the emancipation movement of the middle class as an instrument to gain self-esteem and to articulate its human demands against the absolutist state and the hierarchical society.
>
> (Hohendahl 1982: 52)

It is clear and relatively uncontentious that the early periodicals such as *The Tatler* and *The Spectator* had a central role in this respect, negotiating a cultural alliance between the gentry, the Court and the town through the formation of an inclusive, refined public gently coerced with a mixture of satire and example, into the ways of tolerance and good manners. Naturally this mixture, in which aristocratic values and leadership were combined in a complex and uneven manner with the conservative desires of the squirearchy and the aspirations of the bourgeoisie in the City and the professions, could never be an homogeneous one (see Cannon 1985). Yet the containment of dispute, its restriction to discursive expressions of nominally free critical judgement, was undoubtedly carried through in and by the public sphere.

Its grounding conditions, which enabled Addison and Steele to pursue their totalizing project of moral education, are to be found in the general transformation of the sites of discourse in the early eighteenth century. This general transformation marked out a number of changes in the interrelationship of place, body and discourse during the period. Concomitant with the establishing of the 'refined' public sphere and its distinct notion of professional authorship was a widespread attempt to regulate body and crowd behaviour so as to create conditions favourable to the operation of the sphere. This was not merely an incidental act of social hygiene. As new sites of assembly appeared these were regulated according to manners and norms significantly different from those of the places they were displacing. Furthermore, traditional places such as the theatre, which had always appeared suspect and unstable, were subjected once again to the onslaught of 'the civilizing process' in a renewed attempt to clean up plays and their unruly audiences.

•

In his prologue to *Cleomenes* (1692) Dryden, a crucial figure in this 'cleansing' process, can be seen polemically engaged in attempting to do for the theatre pit and boxes what the coffee-house was doing for the tavern (of which considerably more below). The prologue is of considerable interest. The rhetorical and metaphorical manoeuvres of the speech reveal how powerfully the transcodings of alien territory (Ireland, Virginia, Jamaica), the carnivalesque and the unruly public body are *produced* as transgressive and taboo-laden categories in the urgent attempt to clear the public sphere. The speech, 'spoke by Mr Mountfort' (and that 'Mr' is important for the underscoring of an ordinary, neutral, middling speaker position, an actor stepping out of role to address the audience as a bourgeois professional on behalf of the literary profession), the speech endeavours to coax and shame the unruly audience of aristocratic Beaux and vulgar groundlings into *keeping still* and *keeping quiet*, transforming them, precisely, into a deferential and receptive bourgeois audience. It is no longer sufficient for Dryden that the theatre-goers participate in the spectacle and enjoy themselves as part of a crowd: they must be disciplined into 'true judges', silent appreciators or critics in short, separating out their individual faculties of evaluation from the visceral pleasures of crowd behaviour:

> I think or hope, at least, the Coast is clear,
> That none but Men of Wit and Sence are here:
> That our Bear-Garden Friends are all away,
> Who bounce with Hands and Feet, and cry Play,
>   Play.

Who to save Coach-hire, trudge along the Street,
Then print our Matted Seats with dirty Feet;
Who, while we speak make love to
    Orange-Wenches,
And between Acts stand strutting on the
    Benches:
Where got a Cock-horse, making vile grimaces,
They to the Boxes show their Booby Faces.
A Merry-Andrew such a Mob will serve,
And treat 'em with such Wit as they deserve:
Let 'em go people *Ireland*, where there's need
Of such new Planters to repair the Breed;
Or to *Virginia* or *Jamaica* Steer,
But have a care of some *French* Privateer;
For if they should become the Prize of Battle,
They'll take 'em Black and White for *Irish* Cattle.
Arise true Judges in your own defence,
Controul those Foplings, and declare for Sence
               (*Cleomenes*, Prologue: 1–20)

As we know from the theatre riots later in the eighteenth century Dryden's exhortation to the audience to 'controul those Foplings' was not to be successful for some decades. The formation of a refined, cosmopolitan public, *internally disciplined*, was something which took place gradually over decades and even centuries; it was an almost geological shift in the cultural threshold of shame and embarrassment which regulates the body in public. Thus in the Regency period a foreign commentator remarked that:

The most striking thing to a foreigner in English theatre is the unheard-of coarseness and brutality of the audience. The consequence of this is that the higher and more civilised classes go only to the Italian Opera, and very rarely visit their national theatre . . . English freedom here degenerates into the rudest licence, and it is not uncommon in the most affecting part of a tragedy, or the most charming 'cadenza' of a singer, to hear some coarse expression shouted from the galleries in a stentor voice . . . It is also no rarity for someone to throw the fragments of his 'goute', which do not always consist of orange-peels alone, without the smallest ceremony on the heads of the people in the pit, or to hail them with singular dexterity into the boxes; while others hang their coats and waistcoats over the railings of the gallery and sit in their shirt-sleeves.

> (*A Regency Visitor. The English Tour of Prince Puckler-Mushau described in his letters 1826–1828* ed. E. M. Butler (Golby and Purdue 1984: 70))

Puckler-Mushau's description of the informality and rowdiness of a Regency theatre audience reveals a degree of change nevertheless, and his affronted response to an audience in shirt-sleeves registers a tangible raising of the threshold of self-regulation, the tossing around of orange-peel and rubbish notwithstanding. Dryden seems to have confronted an even more self-willed and unruly body of spectators in the late seventeenth century.

Clearly, by referring to the rowdy audience elements as 'our Bear-Garden Friends' and by saying that a Merry-Andrew (a popular English fairground and carnival figure) would serve them best, Dryden is trying to lever his audience away from their enjoyment of popular culture. In *Popular Recreations in English Society 1700–1850*, Robert Malcolmson writes:

> The point to bear in mind is that, during the first half of the eighteenth century in particular, many gentlemen were not entirely disengaged from the culture of the common people. They frequently occupied something of a half-way house between the robust, unpolished culture of provincial England and the cosmopolitan, sophisticated culture which was based in London. Most of the country houses were not yet principally seasonal extensions of a polite and increasingly self-conscious urban culture, and many of their occupants remained relatively uncitified.
>
> (Malcolmson 1973: 68)

The 'Booby Squires' of late-seventeenth-century comedy were precisely this provincial breed viewed with contempt by the town in part because they had not yet dissociated 'classical' from popular culture: they actively lived *both* and it is precisely this hybridization, this 'both/and' which is here under massive pressure. A few lines further on in his prologue Dryden attacks this group openly, remarking with a sneer upon the low familiarity shown by the rural squirearchy towards popular culture:

Such Squires are only fit for Country towns,
To stink of Ale; and dust a stand with Clownes
(*Cleomenes*, Prologue: 27–8)

Although we should expect disdain for the populace and its
pastimes from Dryden – never over-fond of what he terms 'the dregs
of a democracy' in *Absalom and Achitophel* – his antagonism
towards the 'Boobies' in this couplet is part of an overall strategy of
expulsion which clears a space for polite, cosmopolitan discourse by
constructing popular culture as the 'low-Other', the dirty and crude
outside to the emergent public sphere. Dryden is doing more than
policing a fundamental opposition between high and popular culture, he is also *constructing* it in this prologue, making sure that his
audience knows that they must chose one or the other – that to
belong comfortably to both realms is a monstrosity. He is enforcing a
choice of self-identity: *either* you belong to the world of bear-baiting,
booths, stalls, Hockley-hole fisticuffs, Merry-Andrews and clowns,
or you belong to my world, which is the realm of Wit (not Folly),
'True Judgement' and 'Sence'.

It is not a new territorial division of course, for it was often
inscribed in the opposition between locus and plataea on the Elizabethan stage (Weimann 1978), but what is new, and contrasts
strongly with the Shakespearean stage, is the urgent attempt to expel
the lower sort altogether from the scene of reception, to homogenize
the audience by refining and domesticating its energy, sublimating its
diverse physical pleasures into a purely contemplative force, replac-
ing a dispersed, heterodox, noisy participation in the *event* of theatre
by silent specular intensity. Although the common assumption
concerning the Restoration audience is that it was largely composed
of the upper classes in contrast to the Elizabethan period (Van
Lennep 1965: clxii) and its pricing largely excluded the 'rabble',
what is really at issue is the symbolic manipulation of the self-image
and the body-image of the audience so that it defines *itself* against
an internalized, negative image of the populace. As Sir William
Davenant censoriously expressed it in *News from Plymouth*:

You are not now amongst your tenants' sons,
Swaggering at a wake, in your own village.

Looking in detail at Dryden's prologue to *Cleomenes* we first
observe him creating, conspiratorially as it were, an intimate liaison

with the 'Men of Wit and Sence'. Favouring their presence he shares with them the hope that the coarser sort – who bang on the chairs and floor, tread street filth all over the seats, chat up the orange-sellers, interrupt the play with banter and run up and down the benches during the interval – will be elsewhere. Of course, Dryden is being disingenuous. He knows that these are in fact not two distinct groups but the very same people and the underlying intent of his words is to make the audience reform and discipline itself by an internal transformation of its collective *and* individual identity.

In his *Outline of a Theory of Practice* Pierre Bourdieu has argued that the apparently superficial reformation of manners is in fact one of the most powerful ways in which a culture inculcates its meta-physical, moral and political scheme of things. He writes:

> If all societies . . . that seek to produce a new man through a process of 'deculturation' and 'reculturation' set such store on the seemingly most insignificant details of *dress*, *bearing*, physical and verbal *manners*, the reason is that, treating the body as a memory, they entrust to it in abbreviated and practical, i.e. mnemonic, form the fundamental principles of the arbitrary content of the culture. The principles em-bodied in this way are placed beyond the grasp of consciousness, and hence cannot be touched by voluntary, deliberate transformation . . . The whole trick of pedagogic reason lies precisely in the way it extorts the essential while seeming to demand the insignificant . . . the concessions of *politeness* always contain *political* concessions.
>
> (Bourdieu 1977: 94–5)

The fact is that Dryden is not so much dividing the audience into two real and opposed kinds, the civilized and the vulgar, as symbolically re-aligning the body and behaviour of each and every one of his listeners into a 'unified' and *self-regulating* bourgeois identity. And this is carried through in a relentless series of *exclusions*. 'The Coast is clear', he begins, establishing from the first a rhetorical inside which will gradually envelop his listeners in a symbolic community defined *implicitly* by those it rejects: those who frequent the bear-garden and the fairs; those who infect the space of the play with sexuality, rhythm, noise and the obtrusive presence of their bodies. Then, in a sudden turn, all such barbaric behaviour is projected onto colonials and provincials: the Irish, Virginians, Jamaicans and the

Booby Squires. The civic body is *topographically* reformed by the unceremonious exportation and dumping of libido in the country-side and in the far colonies, where, at the end of the next century, it will be miraculously rediscovered and hailed as a new life-source. Dryden played his small part in that alienation of 'nature' which, concealed from itself, was the precondition for its triumphant return in the prodigal celebrations of the Romantics.

What we have here then is a perfect representation of the production of identity through negation, the creation of an implicit sense of self through explicit rejections and denials, 'No, not *that*, and not *that*'. The public sphere is neither pure ideation nor something which existed only in and for itself: it is, like any form of identity, created through negations, it produces a new domain by taking into itself as *negative introjections* the very domains which surround and threaten it. It thus produces and reproduces itself through the process of denial and defiance. 'Controul those Foplings and declare for Sence' is an internalizing imperative which yokes self-control with crowd control, cosmopolitan identity with colonial identity, suppression with repression.

In *The History of Manners* (*The Civilizing Process*, I) Norbert Elias uses a host of specific examples to show how the social control of body functions such as eating, yawning, spitting, ejecting mucus, fidgeting, touching, inflicting pain and so forth, has a long and complex history. His contention is that public regulation of the body (as in Dryden's prologue) is a restructuring of personality with enormous consequences. Referring to the early eighteenth century and the conduct books of the period he writes:

> Now habits are condemned more and more as such, not in regard to others. In this way, socially undesirable impulses or inclinations are more radically repressed. They are associated with embarrass-ment, fear, shame, or guilt, even when one is alone . . . Moulding by such means aims at making socially desirable behaviour auto-matic, a matter of self-control, causing it to appear in the con-sciousness of the individual as the result of his own free will, and in the interest of his own health or human dignity. And it is only with the advent of this way of consolidating habits, or conditioning, which gains prominence with the rise of the middle classes, that conflict between the socially inadmissible impulses and tendencies, on the one hand, and the pattern of social demands

anchored in the individual, on the other, takes on the sharply defined form central to the psychological theories of modern times – above all, to psychoanalysis. It may be there have always been 'neuroses'. But the 'neuroses' we see about us today are a specific historical form of psychic conflict which needs psychogenetic and sociogenetic elucidation.

(Elias 1978: 150)

Thus whilst Bourdieu connects the regulation of manners to the operation of the whole metaphysical and ideological outlook of a culture, Elias connects manners to the internal construction of the subject, to the historical formation of self, repudiating any possibility of a separation of the psychical and the social. Manners, regulations of the body, thus become the site of a profound interconnection of ideology and subjectivity, a zone of transcoding at once astonishingly trivial and microscopically important. Traversed by regulative forces quite beyond its conscious control, the body is territorialized in accordance with hierarchies and topographical rules which it enacts automatically, which come from elsewhere and which make it a point of intersection and flow within the elaborate symbolic systems of the socius.

The Restoration is strewn with the evidence of a great reform, a re-territorialization of places and bodies, a realignment of domains, discourses, manners and states of mind. Whatever the party-political complexion of events after 1660, a considerable recoding of the significant sites of assembly was under way and it was there, as much as in the narrowly political utterance of Whig and Tory, Court or Country, that hegemonic rule was established. Dryden, we have seen, moves easily and naturally outwards from the question of standing on the theatre benches with muddy feet to the inferiority of the colonies and the cultural superiority of the urban play-goer over the country squire. He ranks classes through places and bodies and he inscribes a politics in the glance of the orange-seller, the grimace of the fop, the foot-banging of the 'critick'. But Dryden was only one of many engaged in this re-territorialization and reform. The Restoration theatre became one of the principal places in which a host of writers took up the task of transforming the mixed and unruly public body inherited from the Renaissance into attentive citizens.

In his *Diary* for 18 February 1666/7 Pepys describes how, whilst attending the King's Theatre to see *The Mayds Tragedy* he was vexed all the while with two talking ladies and Sir Ch. Sidly, yet pleased to hear the discourse, he being a stranger; and one of the ladies would, and did, sit with her mask on all the play; and being exceeding witty as ever I heard woman, did talk most pleasantly with him ... but by that means lost the pleasure of the play wholly.

(Pepys 1970–83: VIII, 71–2)

The epilogue to Lee's *Sophonisba* typifies the irritation of the playwright at his ungovernable audience:

> One half o' the Play they spend in noise and brawl,
> Sleep out the rest, then wake and damn it all.

And similarly in the prologue to *The Comical Revenge* (quoted in Van Lennep 1965: clxviii):

> And Gallants, as for you, talk loud i'th' Pit,
> Divert yourself and Friends with your own Wit.

The prologues and the epilogues to the plays of the period often appear as castigating manuals of audience reform, as in this extract from the prologue to *The Ordinary* (1670/1):

> Some come with lusty Burgundy half-drunk,
> T'eat China Oranges, make love to Punk;
> And briskly mount a bench when th'Act is done,
> And comb their much-lov'd Periwigs to the tune
> And can sit out a Play of three hours long,
> Minding no part of't but the Dance or Song.

In their introduction to *The London Stage 1660–1800* (Van Lennep 1965) Avery and Scouten provide several other examples in this vein. The prologue to *The Rival Queens* (1676–7) scorns those who 'with loud Nonsense drown the Stages Wit'; the epilogue to *Sertorius* (1679) 'scorns those little vermin in the Pit,/Who noise and nonsense vent instead of Wit', and Aphra Behn, invoking the same carnivalesque image of the Merry Andrews which Dryden was to use later, writes in her epilogue to *The False Countess*:

> You Sparks better Comedians are than we;
> You every day out-fool ev'n Noakes and Lee.
> They're forc'd to stop, and their own Farces quit,
> T'admire the Merry-Andrews of the Pit.

The most violent attacks came in the plays of the 1680s, perhaps partly motivated by a general fear of insurrection associated with the disturbances of the early 1680s and the Popish Plot. In the prologue to *The Disappointment* (1684) by Southerne the reprimand is a little shriller:

> Last, some there are, who take their first Degrees
> Of Lewdness in our Middle Galleries:
> The Doughty Bullies enter Bloody Drunk,
> Invade and grabble one another's Punk:
> They caterwoul and make a dismal Rout,
> Call Sons of Whores, and strike, but ne'er luggout.

This concerted campaign for moral correctitude was to reach a polemical zenith in 1698 with the publication of Jeremy Collier's *Short View of the Immorality and Profaneness of the English Stage* in which the blunderbuss of puritan zeal blasted plays, players, playwrights and audiences alike for their blasphemy, impiety, indecency and riotous disorder. Collier's notorious attack was undoubtedly another episode in the long history of puritan antagonism to the theatre, but it can also be seen as a part of a more general transformation of manners to which the playwrights themselves subscribed in their reforming prologues. *The Playhouse* (1685) outdid even Collier in its caustic scorn of theatre audience behaviour:

> The Middle Gall'ry first demands our View;
> The filth of Jakes, and stench of ev'ry Stew.
> Here reeking Punks like Ev'ning Insects swarm;
> The Polecat's Perfume much the happier Charm.
> Their very scent gives Apoplectick Fits,
> And yet they're thought all Civit by the Cits;
> Nor can we blame 'em; for the Truth to tell,
> The want of Brains may be the want of Smell.
> Here ev'ry Night they sit three Hours for Sale;
> The Night-rail always cleanlier than the Tayl.

Here the tricks of Jacobean misogyny are reworked in Restoration satire: the smell of the whore is the scapegoating metonymy of general corruption and the 'reeking Punks' are made the embodiment of a contaminating filth. The orange-sellers are made conjunctive figures who connect the theatre not only to the brothel but to the jakes. The antiseptic crusade of the dramatist severs the space of theatre from the market of sexual liaison and proceeds by associating the sexual and the excremental in one malodorous lump. The association was not uncommon. In James Wright's *The Humours And Conversations of the Town* (1693) exactly the same juxtaposition appears as one reason for not attending the theatre, the orange-sellers made guilty by association with the 'Commodes an Ell high':

> What wou'd you go to the play for? . . . to be dun'd all round with the impertinent Discourse of Beardless Fops to the Orange-Wenches, with Commodes an Ell high; and to the Vizor-Masks of the Rake-hells, talking loud to one another; or the perpetual Chat of the Noisy Coquets, that come there to get Cullies, and to disturb, not mind the Play . . . Tho a Play be a generous Diversion, yet 'tis better to read than to see, unless one cou'd see it without these Inconveniences.
>
> (Van Lennep 1965: clxx)

Looking at these texts as segments of a whole cultural movement we can see, as they weave backwards and forwards from the physical body to place, to class and group and back again, the fabrication of an idealized space of consciousness which is being systematically *scoured*. Wright would rather 'read than see' a play: in common with the playwrights and the new coffee-house public he feels his relationship to culture is threatened by outside interference, by the flow of noise and urine and sexual excitation. The flux and heterogeneity of the theatre audience in consuming mood must be discharged elsewhere where it will not contaminate *culture*. This is no mere matter of 'refinement'. It is a transformation of certain material conditions of theatre-going which had been largely, if sometimes grudgingly, accepted and even enjoyed in an unremarked way until the emergence of a bourgeois public sphere and its increasingly phobic relation to the grotesque collective body. Under the increasing threat of democratic promiscuity the channels of communication and the circuits of reception within which 'culture' and 'rationality' now flowed had to be sealed off. Manners and political distinctions become interfused. The creation of a sublimated public body without smells, without coarse laughter, without organs, separate from the Court and the Church on the one hand and the market square, alehouse, street and fairground on the other – this was the great labour of bourgeois culture, complementary to that *institutionalizing inventiveness* of the same period which Foucault has mapped in *Madness and Civilization* and *Discipline and Punish*.

The theatre was not the only site of this process. In *A Dissertation upon Drunkenness* (1727) the author describes what he considers to be the disgusting environment of the typical alehouse:

> The vile obscene talk, noise, nonsense and ribaldry discourses together with the fumes of tobacco, belchings and other foul breakings of wind, that are generally found in an ale-room . . . are enough to make any rational creature amongst them almost ashamed of his being. But all this the rude rabble esteem the highest degree of happiness and run themselves into the greatest straits imaginable to attain it.
>
> (Clark 1983: 341)

This is not to be taken simply as the isolated and excessively severe judgement of an early teetotaller. As we have seen, the terms in which it casts its argument, pitting the desires and habits of 'any rational creature' against those of 'the rude rabble' were key terms in the *will to refinement* which so marked the struggle to establish the public sphere in the period. The author is here objecting not to drunkenness *per se*, but to smells, 'vile obscene talk', 'noise', 'nonsense and ribaldry' and habits of the body like belching and breaking wind which he finds disgusting. His attack on drink and the alehouse is part of a wider attack on the 'grotesque body' and the physical conditions and norms of assembly favoured by the lower classes of the time. By implication and contrast, 'any rational creature' will favour polite and decent conversation, quietness, no nonsense, ribaldry or drunkenness, and a much stricter control of the body.

Just such a place of assembly for the 'rational creature' was the coffee-house. According to Aytoun Ellis in his book *The Penny Universities* (Ellis 1956) (which we draw upon substantially for the following material), the first coffee-house in Christendom was opened in Oxford in 1650 by Jacob the Jew 'at the Angel in the parish of St Peter in the East'. Hermann Kesten claims in his book *Dichter im Café* that actually the first café in Europe was in St Mark's Square in Venice in 1647, but in either case the coffee-house came to Europe from the Middle East around 1650 and spread with astonishing rapidity and success through all the capital cities of Europe: 1652 in London, 1654 in Marseilles, 1660 in Paris with the founding of the famous *Café Procope* by a Sicilian, 1683 in Vienna when *Zur blauen Flasche* the celebrated Viennese coffee-house first opened, and 1689 in Frankfurt. By the end of the seventeenth century the number of coffee-houses in London exceeded *two thousand*, and this was less than fifty years since they had first arrived in the country. The immediate sweeping popularity of the coffee-houses in England led to the fact that by 1700 every trade and profession in the capital had their local coffee-house for a favourite meeting-place.

It is no exaggeration to say that the development of the bourgeois public sphere was consonant with the growth of the coffee-house. The close connection which existed between certain coffee-houses as places of free discussion and key groups of Enlightenment intellectuals is well known. There is every reason to believe that the two Oxford coffee-clubs frequented by Boyle, Christopher Wren and Sprat provided the nucleus of what was to become the Royal Society (see Ellis 1956: 24, 76, 77). *Le Procope* in Paris was the known focal meeting-place for the Encyclopaedists and a line-drawing by Kretz shows it hosting Buffon, Gilbert, Voltaire, Piron, Diderot, D'Alembert, Marmontel, Le Kain, J. B. Rousseau and D'Holbach.

The importance of the coffee-house was that it provided a radically new kind of social space, at once free from the 'grotesque bodies' of the alehouse and yet (initially at least) democratically accessible to all kinds of men – though not, significantly, to women. Montesquieu wrote:

> It is a merit of the coffeehouse that you can sit there the whole day and half the night amongst people of all classes. The coffeehouse is the only place where conversation may be made to come true, where extravagant plans, utopian dreams and political plots are hatched without anyone even leaving their seat.
>
> (Kesten 1959: 129)

This specific combination of 'democratic' accessibility with a cleansed discursive environment, a new realignment of the male public body and status, was the basis of the coffee-house's importance. The new coffee-house was a heterodox, contradictory place which provided a mediation between domestic privacy and the grand public institutions of business and the state. At the same time whilst it stoutly and successfully resisted the interventions and interference of the State, it was an important instrument in the regulation of the body, manners and morals of its clientele in the public sphere. When it first appeared it was immediately seized upon by protestants as a counter-force to the tavern and the alehouse. The early coffee-houses sold no alcoholic beverages and indeed they were initially defined in clear opposition to the taverns. Every coffee-house had a list of rules posted and under strong protestant influence the rules (of which copies survive) included no swearing, no profane scripture, no cards, dice or gaming, no wagers over five shillings, no drinking of health. As distinct from the tavern, inn and alehouse, these were *decent* places to go.

Without either party being fully aware of it the coffee-house synthesized aspects of both an upper-class and protestant morality with respect to clean living and refinement. There was of course still plenty of noise and clatter but 'decency was never outraged' and the coffee-houses were thus playing an important role in the disciplining of its particular public to norms of sobriety and polite social inter-change: the norms, in fact, which are the absolute precondition for the establishment of a 'democratic' domain of verbal exchange without violence and without the privileges of rank. The coffee-houses were powerful agents in the promotion of an incipient bourgeois democratic ideology and welcomed a mixed *male* company. These were self-consciously democratic institutions, founded in the middle of the Civil War and carrying some of the egalitarian ideals of the Civil War into the structural conditions of assembly. For one penny *any* man could sit and drink. Much emphasis was placed upon this openness, perceived to be radical and innovative, in the pamphlet literature of the period. One such pamphlet went:

> Pre-eminence of place none here should mind,
> But take the next fit seat that he can find;
>
> Nor need any, if Finer persons come,
> Rise up to assigne to them his room.

In his *Unpublished Remains* (1669) the author of *Hudibras* described the coffee-house as:

> A coffee-market, where people of all qualities and conditions meet to trade in foreign drinks and newes, . . . He (the coffee-man) admits of no distinction of persons . . .

The coffee-house thus combined democratic aspirations with a space of discourse less contaminated by the unruly demands of the body for pleasure and release than that of the tavern. The coffee-house was one of the places in which *the space of discourse was being systematically decathected*. Intoxication, rhythmic and unpredictable movements, sexual reference and symbolism, singing and chanting, bodily pleasures and 'fooling around', all these were prohibited in the coffee-house. The emergence of the public sphere required that its spaces of discourse be *de-libidinized* in the interests of serious, productive and *rational* intercourse. Not least of course because sobriety and profit hang together. In the early eighteenth century James Howell wrote:

> 'tis found already that this coffee-drink hath caused a greater sobriety among the nations ... Whereas formerly Apprentices and clerks, with others, used to take the mornings' draught in Ale, Beer, or wine, which by the dizziness they cause in the brain, made many unfit for business, they use now to play the good-fellow in this wakeful and civil drink. (See also *Coffee-Houses Vindicated* in Ellis 1956: 56)

Howell's wonderful phrase, 'this wakeful and civil drink' epitomizes the value of coffee as a new and unexpected agency in the prolonged struggle of capitalism to discipline its work-force.

The coffee-house was thus a significant institutional instrument in the furtherance of the protestant ethic and its concomitant regulation of the unruly body. It simultaneously undermined feudal rules of social hierarchy and precedence whilst extending within its relatively heterogeneous public the laws of decency and civility which Norbert Elias has rightly seen as playing an important role in the symbolic establishment of power.

This does not mean of course that the coffee-house was free from aggressive and even violent forms of behaviour amongst the literary cliques and critical factions. Parrinder has described the public sphere in the coffee-house as a 'marketplace in which different contenders, by fair means and foul, must vie for dominance' (Parrinder: 1985). Nevertheless the establishment of such a space was achieved against the values of the monarchical and aristocratic ideals of rank and against the suspicions of the élite that unregulated public spaces were the breeding grounds of subversion. In 1675 Charles II decreed the closure of the coffee-houses and even went as far as sending a royal newsletter to the country at large proclaiming that 'the most seditious, indecent and scandalous discourses of these places had at last produced the proclamation for suppressing them'. It is of some importance that this attempt totally and ignominiously failed, for it indicates that the political power of the public sphere had reached the point where it could defy the King in defence of its own territory. Such was the outcry against the proposed closure that it soon became apparent no one was going to obey the proclamation, and the King feared that an attempt to enforce it might result in civil unrest. Within ten days Charles had been forced to withdraw the proclamation. Although a variety of ill-conceived and ill-fated attempts were subsequently made during the Restoration to keep these places under some kind of surveillance using spies, they were totally ineffectual and the coffee-house went from strength to strength.

It is not an exaggeration to say that during the late seventeenth and early eighteenth centuries the coffee-house played a central role in the formation of bourgeois institutions and manners. Its great claim to superiority over the alehouse was that it replaced 'idle' and festive consumption with *productive* leisure. The constant emphasis which we find in the polemical literature of these 'penny universities' underlines the way in which they were systematically and subtly re-texturing the discourses of the alehouse and other public places of assembly to accord with the goals of professionalization, productive economy and 'serious knowledge'. Jokes, chatter and gossip were flanked by serious, ordered meetings of both an academic and commercial interest. In *Coffee-Houses Vindicated* the author remarks:

It is grown, by the ill-influence of I know not what hydroptick stars, almost a general custom amongst us that no bargain can be drove, or business concluded between man and man, but it must be transacted at some public house . . . where continual sippings . . . would be apt to fly up into their brains and render them drowsy and indisposed . . . whereas, having now the opportunity of a coffee-house, they repair thither, take each man a dish or two (so far from causing, that it cures any dizziness or disturbant fumes), and so, despatching their business, go out more sprightly about their affairs than before.

(Ellis 1956: 57)

Dryden presided at Will's at the sign of The Red Cow in Russell Street for nearly thirty years and it became one of the principal centres of literary debate during the reign of Queen Anne. Indeed it was Dryden in his violent anti-Whig and anti-puritan prologue to *The Duke of Guise* who attacked the subversive democratic initiative of the coffee-house:

> Doe what in Coffee-houses you began;
> Pull down the Master and set up the Man.
> (*The Duke of Guise*, Prologue: 45–6)

Literary criticism as a professional activity in the modern sense began in the coffee-houses, and around 1712 Addison set up Daniel Button in a coffee-house in Russell Street and 'Button's' henceforth became the meeting place of a circle generally considered to be the originating group of English criticism in the eighteenth century: Addison, Steele, Davenant, Carey, Budgell and Phillips.

It is not our intention to rehearse these early and well-known relations between the coffee-houses and the literary figures of *The Tatler* and *The Spectator*. What is in question rather is an inculcated imperative that participation in the public sphere – and therefore participation in the serious public realm of debate – demanded a withdrawal from popular culture and its translation into negative and even phobic representations. Although it was an 'addition' to the cultural map, the coffee-house presented itself not so much as an addition as a replacement, an alternative site and part of an alternative and superior network in the stratification of the city. It was a process occurring simultaneously across a number of different terrains which mapped out a quite radical re-alignment of place, body, status and discourse.

One of the problems of this dual and complementary transformation of place was its unstable position at the intersection of the State, civil society and the market. The coffee-houses had a habit of metamorphosing into professional or business institutions. The English Stock Exchange started in a coffee-house; having originally met at Jonathan's in 'Change Alley, it moved to a room in Sweetings Alley which subsequently became known as Stock Exchange coffee-house. It was to Garraway's coffee-house that the Sun Fire office, one of the earliest insurance companies, transferred in 1711. Lloyd's began as a coffee-house for shipping owners and traders some time around 1688 and gradually moved into marine insurance over the next few decades. The Phoenix Assurance Company was established following meetings at the Langbourne Ward coffee-house (Ellis 1956: 117, 126). In this volatile period of re-territorialization the boundaries between the emerging forms of civil society and professional bourgeois institutions were pliable and provisional. It was not clear to anyone at the time quite where the lines of demarcation were drawn. The coffee-house at the outset became an ambiguous site for the production and reproduction of civil society and of business professions such as stockbroking, insurance and banking and for a brief time both discursive exchange networks overlapped in the same channels.

THE GROTESQUE SATIRIC BODY

The decaying, vestigial terms of Renaissance iconography which had associated the Court with classical models and the populace with rural buffoonery were visibly disintegrating after the Civil War, yet they could be neither fully abandoned nor accurately translated to cover new conditions of writing. Neither courtiers nor clowns, yet wishing to be associated with the one and to be dissociated from the other, the writers and artists of that period are to be found furiously manipulating the inherited terms of the old feudal symbolic system in the attempt to make them fit the new conditions of literary production. How frequently in the poetry of the period we find kingship and the low-grotesque boiling together in a mixed satiric brew which is *supposed* to describe poetic life. Vestiges of the inherited court–folly opposition are everywhere to be found in the eighteenth century, satirically mismatched and therefore somehow forced into service to approximate to the felt 'neither up nor down' existence of the writer.

The matter was made more complex by the popular image of Restoration court-society itself. In a sense the traditional terms of high-classical and low-grotesque were not simply rendered anachronistic by the growth of professional middling classes to whom the language of hierarchical extremes was inapplicable: the court of Charles II itself made a farce of the chivalric and classical icons of aristocratic and regal identity. The defiant, transgressive devilry of the Restoration court seemed to betoken a crisis of nobility after the civil wars despite the control and political influence which it had maintained. That delirious immersion in violence, promiscuity, invective, duelling and theatrical excess which characterizes the Court Wits had such an element of desperate effrontery about it that it had of itself given the lie to the complacent tableaux of the masque. The robbery and assassination of a tanner in 1662 near Waltham Cross by Lord Buckhurst, his brother Edward Sackville, Sir Henry Belasye and others was matched by another 'frolic' the following year when Sir Charles Sedley and Lord Buckhurst, both of them stark naked, preached drunkenly to the crowd below from the balcony of Oxford Kate's tavern in Covent Garden.

The Restoration court projected a collective image of living in ironic and even defiant incompatibility with its inherited forms of public representation. It was carelessly demonic, nonchalantly outrageous, cynical in the way that only a class which despises its compromises can be cynical. The mixture of 'frolic' and violent outrage on the part of the Wits seemed to both defy and seek some limit to transgression. In the atheistical amusements of the Restoration court we can detect an intense phase of that aristocratic hell-raking which was to carry 'all the tricks of Aretine' through the eighteenth century and which was to command a mixture of revulsion and admiration from the bourgeois writers of the period.

Thus the inadequacy of pre-Civil War repertoires of iconography for the representation of the emerging republic of letters in the late seventeenth century was compounded by the fact that all its terms were slowly altering. As the world of the Court was brought closer to the town and to the realm of the professional publishers, booksellers, pamphleteers, playwrights and poets, its 'grotesque' incompatibility with its inherited pre-eminence became both more visible and more risible. As early as 1669 Pepys talks of how 'cheap' the King made himself by condoning the behaviour of Rochester, Mulgrave, Killigrew and other members of the 'Merry Gang'. Pinkethman recorded how 'King Charles II, being in company with the Lord Rochester and others of the nobility, who had been drinking the best part of the night, Killigrew came in, – Now, says the King, we shall hear of our faults. – No, faith, says Killigrew, I don't care to trouble my head with that which all the town talks of.'

The notoriety of the Court, its patent iconographic failure to match up to its high office and the decorum, serious refinement and responsibility which that office required, led inevitably to a satirical relationship between Court and town. The Court was *both* classical and grotesque, both regal and foolish, high and low. At the fall of Clarendon Evelyn referred to 'the baffoons and the ladies of pleasure' at Court. With only occasional periods of respite (such as the reign of Queen Anne) the perceived indignities and decadence of the monarchy were to be an obsessive source of graphic and verse satire up to the coronation of Victoria.

This was only partly due to actual behaviour and to the occurrence of specific scandals at Court. Although we can trace periods, such as the decade after the accession of George III, when graphic and verse satire were particularly intense and vitriolic, the extraordinary saturation of eighteenth-century culture with satire cannot be explained by referring to particular personalities or political events, royal or otherwise. The ambiguous iconographic representation of the Court was only one element in a cultural set of high/low dichotomies which through satire, were gradually to restructure the territories and discourses of representation in themselves during the Enlightenment. Swift is characteristically savage in his denunciation of kingship and uses the carnivalesque inversion of high/low, king and footman, king and beast, most maliciously:

> But now go search all Europe round,
> Among the savage monsters crowned,
> (I mean all kings except our own)
> In vain you make the strictest view
> To find a king in all the crew
> With whom a footman out of place
> Would not conceive a high disgrace,
> A burning shame, a crying sin,
> To take his morning cup of gin.
>
> . . . .
> Thus think on kings, the name denotes
> Hogs, asses, wolves, baboons and goats,
> To represent in figure just
> Sloth, folly, rapine, mischief, lust.
> (Swift: *On Poetry: A Rhapsody*)

But just as the Court was a source of troubled and troubling representations after the Restoration, so too was the other pole of the dichotomy, the realm of the rustic buffoon, the realm of Folly.

We can analyse a contradictory process taking place. On the one hand the period appears to mark an intensification of certain carnivalesque and popular festivities after the Civil War and this increase and intensification precipitated a conservative desire on the part of the upper classes to separate themselves more clearly and distinctly from these popular activities. In 1738 The Society for the Reformation of Manners was formed and although it only lasted a short while a second society was set up in 1757 in an attempt, mainly under the auspices of the clergy, to regulate popular morality and custom (Curtis and Speck 1976: 45–64; Golby and Purdue 1984: 50).

Perhaps on account of the renewed vitality of the fairs and festivities (Bartholomew Fair undoubtedly enjoyed a period of expansion at the turn of the eighteenth century) there was a commensurate increase in the desire to remove or at least disperse the sites and times of popular carnivalesque pleasures – the fairs, the farces, the games and entertainments (Bushaway 1982; Malcolmson 1973; Golby and Purdue 1984). Many attempts were made to curtail or shorten the duration of the big fairs: in 1750 for example, after years of struggle by the authorities, Bartholomew Fair was cut down from fourteen days to three and its importance drastically reduced.

But as the realm of Folly was being restructured within bourgeois consciousness as precisely that *other realm* inhabited by a grotesque body which it repudiated as a part of its own identity and disdained as a set of real life *practices and rituals*, so it seemed to become more and more important as a set of *representations*. The symbolic energy of carnival festivity spills out uncontrollably from over-stuffed couplets of Augustan satire and the crowded, bustling prints of Hogarth and his contemporaries. The Smithfield Muse was on the move. We find a not dissimilar movement in Paris when, even as the Commedia dell'Arte is being dismissed and exiled in 1697 and its theatre is being closed, there is a veritable explosion of artistic *representations* of the pierrots, players, tumblers and rope-dancers by painters of the time – by Gillot and Watteau in particular. A sort of refined mimicry sets into the salons and ballrooms of Europe in which the imagery, masks and costumes of the popular carnival are being (literally) put on by the aristocracy and the bourgeoisie in order to simultaneously express and conceal their sexual desire and the pleasures of the body.

Thus in a brilliant recent essay Terry Castle has shown the

symbolic centrality of the masquerade in eighteenth-century fiction (Castle 1984), its focusing of sexual and class transgression in a purely vicarious way such that, for the novelists of the period, 'invoking the world of masquerade is typically a way of indulging in the scenery of transgression while seeming to maintain didactic probity' (Castle 1984: 912).

It is wrong, therefore, to assume that the attack on popular culture is simply the story of oppression from above. The grotesque body of carnival was being re-territorialized, it was being appropriated, sublimated and individualized to code refined identity, to give the eighteenth-century nobility and the bourgeoisie masks and symbols to think with at the very moment when they were repudiating the social realm from which those masks and symbols came. These masks and symbols, the motley paraphernalia of the Smithfield Muse and the Venetian carnival, were being systematically *severed* from their anchorage in the annual calendar of contemporary festive life, from the fixed places and times of the year which sustained them as communal events, and they were being discursively reformed and redistributed to supply most powerful symbolic repertoires for the expression of individual body/subjects – the body/subjects of the coffee-house and the cleaned-up theatre, the spa, the pleasure garden, the country house, the ballroom and the assembly room: *not* those body/subjects of the street, market square, fairground, common and village green.

Swift and Pope perpetually identify the scene of writing with the fairground and the carnival and in both writers the festive repertoire is satirically deformed by the vicious competitive circumstances of the literary market. The 'marketplace' has become 'the market' and the individual aspiring poets denigrate each other by trying to associate *everyone else* with the vulgarity of the fair whilst repudiating any connection which they themselves might have with such a world. Spite, repulsion and envy, the very marks of *ressentiment*, recode the figures of carnival in the satiric poetry of the eighteenth century to capture the 'grotesque' new competitive scene:

> As a thorn-bush, or oaken bough,
> Stuck in an Irish cabin's brow,
> Above the door, at country fair,
> Betokens entertainment there,
> So, bays on poet's brows have been

> Set, for a sign of wit within.
> And as ill neighbours in the night,
> Pull down an alehouse bush, for spite,
> The laurel so, by poets worn,
> Is by the teeth of envy torn,
> Envy, a canker-worm which tears
> Those sacred leaves which lightening spares.
> (Swift: *On Paddy's Character*
> *of the 'Intelligencer'*)

The use of the fairground as a slur in Augustan satire is so common that the poetry and pamphlet literature becomes a riot of *tu quoque*, little different in tone from the Punch and Judy shows with which Augustan poets habitually tried to identify each other:

> Two bordering wits contend for glory;
> And one is Whig and one is Tory.
> And this, for epics claims the bays,
> And that, for elegiac lays.
> Some famed for numbers soft and smooth,
> By lovers spoke in Punch's booth.
> And some as justly fame extols
> For lofty lines in Smithfield drolls.
> (Swift: *On Poetry: A Rhapsody*)

Precisely because the suppression and distancing of the physical body became the very sign of rationality, wit and judgement, the grotesque physical body existed as what Macherey calls a 'determining absent presence' in the classical body of Enlightenment poetic and critical discourse, a raging set of phantoms and concrete conditions to be forcefully rejected, projected or unacknowledged. Hence the apparent paradox that writers who were the great champions of a classical discursive body including Dryden, Swift and Pope spent so much time writing the grotesque, exorcising it, charging it to others, using and adopting its very terms whilst attempting to purify the language of the tribe. The production and reproduction of a body of classical writing required a labour of suppression, a perpetual work of exclusion upon the grotesque body and it was that supplementary yet unavoidable labour which troubled the identity of the classical. It brought the grotesque back into the classical, not so much as a return of the repressed as a vast labour of exclusion requiring and generating its own equivocal energies. *Quae negata, grata* – what is denied is desired: Augustan satire was the generic form which enabled writers to express and negate the grotesque simultaneously. It was the natural site for this labour of projection and repulsion upon which the construction of the public sphere depended.

The excremental obsession and carnivalesque imagery of a language resolutely classical may now seem less strange. What Pope refers to as the 'Smithfield Muse' was a popular deity governing traditional feast days, carnival, Saints' Days, the Lord Mayor's Procession (an enormously popular holiday which Pope makes the basis for *The Dunciad* and to which we return below), fairs, wakes, shroving, wassailing and parish feasts. These regular cycles of festivity embodied a diacritical symbolic logic (see Introduction, p. 15): the rhythmic ritual oscillation enabled groups to play out a set of body categories particularly to do with expenditure, consumption and pleasure. What this meant in practice was a *diachronic* separation of the normative and its obverse, of structure and anti-structure into an historical series of alternating binary terms. The *disjunctive* relation of classical and grotesque was thus mediated by temporal switching from one to the other. At set times the 'dirty', the 'excessive', the transgressive and the body as pleasurable subject of consuming and discharging were celebrated in corporate ritual.

Augustan England witnesses a particular phase of the change of mediating form, an act of inner self-regulation and internal distancing on the part of the middling sort. The festive calendar was altogether too dirty, too disruptive, and rooted in a network of sites and places which the urban bourgeoisie was rejecting in favour of new sites of assembly, like the coffee-house and the spa. Rational enjoyment and classical pleasures developed in a network of locations which not only displaced the carnivalesque topography with alternative constructions of 'rational pleasures' but which grew rapidly alongside the older network and defined itself over against that topography.

To a certain extent this was a move from outdoors to indoors, a farewell to the street, fondly ironic such as we find in Gay's *Trivia*, or full of repellent phobias such as in Swift's *A Description of a City Shower*, or full of malicious disdain, such as we find in *The Dunciad*. Street culture, in the eighteenth century, is a source of fascination and fear on the part of a bourgeois culture which must risk contamination by the low-Other, dirt, and danger whenever it steps down into the street ('Ah where must needy poet seek for aid / When dust and rain at once his coat invade?'). Indeed in the first stanza of Swift's *City Shower* the coffee-house is imaged as the haven where the saunterer can escape the stink and inconvenience of the street and complain in comparative comfort. As Pat Rogers has convincingly shown in *Grub Street: Studies in a Subculture*, the urban topography of London was a fundamental symbolic resource in Pope's time and 'Grub Street' is related to an actual place and cannot be treated as a purely abstract image. The reviling of Grub Street took much of its force from the specific and local conditions of the real Grub Street as Rogers shows, but it also gained from a general cultural movement out of the streets and into other more protected middleclass enclaves as the popular urban culture of the street and market square was repudiated. One network of sites, times and bodies was being supplanted by another: the consequences were enormous.

The Enlightenment strengthened and extended the Reformation desire to destroy the popular festive tradition. Yet in the present context it is not so important to establish whether in historical fact the festive calendar was temporarily strengthening itself or in decline. There is evidence that the early eighteenth century saw something of an increase, both in fairground culture and in attacks upon it. What is in question for our present purposes is rather the *self-exclusion* of certain middling and professional classes from that popular ritual culture, irrespective of whether that culture was waxing or waning. The *symbolism* of that tradition remained extraordinarily important in 'high' culture: even as writers were attacking the events and rituals of this festive calendar they were appropriating its symbols, imagery and imaginative repertoires for their own distinct purposes. It was the *form of mediation* which was changing, gradually giving way to other kinds of mediation less inimical to the rules of purity, propriety and continuous production which govern bourgeois reason. As sites of assembly were decathected and cleaned up to provide the material productive network for public discourse and as the carnivalesque rituals of the open air were ironized and sentimentalized in the 'soft culture' of the masquerade, pleasure garden, opera and theatre pantomime, so the ritual oscillation was displaced by 'transduction', a form of mediation between classical and grotesque adhering more closely to the demands of the classical.

The Augustans laboured to translate what they were designating as grotesque (in Bakhtin's special sense) into discourse more in line with the classical: discourse which is elevated, serious, refined, tending to relate to genres of epic and tragedy, pure, homogeneous, closed, finished, proportioned, symmetrical, dignified and decorous. At the same time and just as important, they appropriated symbolic elements of the grotesque and deployed them as the focal imaginative and revivifying elements of their own discourse. This two-way transaction thus begins by creating a discursive hierarchy with itself at the top and a number of inferior realms beneath it where language is deemed to be 'grotesque': impure, vulgar, of lesser epistemological clarity, masked and muddied, irresponsibly protean, indecent and exorbitant. In the act of reforming or rejecting these 'inferior' content-discourses, holding them subject to new kinds of abstract restraining device (such as the rhyming couplet), Dryden, Swift and Pope tried to incorporate them within classical norms.

Thus whilst Augustan poetry witnesses an unprecedented labour of transduction in which it battled against the Smithfield Muse to cleanse the cultural sphere of impure and messy semiotic matter, it also fed voraciously and incessantly from that very material. It nourished and replenished its refined formalisms from the symbolic repertoire of the grotesque body *in the very name of exclusion*. It took the grotesque within itself so as to reject it, but this meant only that the grotesque was now an unpalatable and interiorized *phobic* set of representations associated with avoidance and with others. It could never be owned. It was always someone else who was possessed by the grotesque, never the self. In this way the bourgeois public sphere, that 'idealist' realm of judgement, refinement, wit and rationalism was dependent upon disavowal, denial, projection.

By disowning the grotesque body the Enlightenment rendered itself peculiarly vulnerable to the shock of its continued presence or to its unexpected rediscovery. Swift is never to be taken as normative in anything, but his description of the critic in *A Tale of a Tub* cannot be entirely dismissed as a matter of an insane individual excremental obsession – the fascinated disavowal in the name of cleanliness is too prevalent in the whole culture. The critics, he writes,

In their common perusal of books singling out the errors and defects, the nauseous, the fulsome, the dull, and the impertinent, with the caution of a man that walks through the Edinburgh streets in a morning, who indeed is as careful as he can to watch diligently and spy out the filth in his way; not that he is curious to observe the colour and the complexion of the ordure, or take its dimensions, much less to be paddling in or tasting it; but only with a design to come out as cleanly as he may.

(Swift 1704: 64)

The excremental interest then is dissociative: the sole avowed reason for such close observation, in all bad faith, is avoidance, 'to come out as cleanly as he may'. And Edinburgh, like Ireland and Virginia, is made the suitable site for such exercises of avoidance, once more illustrating the way that the grotesque body may be topographically coded. Why Edinburgh? Not simply because it was a town renowned for mean critics, nor because, as A. L. Rowse once remarked, it was a second-rate Presbyterian city, but because a clean ideal sphere of judgement was being constructed and defined in terms of a low and dirty periphery, a notional and literal 'outside' which guaranteed a coherence and privilege to the 'inside'. Similarly in Pope's *Dunciad*, the use of 'low and base' matter in Book II is legitimated in the footnote with the remark that 'the politest men are sometimes obliged to *swear*, when they happen to have to do with porters and oyster-wenches'. The co-ordinates of geography and class intersect as a network of exclusions which underpin and guarantee the status of the refined sphere, enabling it *both* to speak about that which was rapidly becoming unspeakable *and* to define its class identity by projecting the grotesque body onto the low, foreign courts, the provinces and frequently, as in Swift, onto women.

This refined public sphere occupied the centre. That is to say, it carved out a domain between the realm of kings and the world of the alley-ways and taverns, and it did so by forcing together the high and the low as contaminated equivalents, somehow in league with each other and part of a conspiracy of exchange and promiscuity in which the low was ebbing higher to flood the court and the court was sinking into the filthy ways and pastimes of the low. In Book IV of *The Dunciad* Pope satirizes the Grand Tour, upon which the young son of Dulness:

> Saw ev'ry Court, heard ev'ry King declare
> His Royal Sense of Op'ra's or the Fair;
> The Stews and Palace equally explor'd,
> Intrigu'd with glory, and with spirit whor'd;
> (Pope, *The Dunciad* IV: 312–16)

Indeed the whole conception of *The Dunciad*, which makes Dulness at once a Monarch *and* the embodiment of the fairground spirit, guided by her own muse from Smithfield, this conception of the regal and the lumpen promiscuously compounded is the foundational structure of the poem. At the very outset Pope establishes the circuit of corruption which connects the extremes of Court and marketplace in a single figure. Even the very phrase 'The Smithfield Muse' is a dislocating and ironic compound of high classical and low grotesque which perfectly symbolizes the poetics of transgression at the heart of Pope's project:

> The Mighty Mother, and her Son who brings
> The Smithfield Muses to the ear of Kings,
> I sing.
> (Pope, *The Dunciad* I: 1–3)

The Poet Laureate is a contaminating mediator who brings the carnivalesque to the Court, perversely muddling and enmiring the polar terms of the classical system. In Book III Pope envisages Dulness irrevocably rising from the fairground stalls and passing through the theatres to finally take her place at Court:

> 'Till rais'd from booths, to Theatre, to Court,
> Her seat imperial Dulness shall transport.
> Already Opera prepares the way,
> The sure fore-runner of her gentle sway.
> (Pope, *The Dunciad* III: 299–302)

Here 'Dulness' seems to be a synonym for carnivalesque or popular culture and nothing else. It illustrates that pervasive organizational antimony between 'Folly' and 'Wit' which, at least since Dryden, had served as the trigger words in the struggle to carve out the intermediate domain of 'judgement and sense' (Wit) from the popular culture of the period (Folly). It is also important to realize, as Robert M. Krapp has indicated in 'Class analysis of a literary controversy: Wit and Sense in seventeenth-century English literature' (1946), that the terms 'Wit' and 'Sense' were also polarized against each other towards the end of the seventeenth century in the attack by predominantly middle-class writers ('Sense') upon the aristocratically inclined writers ('Wit'). But for Pope in *The Dunciad* Dulness is Folly and he attacks those writers who are its bearers, those vanishing mediators in the conspiracy of history who (Theobald or Cibber, does it really matter which?) carry the plague of Bartholomew Fair to reach, with infectious consequence, the very ears of Royalty:

> 2. *Smithfield* is the place where Bartholomew Fair was kept, whose shews, machines, and dramatical entertainments, formerly agreeable only to the taste of the Rabble, were, by the Hero of this poem and others of equal genius, brought to the theatres of Covent Garden, Lincolns-inn-fields, and the Haymarket, to be the reigning pleasures of the Court and Town. This happened in the Reigns of King George I and II.
>
> (Pope, *The Dunciad* I: n. 2)

After Charles II's return, Bartholomew Fair was extended from a market officially lasting three days to a fair of two weeks and at one time possibly six weeks' duration. And as the fair grew and flourished it drew the theatres into its orbit. The traffic in ideas, plays, personnel, actors and managers between the fair-booths and the theatres was considerable in the eighteenth century, not least because the fairs offered theatre people the chance of employment during the summer period when the theatres were closed. Actors could often hope to make more money in the fortnight of Bartholomew Fair than they could hope to make in a much longer period in the town theatres (Rosenfeld: 1960). Actors came from the fashionable theatres to perform at the fair's booths. Henry Woodward for example, a well-known actor of the period who appeared in Rich's Lilliputian troupe and played Harlequin Macheath in 1737 in *The Beggars' Pantomime*, made a great part of his reputation in playing Harlequin at the fair. In the opening lines of Churchill's *Rosciad* which satirized contemporary actors, Shuter (*c.* 1728–76) and Yates (1706–96), two reasonably renowned actors, are both remarked for playing booths at the fairs:

> Shuter keeps open house at Southwark fair,
> And hopes the friends of humour will be there;
> In Smithfield, Yates prepares the rival treat
> For those who laughter love, instead of meat.
> (Churchill, *Rosciad*: 29–32)

William Pinkethman, a member of the Drury Lane Company, ran a booth at Smithfield with two or three other actors, thereby earning himself the contempt of a pamphleteer who wrote 'A Comparison between the Two Stages':

> SULLEN: But Pinkethman, the flower of –
> CRITIC: – Bartholomew Fair, and the idol of the rabble.
> (Morley 1859: 364)

As the fair and the theatre became interfused the fear of a general contamination grew and to be associated with Bartholomew Fair was recognized by critics as a mark of inferiority. It indicated that the writer concerned was a *hybrid* creature trying to straddle the world of popular fairground culture and the 'higher' world of humanistic ethics and ideals. Since, as we have seen, it was precisely self-exclusion from the sites of popular festivity which was a major symbolic project for the emergent professional classes, such hybridization appeared as especially grotesque. The *separation* of the two cultural spheres was a specific and quite self-conscious labour for the Augustan élite, particularly since the two realms appeared to be getting closer together. There is something of a moral panic in the period about the promiscuous mingling of the high and the low on the site of the fair. Pope in particular seems to fear

> A motley mixture in long wigs, in bags,
> In silks, in crapes, in Garters and in rags,
> From drawing rooms, from colleges, from garrets,
> On horse, on foot, in hacks, and gilded chariots:
> (Pope, *The Dunciad* II: 21–4)

– a motley crew who are to gather 'where the tall may-pole once o'er-look'd the Strand'. Indeed a recurrent line of invective aimed at Cibber underscores the intolerable social mix and range of his supporters and Pope refers to him as 'This Mess, toss'd up of Hockley-hole and White's / Where Dukes and Butchers join to wreathe my crown'. Any transgression of the high–low domains creates a grotesque hybrid right at the social threshold, a neither/nor creature, neither up nor down, which repels and fascinates Pope and which guards, like the hydra, the pathways and meeting-places between high and low. And the effect is not merely that predictably anti-democratic polemic we should expect from Pope. It is of graver consequence, a closure of identity which in attempting to block out somatic and social heterodoxy is fated to rediscover it everywhere as Chaos, Darkness and 'Mess'. The classical body splits precisely along the rigid edge which is its defence against heterogeneity: its closure and purity are quite illusory and it will perpetually rediscover in itself, often with a sense of shock or inner revulsion, the grotesque, the protean and the motley, the 'neither/nor', the double negation of high and low which was the very precondition for its social identity.

Hence, perhaps, Pope's special mistrust of Alkanah Settle who had been Poet Laureate to James II, who later became the salaried dramatist of Mrs Mynns and her daughter Mrs Leigh at Bartholomew Fair (Morley 1859: 358) and who supposedly ended up acting as a dragon in one of his plays about St George – the grotesque body indeed. In *The [1729] Dunciad* Settle is given the following lines to speak:

> Yet lo in me what authors have to brag on
> Reduc'd at last to hiss in my own dragon.
> Avert it heav'n that thou or Cibber e'er
> Should wag two serpent tails in Smithfield Fair.
> Like the vile straw that's blown about the streets
> The needy Poet sticks to all he meets,
> Coach'd, carted, trod upon, now loose, now fast,
> In the Dog's tail his progress ends at last.
> (Pope, *The Dunciad* III: 287–94)

In 1733 the Poet Laureate Cibber, later to be pilloried as the 'hero' of the 1743 *Dunciad* moved from the Drury Lane to act as Bajazet in *Tamerlaine the Great* at Bartholomew Fair. Cibber's daughter, who also performed at the fair, was later said to be keeping a puppet show and selling sausages.

The 'crime' of Theobald, Cibber, Settle and others is the act of mediation: they occupy a taboo-laden space *between* the topographical boundaries which mark off the discrete sites of high and low culture. They transgress domains, moving between fair, theatre, town and court, threatening to sweep away the literary and social marks of difference at the very point where such differences are being widened.

It was not only through Bartholomew Fair that such differences were made. Aubrey Williams has made a convincing case for the idea that *The Dunciad* is a symbolic commentary upon the Lord Mayor's Show and that, not only is it a satire on the hacks of Grub Street but a simultaneous satirical onslaught on the 'antics' of the trading classes and their procession which formed a popular holiday show celebrating the power of the city (Williams 1955: 30–41). He writes that the specific details of the poem –

> its setting of a particular Lord Mayor's Day [October 28th], the numerous references to the mayoral pageantry, the precision with which the poet designates the geographical location of various events and movements – would appear to support an attempt to make sense out of the similarities which obviously do exist.
>
> (Williams 1955: 33)

The Lord Mayor's Pageant had come back with renewed splendour after the Restoration, 'there being twice as many pageants and speeches as have formerly shewn' in 1660, remarked John Tatham, and the 'gaudy day' was one which mingled ostentatious display of wealth by the commercial City interest with a rowdy holiday for the populace of London. The event was remarked for its loose familiarity towards the Court – in 1662 Charles and his Queen were greeted thus by the speaker in the waterman's barge:

> God blesse thee, King Charles, and thy good woman there; and blest creature she is, I warrant thee, and true. Go thy way for a wag. thou hast had a merry time on't in the west; I need say no more. But do'st hear me, don't take it in dudgeon that I am so familiar with thee; thou may'st take it kindly, for I am not alwayes in this good humour; though I *thee* thee and *thou* thee, I am no Quaker, take notice of that.
>
> (Chambers 1863–4, II: 564)

It was the one day above all when the world of trade and commerce showed its material power and put on a gorgeous symbolic entry – the concluding plate of Hogarth's *Industry and Idleness* gives a vivid picture of the proceedings. From 1691 to 1708 Settle was the city-laureate and he is reputed to have pleased the crowds well enough with his sense of display at the Show (Fairholt 1843). Pope, as we noted above, heaped especial ridicule upon him in *The Dunciad* for his association with popular custom and his last days spent acting at Bartholomew Fair. Associated with *both* the Lord Mayor's Show *and* with Bartholomew Fair poor Settle was doubly damned. Within this context Williams' interpretation seems most persuasive:

> Since the Lord Mayor's Procession journeyed from that symbol of City interest, Guildhall, to the world of the Court represented by Westminster Hall, this progress could be seen by Pope as offering an analogy to the spreading influence of dulness, the translation of empire, the deterioration of arts and morals, that his poem postulates.
>
> (Williams 1955: 33)

The social and aesthetic interfusion of high and low has its counterpart at the linguistic level where a grotesque hybridization threatens to subvert the distinction between words and genres. In Rag-Fair where 'old cloaths and frippery are sold' Dulness watches

> a Mob of Metaphors advance,
> Pleas'd with the Madness of the mazy dance:
> How Tragedy and Comedy embrace;
> How Farce and Epic get a jumbled race.
> (Pope, *The Dunciad* I: 65–8)

The Dunces' writing is here conceived of first as *socially* grotesque, bearing the emblems of poverty, of plebeian politics (the 'Mob') and of Bedlam (the madness of the mazy dance), and this social grotesque is itself inscribed in the mixing of genres.

This correlation of the mixing of genres with the subversion of social hierarchy was not, of course, invented by Pope. Indeed, it had underpinned the stock accusation against the popular stage as early as the sixteenth century when Sidney attacked 'mongrell Tragi-comedie' which mingled kings and clowns and allowed the clown 'to play a part in majesticall matters' (Sidney 1907: 54). Joseph Hall pressed similar charges in his *Virgidemiarum* (1957):

> A goodly hotch-potch: when vile Russetings
> Are matched with monarchs, and with mighty kings.
> A goodly grace to sober Tragic Muse,
> When each base clown, his clumbsie foot doth bruise,
> And show his teeth in double rotten row
> For laughter at his selfe-resembled show.

What *was* novel in Pope was the sheer scale of the onslaught against the authors, audiences, places and linguistic practices which he condemned. He attempted to construct a transcendent position for the master-poet by a feat of negation more absolute and comprehensive than anything we can find in Ben Jonson.

Yet as his critics were amply to demonstrate Pope's act of negation could itself be turned against its author so as to reveal Pope's own features in the hybridization of the fair. As Pope scorned the social promiscuity which raised Smithfield to the ear of kings he was in turn pilloried as a social hybrid, 'furnish'd with a very good Assurance, and a Plausible, at least Cringing Way of Insinuation' (Gildon 1718: 71). As he accused the dunces of low manners so he was accused of low birth: Curll claimed that 'his Father was but a Husbandman on Windsor-Forest' and that 'being of Consumptive Constitution, and an only Son, he was by the Indulgence of his Parents, excus'd from the labouring Work of the Field' (Curll 1728: 154). As Pope sneered at the contamination of others by the fair he himself could be imagined as a Smithfield freak, 'a little diminutive Creature', 'a little Aesopic sort of an animal in his own cropt Hair, and dress agreeable to the Forest he came from' (Gildon 1718: 71). As he imagined his dunces fishing in the 'nether realms' of the sewer for 'ordure's sympathetic force' he was attacked for working 'in Terms so Coarse and Filthy, that few Readers can forbear puking at his bare Ideas' and it was mockingly claimed that if one deleted the poem's filth there would be nothing left but the filthy poet himself:

> For take away the filthy Part,
> Of T—rd, and Spew, and Mud, and Fart:
> (Words which no Gentleman could use,
> And e'en a Nightman would refuse)
> There nought remain'd save to the Elf
> A Disemboguement of himself.
>
> (Curll 1728: 155)

Thus the social and linguistic debasements of which Pope accused others were said to be characteristic of *The Dunciad* itself and in *Tom O'Bedlam's Dunciad: or Pope Alexander the Pig*, John Henley wrote:

> O wonder not, that he such flights has shown,
> He shines in borrow'd Beauties, not his own.
> Well might his Smithfield Muse so sweetly sing,
> Since Watermen their due Assistance bring.
>
> (Henley 1723: 171)

Later in Henley's poem Pope threatens suicide but his friends comfort him with the prospect of Billingsgate which is described as the imaginative source of Pope's writing – a not entirely unwarranted ascription:

> There's Billingsgate! an unexhausted Spring,
> Whence we our Flights and Witticisms bring.
>
> (Henley 1723: 171)

Similarly a pamphlet published in 1743, *Why How Now, Gossip Pope*, claimed that *The Dunciad* was a distillation of Billingsgate, remarking that 'Your whole piece is only refining on the low Jests of Porters and Fish-women, as you live by the Water-side; or dressing the insolent scurrility of Link-Boys and Hackney-Coachmen in something (not much) genteeler language' (Henley 1743: 315).

The mitigating fact of Pope's superior poetic ability could not save him from being immersed in the very process of grotesque debasement which he scorned in others. Of course it was against the 'bastard pleasure' of critics, laureates and hacks which Pope wrote. Jonson, we argued, consolidated his 'authorship' as an act performed *on* and *against* theatrical scripts (both his own and others'). At Twickenham Pope could eventually aspire to take a more distant view of the literary marketplace and yet his work suggests that even more than Jonson he could envisage authorship only as a system of competitive differentiation which could put him above the Theobalds, the Cibbers and the Grub Street hacks. Indeed Pope could not even imagine the union of knowledge and power, poet and prince which Jonson sometimes believed might stabilize differentiation through its relation to a single, fixed place of authority. In the absence of any guarantee of higher authority Pope's obsessive negation drew attention inevitably to the arch-negator himself, who was no more able than those whom he attacked to climb outside or above the marketplace. For, as Stanley Fish argues, 'the self of the professional' – and of the professional writer above all – 'is constituted and legitimized by the very structures – social and institutional – from which it is supposedly aloof' (Fish 1984: 26).

SURVEYING THE FAIR AND PROBLEMS OF DIFFERENCE

In 1685, Sir Robert Southwell wrote a letter from Kingsweston to his son, Edward, who was in London with his tutor. In the letter he advised Edward 'to consider the great theatres of Bartholomew Fair' and to 'convert that tumult into a profitable book':

> You would certainly see the garboil there to more advantage if Mr Webster and you wou'd read, or could see acted, the play of Ben Jonson, called Bartholomew Fair.
>
> (Morley 1859: 288)

Southwell tells his son to take with him to the fair his 'impressions of that play', and once at Smithfield, he continues, 'I should think it not amiss if you then got up in some high window to survey the whole pit at once'. The father goes on with his paternal guidance to provide a kind of conceptual grid through which his son should view and make sense of the fair. Edward should note the rope-dancers, the fools, the drunkards, the madmen, the monsters, the pickpockets (the account of whom Southwell senior draws from Ben Jonson's play); he should then notice the 'places devoted to the eating of pig' and the various corners of 'lewdness and impurity'. But what benefit can be gained from this 'sort of Bacchanalia, to gratifie the multitude in their wand'ring and irregular thoughts'?

The benefit, he argues, is that in watching the fair Edward will learn the rules of resemblance and differentiation, and, having learned them, he will be able to 'convert that tumult into a profitable book':

> I have formerly told you that I look'd upon human nature as a great volume, wherein every man, woman, and child, seem'd to be a distinct leaf, or page, or paragraph that had something in it of diversity from all the rest, not but that many humours, natures, and inclinations, might fall under the same chapter, or be rang'd

under the same common head. Yet still there is such distinction of one from the other, as a discerning mind will find out. And, indeed, it never was otherwise, even in the whole mass of things, since the creation; for two things, if they did not differ, would not be two, but the same.

(Morley 1859: 291)

The banality of the philosophical conclusion notwithstanding, Southwell has shown throughout his letter how a plebeian event can be transformed into a literary text for the educated élite. This act of transformation depends upon the social and physical separation of the observer. By reading Jonson first, the young gentleman will not only have already aestheticized the fair, he will have placed himself above the crowd which he has come to watch. And his mental elevation will in turn be secured by his physical elevation: he should 'get up into some high window' so as 'to survey the whole pit at once'. That theatrical allusion to the pit and the 'at once' are crucial. For it is through seeing the fair as a simultaneous whole outside of himself that he will enclose all the distinct pages in the 'great volume' which is constituted by his gaze. He will have made himself into a specific kind of transcendental cognitive ego by the act of partition and observation.

But the coherence of the 'great volume' is threatened from two opposite directions. Firstly there is the danger that without the active process of 'distinction' by the observer, the whole fair will 'fall under the same chapter'. Secondly it is possible that the 'discerning mind' will lose itself in the endless distinctions which cannot be bound up into a 'profitable book'. Both of these dangers seem remote from the secure and affable rhetoric of Sir Robert Southwell. Yet it is precisely these dangers which press in upon the last part of Book VII of Wordsworth's *The Prelude* (1805), in which the poet contemplates the 'blank confusion' of Bartholomew Fair.

At one level, Wordsworth's description suggests the excitement of the fair, which Charles Lamb had taken Dorothy and him to see in September 1802. However 'monstrous' he finds it, the poet seems to revel in the 'colour, motion, shape, sight, sound' (VII. 661):

> All moveables of wonder from all parts
> Are here, Albinos, painted Indians, Dwarfs,
> The Horse of Knowledge, and the Learned Pig,

> The Stone-eater, the Man that swallows fire,
> Giants, Ventriloquists, the Invisible Girl,
> The Bust that speaks, and moves its goggling eyes,
> The wax-work, Clock-work, all the marvellous craft
> Of modern Merlins, wild Beasts, Puppet-shows,
> All out-o'-th'way, far-fetch'd, perverted things.
> All freaks of Nature, all Promethean thoughts
> Of Man; his dulness, madness, and their feats,
> All jumbled up together to make up
> This Parliament of Monsters. Tents and Booths
> Meanwhile, as if the whole were one vast Mill,
> Are vomiting, receiving, on all sides,
> Men, Women, three-years' Children, Babes in arms.
> (Wordsworth, *The Prelude* VII: 679–94)

The carnivalesque ambivalence of 'praise and abuse' still hovers about this passage, and yet there are also traces of a disgust, a horror of contamination, which bear a striking resemblance to Pope's. As Pope attacked 'the Madness of the mazy dance' so Wordsworth sees in the fair Man's 'dulness, madness, and their feats, / All jumbled up together ...'. Carnivalesque hybridizing is reinscribed by Wordsworth, as by Pope, as a fascinating but repellent *perversion* in such a way that an insane darkness seems to inhabit the fair, not communal folly but the collapse of language into itself. The boundaries between all categories are confused and transgressed: animals become human, humans become animals, freaks and monsters, buildings become open orifices which vomit forth and consume people simultaneously, fair-goers of different ages and genders are muddled up together.

Wordsworth concluded the previous book of *The Prelude* on 'Cambridge and the Alps', by noting how he had responded on the continent to the armies which were on the move 'in the cause of Liberty':

> A Stripling, scarcely of the household then
> Of social life, I look'd upon these things
> As from a distance, heard, and saw, and felt,
> Was touch'd, but with no intimate concern ...
> (VI: 693–6)

Wordsworth's remote and observant solitude, his lack of intimate concern for the collectivity, contrasts remarkably with the feelings of the French intellectuals whose writings had helped put the revolutionary armies on the move. Both Rousseau and Diderot cultivated a nostalgic and utopian view of the festivals of the Ancients and of contemporary popular festivities. 'How fine humanity is at the spectacle', enthused Rousseau, 'why should they separate so quickly. Men are so good, so happy, when courtesy unites their separate wills, merges them, makes them one.' In the *Lettre sur les spectacles* he attacks the exclusivity and individuated passivity of the theatrical audience in the name of democratic festivity, inaugurating a bourgeois progressive and idealist strand of thinking about popular festivity to which Bakhtin himself undoubtedly belongs. It is a populism which, despite his *own* kind of avowed democratic populism, is alien to Wordsworth. It registers a difference in constitution, in the internalized image of collective–individual representations, which is of some consequence. Rousseau writes:

> But what shall be the objects of the spectacle? What shall be shown? Nothing, if you so wish. Wherever there is liberty and public concourse, there too will be well-being. Set up a pole, crowned with flowers in the middle of the public square, have the people assemble – and you will have a festival. Better still, let the spectators partake in the spectacle, make them actors themselves, let each person see himself and love himself in the others, and they will be more closely united.
>
> (Starobinski 1964: 100)

What is evident in much continental writing on popular festivity at this time is just that strain of republican enthusiasm which was so short-lived in Wordsworth. In some ways the continental carnival had become the most positive image of democratic freedom available up to the time of the French Revolution and was habitually associated with republicanism, often indeed with the 'Great Republic' of Venice:

> A strip of white satin over your face, and on your shoulders a hood of black lace or taffeta, reaching down to the flowing folds of the mantle, and by means of this ridiculous disguise, aristocratic Venice becomes democratic ... But the mask is more than a disguise, it is an incognito. It is secrecy, anonymity, confident

impunity, it is licensed folly and licit nonsense ... you can recognize no one, and no one recognizes you.

(Phillipe Monnier 1920, quoted in Starobinski 1964: 90)

Byron is closer to this set of associations than other English writers of this period and when asked for his impression of Italy and the Italians replied that 'their best things are the Carnival balls and the masquerades, where everyone runs mad for six weeks'. Distinctly not a Wordsworthian enthusiasm: in Book VII of *The Prelude* he flees in panic from the festive scene:

> For once the Muse's help will we implore,
> And she shall lodge us, wafted on her wings,
> Above the press and danger of the Crowd,
> Upon some Showman's platform: what a hell
> For eyes and ears. What anarchy and din
> Barbarian and infernal.
>
> (VII: 655–60)

As in Sir Robert Southwell's letter, so here the desire is to survey the fair both physically and metaphysically, though there is a degree of neurotic anxiety in Wordsworth's flight quite absent from Southwell's easy instructions. Just as Southwell recommended climbing into 'some high window', so Wordsworth desires to climb upon some showman's platform; as Southwell advised seeing the fair through the eyes of Ben Jonson so Wordsworth implores the Muse's aid. However, the interplay between distinctions and resemblances which Southwell believed to be the basis for translating the fair into a 'profitable book' threaten to dissolve Wordsworth's text and to put the 'whole creative powers of man asleep' (Wordsworth 1805, VII: 654). The fair becomes a type of the city itself, a 'blank confusion', an 'undistinguishable world'. From his perspective of visionary aloofness Wordsworth surveys the city-dwellers who appear as 'slaves ... of low pursuits',

> Living amid the same perpetual flow
> Of trivial objects, melted and reduced
> To one identity, by differences
> That have no law, no meaning, and no end.
>
> (VII: 700–4)

Southwell had assured his son that 'a discerning mind' would find 'distinction of one from the other', but for Wordsworth it is the boundaries which separate word from word, object from object and observer from observed which are at stake. In the city, as in the fair, differences proliferate and at the same time melt into one identity so that the observer, cast loose in a chain of signifiers which have 'no law, meaning, and no end', finds his own identity dissolving into the 'blank confusion'.

In the final lines of Book VII, Wordsworth discovers a cure for this confusion in his 'early converse with the works of God' (VII: 718) which enables him to 'diffuse', even into 'transitory things', 'Composure and ennobling Harmony' (VII: 740). But that line, with which he concludes the book, is perplexing. On the one hand, it points us back to the mountains and the 'ancient hills' of Wordsworth's childhood. But on the other, it suggests how far the poet has moved away from his radical programme as a 'man speaking to men'. In recuperating the fair and the city as his subject matter, Wordsworth is drawn back into the *neo-classical* rhetoric of Dryden according to which the 'lowest' forms could, and should, be raised up or ennobled by the poet. But the low forms could only be ennobled if the poet was, in both social and literary terms, *superior to his subject*.

The fair thus prompts Wordsworth to transcend 'the press and danger of the crowd'. To achieve that transcendence he turns to the machinery of the classical canon which he had deliberately set his face against in the *Lyrical Ballads*. 'For once' – at this particular moment of crisis, in the turbulent throng of Bartholomew Fair – he turns not to the imagination, nor to Nature, but to the classical 'Muse' to 'implore' help. In invoking the Muse, Wordsworth also invokes the linguistic and generic hierarchies of a classical aesthetic which can separate into discrete categories all that has been 'jumbled up together'. It is as if the fair's threat to authorship and identity alike could only be contained by returning to the poetics, and also the politics, of the old classical dispensation – a return to the categorical distinctions which *The Prelude* as a whole tries to dissolve.

In this chapter we have seen how a division of culture was inscribed into the definitional structure of poetic authorship. Jonson, Dryden, Pope and Wordsworth, each sought to legitimate his claim to the vocation of master-poet by disengaging himself from the carnivalesque scene so as to stand above it, taking up a singular position of transcendence. The traces of this labour, of this act of discursive rejection, are marked out by nothing so much as the poet's attempt to found an illusory unity above and beyond the carnival. In each case however, this apparently simple gesture of social superiority and disdain could not be effectively accomplished without revealing the very labour of suppression and sublimation involved. Such a project is constitutive, not contingent.

The ambivalence of the poetic 'I' is thus inscribed in its ineluctable return *in writing* to that very scene from which it persistently declared its absence. Like the scene of seduction, Bartholomew Fair contained a phobic enchantment which, at least in Wordsworth, might well be called traumatic. 'Wo es war soll ich werden' could be the apt description of a poet-subject repulsed by social practices destined to become the very content of the bourgeois unconscious. Indeed, as we shall see below, it is not too much to claim that as the fair and the carnival were scripted as the alien space of undifferentiation, filth and excess, they simultaneously encoded the most powerful linguistic repertoires of the 'Imaginary'.

3

The City:
the Sewer, the Gaze and
the Contaminating Touch

In the previous chapter, we looked at the return in writing to the scene of 'blank confusion' from which the author obsessively declared his absence. In the nineteenth century that fear of differences that 'have no law, no meaning, and no end' was articulated above all through the 'body' of the city: through the separations and interpenetrations of the suburb and the slum, of grand buildings and the sewer, of the respectable classes and the lumpenproleteriat (what Marx called 'the whole indefinite, disintegrated mass thrown hither and thither' (Marx 1951, I: 267)). In this chapter, we will move from the theatre, the poem and the scenes of 'authorship', to trace the transcodings of psychic desire, concepts of the body and the structuring of the social formation across the city's topography as this was inscribed in the parliamentary report, the texts of social reform, the hysterical symptom of the psychoanalyst's patient, as well as in the poet's journal and the novel.

It was in the reforming text as much as in the novel that the nineteenth-century city was produced as the locus of fear, disgust and fascination. Chadwick's *Report ... on an Inquiry into the Sanitary Conditions of the Labouring Population of Great Britain* (1842), for instance, was an instant best-seller, and more than 10,000 copies were distributed free (Chadwick 18; Finer 1952: 209–10; Hennock 1957: 117). In Chadwick, in Mayhew, in countless Victorian reformers, the slum, the labouring poor, the prostitute, the sewer, were recreated for the bourgeois study and drawing-room as much as for the urban council chamber. Indeed, the reformers were central in the construction of the urban geography of the bourgeois Imaginary. As the bourgeoisie produced new forms of regulation and prohibition governing their own bodies, they wrote ever more loquaciously of the body of the Other – of the city's 'scum'.

The body of the Other produced contradictory responses. Certainly, it was to be *surveyed*, as Southwell and Wordsworth surveyed the fair, from 'some high window' or superior position. Chadwick insisted that satisfactory regulation depended upon breaking down those architectural barriers which kept the immoral 'secluded from superior inspection and from common observation' (Chadwick 1842: 243). At the same time, new forms of propriety must penetrate and subjugate the recalcitrant body: hence, the insistence upon 'regularity of diet', 'clean or respectable clothes', even *drill-masters* to restrain 'bodily irritability, and thence uncontrollable mental irritability' (Chadwick 1842: 246, 248; 1880: 274). Chadwick argued that calisthenics, 'which to the common eye are expensive and misbefitting luxuries, are in the experience of Sanitary Science, "formatives", necessary to impart mobility to all parts of the frame, to get rid of clumsiness and to augment health and productive force: – the objects of an economical administration' (1880: 275). But even as the bourgeoisie speculated upon new regimes for the body, they obsessively returned to the 'unutterable horrors' of the city, where there were no 'architectural barriers or protections of decency and propriety', to the imaginary place whose empirical existence a Scottish police superintendent asserted was a place where there lived 'a thousand children who have no names whatever, or only nick-names, like dogs' (Chadwick 1842: 124, 131–3).

SLUM AND SEWER

The relation of social division and exclusion to the production of desire emerges with great clarity in the nineteenth-century city. New boundaries between high and low, between aristocrat and rag-picker, were there simultaneously established and transgressed. On the one hand, the slum was separated from the suburb: 'the undrained clay beneath the slums oozed with cesspits and sweated with fever; the gravelly heights of the suburbs were dotted with springs and

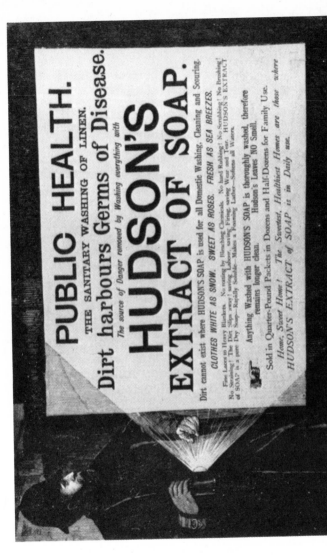

5   An advertisement for Hudson's soap, printed in *The Graphic*, 1 August 1891

bloomed with health' (Dyos and Reeder 1973: 370). On the other hand, the streets were a 'mingle-mangle', 'a hodge-podge', where the costermonger, the businessman, the prostitute, the clerk, the nanny and the crossing-sweeper jostled for place.

Henry Mayhew's *London Labour and the London Poor* (1861) is traversed and fractured by contradictory formulations of these relations of high to low. His work begins with a Chapter 'Of wandering tribes in general' in which he separates out two distinct 'races': 'the wanderers and the civilized tribes' (Mayhew 1861–2: I, 1). Mayhew's definition of the nomadic is a demonized version of what Bakhtin later defined as the grotesque. The nomad, Mayhew writes, is distinguished from the civilized

> by his repugnance to regular and continuous labour – by his want of providence in laying up store for the future . . . – by his passion for stupefying herbs and roots, and, when possible, for intoxicating fermented liquors . . . – by his love of libidinous dances . . . – by the looseness of his notion as to property – by the absence of chastity among his women, and his disregard of female honour – and lastly, by his vague sense of religion.
> (Mayhew 1861–2: I, 2)

Mayhew constructs the nomad in terms of his desires ('passion', 'love', 'pleasure') and in terms of his rejections or ignorance ('repugnance', 'want', 'looseness', 'absence', 'disregard'). In the slum, the bourgeois spectator surveyed and classified *his own antithesis*.

The nomads are improvident: 'like all who make a living as it were by a game of chance, plodding, carefulness, and saving habits cannot be reckoned among their virtues' (Mayhew 1861–2: II, 152). Their habits are 'not domestic': for those who inhabit the markets, streets, beer shops, dancing-rooms and theatres, 'home has few attractions' (1861–2: I, 11). They are indifferent to marriage: '[only] one-tenth – at the outside one-tenth – of the couples living together and carrying on the costermongering trade are married. Of the rights of 'legitimate' and 'illegitimate' children the costermongers understand nothing, and account it a mere waste of time and money to go through the ceremony of wedlock' (1861–2: I, 20). They are opposed to constituted authority and above all to the police: 'the hatred of a costermonger to a "peeler" is intense, and with their opinion of the police, all the more ignorant unite that of the governing power' (1861–2: I, 20); 'in their continual warfare with the force, they resemble many savage nations, from the cunning and treachery they use' (1861–2: I, 16). They are ignorant of religion 'not 3 in 100 costermongers had ever been in the interior of a church, or any place of worship, or knew what was meant by Christianity' (1861–2: I, 21), whilst a 9-year-old mud-lark 'did not know what religion was. God was God, he said. He had heard he was good, but he didn't know what good he was to him' (1861–2: II, 156). Above all, the 'nomads' confront the bourgeois observer as a spectacle of filth.

As the nomads transgress all settled boundaries of 'home', they simultaneously map out the area which lies beyond cleanliness. However much Mayhew attempts to separate 'moral wickedness' from 'physical filthiness' (1861–2: II, 394), the very categories of his work (excluding as they do the railway man, the factory worker and the domestic servant) foreground the connections between topography, physical appearance and morality. The emergent proletariat is displaced by the lumpenproletariat whom Marx describes in *The Eighteenth Brumaire*:

> Alongside decayed *roués* with dubious means of subsistence and of dubious origins, alongside ruined and adventurous off-shoots of the bourgeoisie, were vagabonds, discharged jailbirds, escaped galley slaves, swindlers, mountebanks, *lazzaroni*, pickpockets, tricksters, gamblers, *maquereaus*, brothel-keepers, porters, *literati*, organ-grinders, ragpickers, knife-grinders, tinkers, beggars, – in short, the whole indefinite, disintegrated mass thrown hither and thither, which the French call *la bohème*.
>
> (Marx 1951, I: 267)

Like Mayhew, Marx here concentrates on those who are marginal to the forces of production. And, paradoxically, it is this very group which stimulates his linguistic productivity. Marx ransacks French, Latin and Italian in his attempt to grasp this 'indefinite, disintegrated mass'. Marginal in terms of production, the lumpenproletariat are yet central to the 'Imaginary', the object of disgust and fascination.

Mayhew's *London Labour*, then, covers not *all* forms of labour but those forms which, lying on the margins of the nameable ('dubious', 'indefinite', 'disintegrated'), characteristically embody the carnivalized picturesque. Mayhew fixates upon bone-grubbers, rag-gatherers, 'pure'-finders (collectors of dog shit), sewer-hunters, mud-larks, dustmen, scavengers, crossing-sweepers, rat-killers, prostitutes, thieves, swindlers, beggars and cheats. And his attempt at social analysis is inseparable from his scopophilia.

The emphasis upon dirt was also central to the discourse which traced the concealed links between slum and suburb, sewage and 'civilization'. In *The Condition of the Working Class in England* (Engels 1971), for instance, Engels analysed the planning of a city whereby the 'dirty' was made invisible to the bourgeoisie. (We are particularly indebted to Steven Marcus's essay on Engels (Marcus 1973).) Manchester, he argued, was divided into three circles: an inner ring of commerce, where warehouses and offices were already partially concealed behind the expensive shops of the main thoroughfares; a second ring of working-class housing; and an outer ring of suburbs inhabited by the bourgeoisie. The inner and outer rings were joined by main thoroughfares along which a 'good' class of shops developed so as to service the bourgeoisie on their way to and from work. In the process, the working-class housing 'disappeared' behind a respectable front.

Engels represented the second ring, where the poor lived, in grim detail. In a Salford cow-shed, he found a man 'too old for regular work' who 'earned a living by removing manure and garbage with his handcart. Pools of filth lay close to his shed' (Engels 1971: 75). Off Long Millgate, Engels visits a court where 'the privy is so dirty that the inhabitants can only enter or leave the court if they are prepared to wade through puddles of stale urine and excrement' (Engels 1971: 58). From Ducie Bridge, he observes the River Irke, 'a narrow, coal-black, stinking river full of filth and rubbish' and of 'the liquid and solid discharges' from factories as well as of 'the contents of the adjacent sewers and privies' (Engels 1971: 60–1). (One might compare Dickens's vision of London in *Little Dorrit*: 'Through the heart of the town a deadly sewer ebbed and flowed, in the place of a fine river', whilst in 'fifty thousand lairs . . . the inhabitants gasped for air' (Dickens 1857: 29).)

But although Engels and Dickens attempt to analyse the city by tracing the sewer back to the suburb, the representation of filth which traverses their work is unstable, sliding between social, moral and psychic domains. At one level, the mapping of the city in terms of dirt and cleanliness tended to repeat the discourse of colonial anthropology. In 1881, Captain Bourke, a cavalry officer in the US

Army, observed the 'characteristic dances' of the Zuni Indians in New Mexico. He watched the 'filthy brutes' drinking urine; he heard one dancer relate how they normally 'made it a point of honour to eat the excrement of men and dogs'; finally, when the dance which had taken place indoors was over, he ran from the room which had become 'foul and filthy' from the presence of a hundred Indians (quoted in Greenblatt 1982:1). (Here as elsewhere, we are indebted to Stephen Greenblatt's fine essay, 'Filthy rites' (Greenblatt, 1982).) Ten years later, Bourke published *Scatologic Rites of All Nations* (1891) in which he obsessively dwelled upon the filth of 'savages', contrasting them with Christians and Hebrews who were 'now absolutely free from any suggestion of this filth taint' (quoted in Greenblatt 1982:2). In Bourke's work the division between cleanliness and filth, purity and impurity, is that between Christian and pagan, the civilized and the savage. But the nineteenth-century sanitary reformers mapped out the same division across the city's topography, separating the suburb from the slum, the respectable from the 'nomad' along the same lines. Chadwick, the leading exponent of 'the sanitary idea' in Britain, asked 'how much of rebellion, of moral depravity and of crime has its root in physical disorder and depravity' and he argued that '[the] fever nests and seats of physical depravity are also the seats of moral depravity, disorder, and crime with which the police have most to do' (Chadwick 1874: 274). Chadwick connects slums to sewage, sewage to disease, and disease to moral degradation: 'adverse circumstances' lead to a population which is 'short-lived, improvident, reckless, and intemperate, and with an habitual avidity for sensual gratifications' (Chadwick 1842: 369–70). Like most of the sanitary reformers, Chadwick traces the metonymic associations between filth and disease: and the metonymic associations (between the poor and animals, between the slum-dweller and sewage) are read at first as the signs of an imposed social condition for which the State is responsible. But the metonymic associations (which trace the *social* articulation of 'depravity') are constantly elided with and displaced by a metaphoric language in which filth stands in for the slum-dweller: the poor *are* pigs.

In Mayhew, we can observe the same sliding between the metonymic and the metaphoric. At the beginning of Mayhew's work, the street-people are remarked upon for their 'greater development of the animal than of the intellectual or moral nature of man . . . for their high cheeks and protruding jaws' (Mayhew 1961: I, 2–3), and this vision of innate animality permeates even a sympathetic account of an old woman who had been a 'pure-finder'. She lies like 'a bundle of rags and filth stretched on some dirty straw' in a place 'redolent of filth and pregnant with pestilential diseases, and whither all the outcasts of the metropolitan population seem to be drawn' (1861–2: II, 144). That last phrase is troubling, implying that the 'filthy' are *drawn* to the filth (as pigs were said to be drawn to the mire). To the extent that the poor are constituted in terms of bestiality, the bourgeois subject is positioned as the neutral observer of self-willed degradation.

Transgressing the boundaries through which the bourgeois reformers separated dirt from cleanliness, the poor were interpreted as also transgressing the boundaries of the 'civilized' body and the boundaries which separated the human from the animal. Even Engels, despite his desire to demonstrate the culpability of the bourgeoisie for the slums, retains an essentialist category of the sub-human 'nomad': the Irish. Engels, indeed, works within a colonial discourse which had been formed in the late sixteenth century and early seventeenth century when the Irish had been constructed as a race living 'beyond the pale' (we witnessed Dryden's use of this construction in Chapter 2): they were said to be 'more hurtfull and wilde' than 'wilde Beastes'; they were accused of 'uncleannesse in Apparrell, Diet and Lodging'; they were said to live in a 'foul dunghill' in their 'swinesteads', snatching food 'like beasts out of ditches' (Davies 1612: 162–3, 181; Spenser 1970: 82–3). Engels particularly develops the association between the Irish and 'swinesteads':

> the Irishman allows the pig to share his own living quarters. This new, abnormal method of rearing livestock in the large towns is entirely of the Irish origin. . . . The Irishman lives and sleeps with the pig, the children play with the pig, ride on its back, and roll about in the filth with it.
>
> (Engels 1971: 106)

Engels was, in fact, quite wrong: there was nothing specifically Irish about keeping pigs in town, which was a common English practice. But by condensing the 'abnormal' practices of the slum into the figure of the savage Irishman, Engels attempted to purify the English proletariat. He insisted upon the contingent, metonymic relation between the English poor and filth, whilst simultaneously establishing a fixed and 'natural' metaphoric relation between the Irish and animality.

Once the metaphoric relations were established, they could be reversed. If the Irish were like animals, animals were like the Irish. One of the sewer workers who talked to Mayhew described the sewers (which Irish labourers had helped to build) as full of rats 'fighting and squeaking . . . like a parcel of drunken Irishmen' (quoted in Wright 1960: 155). More generally, the links which associated the poor with animals and disease could be traced backwards; disease itself could be read as a member of the dangerous classes. In 1864, William Farr of the Registrar-General's Office wrote that 'zymotic poisons, as dangerous as mad dogs, are still allowed to be kept in close rooms, in cesspools and in sewers, from which they prowl, in the light of day, and in the darkness of night, with impunity, to destroy mankind' (quoted in Wohl 1983: 88).

However 'close' and confined the slums were, they were not confined enough. As the orifices of the poor opened to contaminate the purity of bourgeois space (at the turn of the century 44 per cent of poor Glasgow children were defined as 'mouth breathers'), so in the bourgeois imagination the slums opened (particularly at night) to let forth the thief, the murderer, the prostitute and the germs – the 'mad dogs' which could 'destroy mankind' (Wohl 1983: 79). The discursive elision of disease and crime suggested an elision of the means with which to cope with them: like crime, disease could be policed. In 1843, Farr argued that 'the Legislature' should enact 'the removal of known sources of disease, and, if necessary, trench upon the liberty of the subject and the privilege of property, upon the same principle that it arrests and removes murderers' (quoted in Wohl 1983: 144). The notorious Contagious Diseases Acts of 1864, 1866, and 1869 allowed special policemen to arrest women, subject them to internal examination and incarcerate them in lock-hospitals if they were suffering from gonorrhoea or syphilis (Walkowitz 1980: 1–2). Justifying police regulations, W. R. Greg claimed that 'the same rule of natural law which justifies the officer in shooting a plague-stricken sufferer who breaks through a *cordon sanitaire* justified him in arresting and confining the syphilitic prostitute who, if not arrested, would spread infection all around her' (quoted in Walkowitz 1980: 43–4).

In 1901, Charles Masterman published *The Heart of the Empire* in which he described the battle between 'the forces of progress' and 'social diseases'. In his introductory essay on the 'Realities at home', he described how town authorities were 'pushing their activities into the dark places of the earth; slum areas are broken up, sanitary regulations enforced, the policemen and the inspector at every corner' (quoted in Wohl 1983: 330). As the Empire shed light upon the 'darkness' of Africa, so the sanitary regime would shed light upon the city's 'dark places'. The connection between sanitation, light and policing can be seen in a Hudson's soap advertisement of the 1890s. In the picture, a policeman stands in the night holding up his lantern to illuminate a poster of Hudson's 'extract of soap'. At the top of the poster 'PUBLIC HEALTH' is written, and underneath: 'Dirt harbours Germs of Disease'. But the 'source of Danger' will be removed by using 'Hudson's' (in huge letters, occupying the centre of the poster). The bottom half of the poster is given over to the miraculous powers of Hudson's and concludes: 'Home, Sweet Home! The Sweetest, Healthiest Homes are those where HUDSON'S EXTRACT OF SOAP is in Daily use' (Wohl 1983: 71). The policeman and soap are analogous: they penetrate the dark, public realm with its disease and danger so as to secure the domestic realm ('Sweet Home') from contamination. The police and soap, then, were the antithesis of the crime and disease which supposedly lurked in the slums, prowling out at night to the suburbs; they were the agents of discipline, surveillance, purity.

The discipline of policing and sanitation depended in turn upon a transformation of the senses. As Foucault has argued, nineteenth-century policing found its privileged form in Bentham's Panopticon, which ensured the 'permanent visibility' of the inmate (Foucault 1979: 201). The gaze is structured in the Panopticon so that 'in the peripheric ring, one is totally seen without ever seeing; in the central tower, one sees everything without ever being seen' (Foucault 1979: 202). Throughout the nineteenth century, the 'invisibility' of the poor was a source of fear. In Britain, the Select Committee of 1838 noted that there were whole areas of London through which 'no great thoroughfare passed' and, as a consequence, 'a dense population of the lowest classes of persons' were 'entirely secluded from the observation and influence of better educated neighbours' (quoted in Stedman Jones 1971: 166). The 'labouring' and 'dangerous' classes would be transformed, it was implied, once they became visible. On the one hand, there would be surveillance by *policing*; on the other, the inculcation of *politeness* through the benign gaze of the bourgeoisie.

But the bourgeoisie's organization of the gaze was always problematic. If the dominant discourses about the slum were structured by the language of reform, they could not but dwell upon the seductions for which they were the supposed cure. It was, perhaps, as a remedy for the ambivalence of the gaze that there was an increased regulation of *touch*. For even if the bourgeoisie could establish the purity of their own gaze, the stare of the urban poor themselves was rarely felt as one of deference and respect. On the contrary, it was more frequently seen as an aggressive and humiliating act of physical contact.

Thus even as the separation of the suburb from the slum established a certain class difference, the development of the city simultaneously threatened the clarity of that segregation. The tram, the railway station, the ice rink, above all the streets themselves, were shockingly promiscuous. And the fear of that promiscuity was encoded above all in terms of the fear of being touched. 'Contagion' and 'contamination' became the tropes through which city life was apprehended. It was impossible for the bourgeoisie to free themselves from the taint of 'the Great Unwashed' (an English expression which emerged in the 1830s). Even money bore their stain. One government official paid Freud in paper florins which had been ironed out at home. 'It was a matter of conscience with him, he explained, not to hand anyone dirty paper florins: for they harboured all sorts of dangerous bacteria and might do some harm to the recipient' (Freud 1909: 77). The capitalist commodity itself permitted, and even encouraged, alarming conjunctions of the élite and the vulgar. In late nineteenth-century Holland, the bourgeois Versehoors would clandestinely burn the packages which *Jürgens Solo Margerine* came in, so that the neighbours would not discover them in the garbage can (Wouters 1979: 10).

If the vulgar commodity could contaminate the home, the sorties of the home into the street were even more dangerous. In her book on good manners (*Goede Manieren*), Mrs Van Zutphen van Dedem devoted a whole chapter to the 'act of avoiding and excluding'. She listed places to be avoided which included slums, local trains and streetcars, third-class pubs, cheap seats at movie theatres, and crowds or celebrations in the streets (Wouters 1979: 11). But since the promiscuity of public space was unavoidable, one must make all the greater effort not to *touch* any 'undesirable'. The 'more refined person' was to avoid even

> the slightest contact, so far as possible, with the bodies and garments of other people, in the knowledge that, even greater than the hygienic danger of contamination, there is always the danger of contact with the spiritually inferior and the repugnant who at any moment can appear in our immediate vicinity, especially in the densely populated centres of the cities, like germs in an unhealthy body.
>
> (Quoted in Wouters 1979:11)

The 'healthy' body is *refined*, uncontaminated by the 'germs' of 'the spiritually inferior', yet it is constantly assailed by them.

The gaze/the touch: desire/contamination. These contradictory concepts underlie the symbolic significance of the *balcony* in nineteenth-century literature and painting. From the balcony, one could gaze, but not be touched. The gentleman farmer who presided over a harvest feast would commonly arrange the table so that he could sit at its head *inside the house*, distributing hospitality through an open window or door. Similarly, the bourgeoisie on their balconies could both participate in the banquet of the streets and yet remain separated.

The flâneur, on the contrary, appalled by the 'horror of one's home', sought out the urban carnival. 'Even when he flees from town', wrote Baudelaire, 'he is still in search of the mob' (Baudelaire 1983: 71). Yet when he mingles with the crowd, he does not feel one of them. Indeed, Baudelaire sneered at George Sand's 'love for the working classes', and argued that 'it is indeed a proof of the degradation of the men of this century that several have been capable of falling in love with this latrine' (Baudelaire 1983: 67). Preferring 'harlots to Society women', Baudelaire nevertheless talked of 'contaminated' women and wrote obsessively of 'Hygiene Projects', 'Hygiene Morality', 'Hygiene. Conduct. Morality' (Baudelaire 1983: 70, 96–102). He tried to abstain from 'all stimulants' by obeying 'the strictest principles of sobriety', yet his sobriety at home was the spur to ever greater excesses in the city. The silenced desires of the bourgeois citizen ('A summary of wisdom: Toilet/Prayer/ Work' (Baudelaire 1983: 99)) found their loquacious expression through the topography of Paris.

Within this social and psychic economy, a key figure was the prostitute. 'There is, indeed, no exalted pleasure which cannot be related to prostitution', wrote Baudelaire (1983: 21). It was above all around the figure of the prostitute that the gaze and touch, the desires and contaminations, of the bourgeois male were articulated. From the perspective of the righteous patriarch, every young man was 'meeting with, and being accosted by, women of the street at every step':

> His path is beset on the right hand and on the left, so that he is . . . exposed to temptation from boyhood to mature age, his life is one continued struggle against it.
>
> (Quoted in Walkowitz 1980: 34)

And the 'contamination' of the prostitute seeped into the respectable home. In 1857, a writer in the *Lancet* complained that

> The typical Pater-familias, living in a grand house near the park, sees his son allured into debauchery, dares not walk with his daughters through the streets after nightfall, and is disturbed in his night-slumbers by the drunken screams and foul oaths of prostitutes reeling home with daylight. If he look from his window he sees the pavement – his pavement – occupied by the flaunting daughters of sin, whose loud, ribald talk forces him to keep his casement closed.
>
> (Quoted in Trudgill 1973: 694)

In the 1850s, the fears of the 'respectable' increasingly concentrated upon 'the great social evil', prostitution. But through the discourse on prostitution they encoded their own fascinated preoccupation with the carnival of the night, a landscape of darkness, drunkenness, noise and obscenity.

This is not, of course, to deny the *regulatory* aspect of the construction of prostitution as 'the great social evil'. Following the Contagious Diseases Acts of the 1860s, there was undoubtedly an increased categorization and surveillance of the 'unrespectable' poor. A new disciplinary regime could be inscribed upon the bodies of prostitutes once they had been classified and confined. In 1873, Inspector Sloggett recorded that the women in the Royal Albert Hospital in Southampton were 'clad alike in blue serge dresses, their hair neatly draped and wearing muslin caps' and seemed 'rather like a number of respectable young women in domestic service than registered prostitutes'. And William Acton claimed that the women in Aldershot Lock Hospital were 'most respectful; there was no noise, no bad language, no sullenness, no levity' (quoted in Walkowitz 1980: 223). (Undoubtedly, these were idealized accounts of 'reformation'. In Portsmouth, women in the lock-hospital rioted and smashed windows, and one commentator complained that they were given to 'insane frenzy', 'singing, dancing, swearing, or destroying the blankets and rugs given them to sleep in' (quoted in Walkowitz 1980: 216, 224).)

The 'prostitute', though, was just the privileged category in a metonymic chain of contagion which led back to the culture of the working classes. The social-purity crusade of Ellice Hopkins in Plymouth aimed not only at inculcating new standards in young men but also at establishing legal and institutional programmes to combat working-class 'immorality'. During the attempt to suppress Plymouth's Fancy Fair in 1886, Sergeant-Major Young claimed that numbers of young girls 'were being ruined in that place every week, and afterwards bringing contamination into the homes of the well-to-do as nurse girls, and servants' (Walkowitz 1980: 242, 244). When a girl disappeared at the fair, a migratory fiddler, Henry Greenslade, was prosecuted, but the trial was almost entirely devoted to 'the immoral influence of the fair' which, it was claimed, had destroyed the girl's character. Purity crusaders set up the Girls' Evening Home Movement (which emphasized reading, music, and cooking lessons) in opposition to the 'aimless street saunters' of working girls who could too easily stray 'to such places as the fancy fair' (Walkowitz 1980: 244). Similarly, Trinity Fair in Southampton was limited to one day whilst the Above-Bar Fair was abolished because of its 'moral delinquencies' and 'customary origins' (Walkowitz 1980: 245). Like the prostitute, the fair was conceptualized as the breeding ground of physical and spiritual germs which, through the mediation of servants, would bring 'contamination into the homes of the well-to-do'.

It is surely no coincidence, though, that the zeal for reform was so often accompanied by a prolonged, fascinated gaze from the bourgeoisie. In the 1830s, for instance, the plans to construct 'great thoroughfares', by means of which the 'civilized' would, by their mere visibility, improve the 'normally degraded', coincided with a flood of books which titillated the middle-class reader with tales of 'a hardened, semi-criminal race of outlaws, safe from public interference within ancient citadels of crime and vice' (Stedman Jones 1971: 180). Pierce Egan's *Life in London* (1812), for instance, was avidly consumed both as a book and as a play in the 1820s and 1830s. In the book, Tom and Jerry find 'life' (i.e. drinking, dancing, swearing) in the East End of London, where 'lascars, blacks, jack-tars, coal heavers, dustmen, women of colour, old and young, and a sprinkling of the remnants of once fine girls, etc., were all *jigging* together'. It was common during this period for young bloods, sometimes protected by detectives, to visit Ratcliffe Highway ('a Babel of Blasphemy') to gaze at the sailors and prostitutes (Keating 1973: 587–8). Similarly in the 1880s, a time of crisis for the poor and of renewed moral panic amongst the bourgeoisie, there was 'an epidemic of slumming' (Stedman Jones 1971: 285). And again, there was a flood of writing *about* the slums which could be consumed within the safe confines of the home. Writing, then, made the grotesque *visible* whilst keeping it at an *untouchable* distance. The city however still continued to invade the privatized body and household of the bourgeoisie as *smell*. It was, primarily, the sense of smell which engaged social reformers, since smell, whilst, like touch, encoding revulsion, had a pervasive and invisible presence difficult to regulate.

Chadwick, the great sanitary reformer of the early nineteenth century, worked in Benthamite circles in the 1820s and from 1830–2 worked closely with Bentham himself (Schoenwald 1973: 676). In 1846, Chadwick wrote: 'all smell is, if it be intense, immediate disease, and eventually we may say that, by depressing the system and making it susceptible to the action of other causes, all smell is disease' (quoted in Schoenwald 1973: 681). Smell was organized above all around *disgust*. George Buchanan, a Medical Officer of Health, attributed to 'the influence of stink' not only 'loss of appetite, nausea' but also 'a general sense of depression or malaise'; another Medical Officer, John Liddle, found the smell of the poor's linen, even when just washed, 'very offensive' (Wohl 1983: 81, 64). The Great Stink of 1858 only focused more intensively the bourgeoisie's obsessive concern with 'the unmistakeable and most disgusting odour of living miasm' (Wohl 1983: 81).

At one level smell was re-formed as an agent of class differentiation. Disgust was inseparable from refinement: whilst it designated the 'depraved' domain of the poor, it simultaneously established the purified domain of the bourgeoisie. The process is similar to that which we have already observed in Mayhew. Depicting the 'nomad', Mayhew was able to construct by back-formation the 'civilized': 'regular and continuous labour', 'providence', 'property', 'chastity', 'religion' (Mayhew 1861–2: I, 2). Yet the imagined pleasures of the nomadic (including the smells) remained to undermine the 'civilized'. Mayhew's text, like the sanitary reports, testifies to one of the ways by which the nomad and the slum made their way into the bourgeois study and drawing room, to be *read* as objects of horror, contempt, pity, and fascination. Texts which were structured by antithetical thinking became gaps in the domestic scene through which contaminating desires leaked.

Like Chadwick, Mayhew was aware of the practical problems of sanitation. The subject of 'London Sewerage and Scavengery' was, he wrote, 'vast', concerning 'the cleansing of the capital city, with its thousands of miles of streets and roads *on* the surface: and its thousands of miles of sewers and drains *under* the surface' (Mayhew 1861–2: II, 179). But in describing the functional process of cleaning, Mayhew articulates the sewers as a symbolic system. Indeed, he repeats one of the dominant tropes of western metaphysics: truth lies hidden behind a veil. But 'truth' is now conceived materially, as excrement. In *Les Misérables*, in what might be called, without irony, one of the most brilliant explorations of the semantics of the sewer, Victor Hugo wrote that there could be 'no false appearance' in the 'vast confusion' of the 'ditch of truth': '[the] last veil is stripped away. . . . This sincerity of filth pleases us and soothes the spirit' (Hugo 1980: 2, 369). What Dickens called 'the attraction of repulsion' is developed and analysed in Hugo's text. Here the attraction is constructed as simply the revelation of the bodily functions, hidden by 'the last veil'.

Curiously, Freud's 'Wolf Man' conceptualized reality through the same image of the veil.

The world, he said, was hidden from him by a veil. . . . The veil was torn, strange to say, in one situation only; and that was at the moment when, as a result of an enema, he passed a motion through his anus. He then felt well again, and for a very short time he saw the world clearly.

(Freud 1918: 340)

The basic constitutive elements of the symbolic system of both 'Wolf Man' and Hugo are the same: the veil, excrement, the 'truth', and pleasure ('he felt well again'). But whereas Freud articulated the *psychic* formation of that system, Hugo represented its *social* formation. The sewer, Hugo wrote was

the conscience of the town where all things converge and clash. There is darkness here, but no secrets. . . . Every foulness of civilization, fallen into disuse, sinks into the ditch of truth wherein ends the huge social down-slide, to be swallowed, but to spread. No false appearances, no white-washing, is possible; filth strips off its shirt in utter starkness, all illusions and mirages scattered, nothing left except what is, showing the ugly face of what ends.

(Hugo 1980: II, 369)

The sewer here represents a *non plus ultra* of naturalist reason, truth itself which, unimaginable '*on* the surface', can only subsist '*under* the surface':

the spittle of Caiaphas encounters the vomit of Falstaff, the gold piece from the gaming house rattles against the nail from which the suicide hung, a livid foetus is wrapped in the spangles, which last Shrove Tuesday danced at the Opera, a wig which passed judgement on men wallows near the decay which was the skirt of Margoton. It is more than fraternity, it is close intimacy.

(Hugo 1980: II, 369)

The melodramatic coercion of extreme opposites into close intimacy here becomes the ultimate truth of the social. For indeed the signs of the sewer could not be confined 'under the surface'. The sewer – the city's 'conscience' – insisted, as Freud said of the hysterical symptom, in 'joining in the conversation'. Hugo imagines a social 'return of the repressed' in terms of the city's topography:

the cloaca at times flowed back into the town, giving Paris a taste of bile . . . The town was angered by the audacity of its filth, and could not accept that its ordure should return.

(Hugo 1980: II, 371)

Hugo, though, was writing about a past when 'the sewerage was opposed to any discipline' and in its 'confusion of cellars' mirrored the 'confusion of tongues': the sewer had been 'the labyrinth below Babel'. But at the moment when Hugo wrote, the sewers had been cleaned up:

Today the sewer is clean, cold, straight, and correct, almost achieving that ideal which the English convey by the word 'respectable'.

(Hugo 1980: II, 375)

Before the cholera outbreaks of the 1830s, the 'excremental crypt' had asserted itself by flooding, and through it had entered 'crime, intelligence, social protest, liberty of conscience, thought and theft, everything that human laws pursue' (Hugo 1980: II, 368). But the sewer had been transformed:

The sewer today has a certain official aspect . . . Words referring to it in administrative language are lofty and dignified. What was once called a sluice is now a gallery, and a hole has become a clearing.

(Hugo 1980: II, 376)

As the sewer was more rigorously segregated from the city above, it was linguistically reformed, absorbed into the discourse of respectability. 'A good sewer', Ruskin declared, was a 'far nobler and a far holier thing . . . than the most admired Madonna ever printed' (quoted in Wohl 1984: 101). The nobility of the Victorian sewer was nowhere more dramatically confirmed than in the opening ceremonies of Bazalgette's intercepting sewers, south and north of the Thames, which were attended by the Prince of Wales, Prince Edeward of Saxe-Weimar, the Lord Mayor, the Archbishop of Canterbury and the Archbishop of York (Wohl 1983: 107). Yet paradoxically the sewer's improved status depended upon its invisibility. In 1865, the *Illustrated Times* depicted 'The Prince of Wales starting up the main-drainage works at Crossness': the pumping station is portrayed as a striking architectural monument and in the foreground of the picture a police sergeant holds a large flag. The sewer was becoming acceptable because it was locked and patrolled to prevent contamination, 'the keyhole and the bolt securely in place', as Hugo wrote, with added protection from 'one of those prison locks' (Hugo 1980: II, 394). The only remaining trace of the sewer was 'a vaguely suspect odour, like Tartuffe after confession' (Hugo 1980: II, 376).

The sewer, however, like all the 'low and grotesque' systems we have here examined, could not entirely be closed off from above. Passing between the sewer ('the conscience of the town' which was now blocked off) and the city (with its 'noble buildings' (Hugo 1980: II, 367)) were the rats: 'and here, in the foetid darkness, the rat is to be found, apparently the sole product of Paris's labour' (Hugo 1980: II, 368). Indeed, Hugo claimed that despite the rebuilding of the sewers the 'immemorial rodent population' was 'more numerous than ever' (Hugo 1980: II, 376). Rats had, of course, been the objects of hatred before the nineteenth century (Zinsser 1985). But just as the meaning of the grotesque body was transformed by its diacritical relation to the emergent notion of the bourgeois body, so the symbolic meaning of the rat was refashioned in relation to the sanitary and medical developments of the nineteenth century. As the connections between physical and moral hygiene were developed and redeployed, there was a new attention to the purveyors of physical and moral 'dirt'. The rat was no longer primarily an economic liability (as the spoiler of grain, for instance): it was the object of fear and loathing, a threat to civilized life. Hence, the stories which Mayhew recorded of sewer rats attacking men 'with such fury that the people have escaped from them with difficulty' (1861–2: II, 151).

The rat, then, furtively emerged from the city's underground conscience as the demonized Other. But as it transgressed the boundaries that separated the city from the sewer, above from below, it was a source of fascination as well as horror. In one of Freud's case studies, Frau Emmy von N. spoke of 'a case of white rats' whilst '[she] clenched and unclenched her hand several times. "Keep still! – Don't say anything! – Don't touch me! – Suppose a creature like that was in the bed!" (She shuddered.) "Only think when it's unpacked! There's a dead rat in among them – one that's been gn-aw-aw-ed at!"' (Freud 1893: 107). It is true that the rat was only one of various animals about which Frau Emmy hallucinated, but her particular fascination with rats is suggested by her 'extreme horror' at the story of Bishop Hatto who was supposedly eaten by them (Freud 1893: 131). (The story implies a dramatic contrast of high and low: the bishop, who preaches of a transcendent heaven, is destroyed by rats, which live in a physical 'hell').

Elsewhere Freud named one of his patients after the rat, and his case permits us to analyse 'the attraction of repulsion' in greater detail. Freud called his patient the 'Rat Man' because of his 'great obsessive fear' which was triggered by a story told him by an army officer about the punishment of a criminal in the East:

> 'a pot was turned upside down on his buttocks . . . some *rats* were put into it . . . and they . . .' [the patient] had again got up, and was showing every sign of horror and resistance – '. . . . bored their way in. . . .' – Into his anus, I helped him out.

> (Freud 1909: 47)

But even as 'Rat Man' recalled this story, Freud observed 'a very strange, composite expression' on his face, 'one of *horror at pleasure of his own of which he himself was unaware*' (Freud 1909: 48, Freud's italics). The pleasure was derived, Freud argued, from the 'anal erotism' (Freud 1909: 93) which his patient had repressed: the pleasure reappeared in the form of a negation and with the eroticism represented by the rat which bored into his anus. Thus, a bourgeois 'of irreproachable conduct' (Freud 1909: 40) found his way back down the axis of his body to the censored realm of excremental ambivalence.

Freud, to be sure, analyses the 'rat' as a sliding signifier within the domain of the psyche, but he nevertheless treats the concept of 'rat' as unproblematically *given*, the 'natural' symbol of his patient's repression. But the process of symbolization is in need of social as well as psychic explication. We would argue that, although symbolic systems are never entirely reducible to each other, one cannot analyse the psychic domain without examining the processes of transcoding between the body, topography and the social formation. We can perhaps clarify our argument with the aid of a highly simplified model, taking the symbolic axes of the bourgeois body analogically mapped by the city's topography.

The vertical axis of the bourgeois body is primarily emphasized in the *education* of the child: as s/he grows up/is cleaned up, the lower bodily stratum is regulated or denied, as far as possible, by the

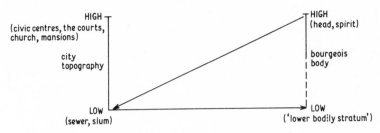

The hierarchy of the body transcoded through the hierarchy of the city.

correct posture ('stand up straight', 'don't squat', 'don't kneel on all fours' – the postures of servants and savages), and by the censoring of lower 'bodily' references along with bodily wastes. But whilst the 'low' of the bourgeois body becomes unmentionable, we hear an ever increasing garrulity about the *city's* 'low' – the slum, the rag-picker, the prostitute, the sewer – the 'dirt' which is 'down there'. In other words, the axis of the body is transcoded through the axis of the city, and whilst the bodily low is 'forgotten', the city's low becomes a site of obsessive preoccupation, a preoccupation which is itself intimately conceptualized in terms of discourses of the body. But this means that the obsessional neurosis or hysterical symptom can never be immediately traced back through the psychic domain. To deconstruct the symptomatic language of the bourgeois body it is necessary to reconstruct the mediating topography of the city which always–already inscribes relations of class, gender, and race.

We would argue, then, that 'Rat Man' 'speaks' his body through the topography of the city, a topography which is in turn shaped and controlled by the divisions of the social formation. Body and social formation are inseparable. 'Rats', 'sewage', 'filth' are not transparent signifiers which lead directly back to some primal moment. If they speak the unconscious, it is only through the mediation of the slum. The vertical axis of the body's top and bottom is transcoded through the vertical axis of the city and the sewer and through the horizontal axis of the suburb and the slum or of East End and West End. Furthermore the topography of the city, as we shall argue in Chapter 4, is represented within the bourgeois household itself through the relation of the family to its servants, through the relation of 'upstairs' to 'downstairs'.

Indeed, an analysis of Rat Man's sociolect requires an examination of the relation between the topography of the city and that of the household. As a child, 'Rat Man' crept up his governess's skirt or stared in fascination at Fraülein Lina's abscesses (Freud 1909: 41–2). But to the analysand, such delights can only be thought of as the obsessions of a rat. Ergo, children themselves must be rats (Freud 1909: 97). This enables the patient with one part of his psyche to adopt the position of his father: he must be punished:

> The notion of a rat is inseparably bound up with the fact that it has sharp teeth with which it gnaws and bites. But rats cannot be sharp-toothed, greedy and dirty with impunity: they are cruelly persecuted and mercilessly put to death by man, as the patient had often observed with horror.
>
> (Freud 1909: 96)

As an adult 'of irreproachable conduct', he must shun not only rats but also those elements with which he associated them. Hence, his disgust at prostitutes (Freud 1909: 39). Knowing that rats were carriers of dangerous infectious diseases, 'he could . . . employ them as symbols of his dread . . . of *syphilitic infection*' (Freud 1909: 94, Freud's italics). And since the penis was itself a carrier of syphilis, 'he could consider the rat as a male organ of sex' (Freud 1909: 94).

But if the symbolization of rats positioned 'Rat Man' with his father as the censor of his own childhood pleasure, it also determined his phantasies of rebelling. When visiting his father's grave, he saw what he took to be a rat (Freud believed that it was really a weasel) and he imagined that it 'had actually come out of his father's grave, and had just been having a meal off his corpse' (Freud 1909: 96). He associated the punishment in which a rat bored its way up the criminal's anus both with his father and with the woman whom he was thinking of marrying (Freud 1909: 48). The German word for 'to marry' ('heiraten') was associated both with '*Ratten*' (rats) and with '*Raten*' (instalments): 'so many florins, so many rats', 'Rat Man' had told Freud. So in his fantasy, the middle-class fiancée was elided with the rat and the prostitute, the sewer and the slum. The rat then was a phobic mediator between high and low, a kind of debased coinage in the symbolic exchange underpinning the economy of the body. The symbolic figure of the rat overran not only the boundaries between city and sewer: it gnawed away at the distinctions which separated patriarch from child, bourgeois beloved from prostitute, mother from abscessed maid, the pure from the contaminated.

Just as the rat was one of the dominant signs through which the bourgeoisie imagined the passage between 'the noble buildings' and 'the foetid darkness', so too the pig was to be transvalued. On the one hand, it was conspicuously present in the cities. In the middle of the wealthy suburb of North Kensington lay the Potteries, a seven-acre slum with open sewers, stinking ditches, and a stagnant, poisonous lake. The 1851 census revealed three pigs for every human there; the pigs provided bacon for the surrounding suburb whilst the inhabitants provided the servants, prostitutes, chimney-sweeps, and night-soil men to 'service' the bourgeois households. Whilst the pig moved up the social scale to the middle-class table, the swill of the suburbs passed down into the slums.

A man 'who had moved in good society' told Mayhew that

> [when] a man's lost caste in society, he may as well go the whole hog, bristles and all, and a low lodging house is the entire pig.
>
> (Mayhew 1861–2: I, 255)

Indeed, the pig could appear in more troubling shapes than 'the entire pig' of the lodging house. Mayhew heard a strange tale from the sewer-hunters

> of a race of wild hogs inhabiting the sewers in the neighbourhood of Hampstead. The story runs, that a sow in young by some accident got down the sewer through an opening, and, wandering away from the spot, littered and reared her offspring in the drain, feeding on the offal and garbage washed into it continually. Here, it is alleged, the breed multiplied exceedingly, and have become almost as ferocious as they are numerous.
>
> (Mayhew 1861–2: II, 154)

This surreal narrative perfectly embodies the phobic inversion of the carnivalesque icon. It participates in the formation of a 'carnival of the night' which was to trouble the dreams of the bourgeoisie. The pig, reared in the slums, is displaced by an imaginary race of sewer pigs, living in darkness, multiplying like rats, eating garbage, threatening the high with the ferocity of the low.

In the symbolic formation of the city, the pig too, like the rat, could figure as recalcitrant Other to trouble the fantasy of an independent, separate, 'proper' identity. It would surely be mistaken to see the pig and the rat here as merely the residual signifiers of a pre-capitalist formation. On the contrary, the reformation of the senses *produced*, as a necessary corollary, new thresholds of shame, embarrassment and disgust. And in the nineteenth century, those thresholds were articulated above all through specific *contents* – the slum, the sewer, the nomad, the savage, the rat – which, in turn, remapped the body. It is important to emphasize that this 'manifest content' was no incidental and contingent metaphor in the structuring of the bourgeois Imaginary. It was not a secondary over-coding of some anterior and subjective psychic content. Indeed it participated in the *constitution* of the subject, precisely to the degree that identity is discursively produced from the moment of entry into language by such oppositions and differences as we have explored here.

4

Below Stairs:
the Maid and
the Family Romance

Now let me call back those who introduced me to the city. For although the child, in his solitary games, grows up at closest quarters to the city, he needs and seeks guides to its wider expanses, and the first of these – for a son of wealthy middle-class parents like me – are sure to have been nursemaids. With them I went to the Zoo . . . or, if not to the Zoo, to the Tiergarten.

(Benjamin 1978: 3)

Thus Walter Benjamin begins his *Berlin Chronicle*, an attempt to set out 'the sphere of life – bios – graphically on a map' (Benjamin 1978: 5). And yet the map turns out to trace loss and transgression. In the city, one can 'lose oneself' amidst 'a maze not only of paths but also of tunnels' (Benjamin 1978: 8–9). There, Benjamin explores 'the limits', in a seedy railway hotel. There, he sits at the Romanische Café amongst artists and criminals, waited on by 'a hunchback who on account of his bad reputation enjoyed high esteem' (Benjamin 1978: 23). There, he observes in the Ice Palace 'a prostitute in a very tight-fitting white sailor's suit (Benjamin 1978: 40) about whom he will dream for years to come. And it is in the streets of the city that he feels 'the first stirrings of [his] sexual urge' (Benjamin 1978: 52). He has been sent by his parents to a relative who will escort him to divine celebrations at the synagogue. But between the secure places of home and synagogue lies the lure of the streets where he discovers 'an immense pleasure that filled me with blasphemous indifference towards the service, but exalted the street in which I stood'

(Benjamin 1978: 53). Desire emerges out of that lapsus, where the timetable of piety intersects with the aimless distractions of the city.

For Benjamin, to write his own biography is to write the city. But he notes the difficulties which simultaneously stand in the way of and construct the transgressive trajectory of the middle-class boy. For he is 'confined' in an affluent ghetto, rarely permitted to hear the 'shameless' music of the brass bands which mingles with the calls and screeches of gnus and vultures, condors and wolves from the zoo (Benjamin 1978: 24–5). Yet from his confinement, he will dream not only of the zoo's exotic animals and the distant places of which his grandmother sends him postcards, but also of the poor, the prostitutes, the criminals who are 'waiting behind' the streets along which he is escorted (Benjamin 1978: 4). And as he stubbornly refuses to walk beside his mother, with pedantic care keeping half a step behind her, he yearns for 'the flight into sabotage and anarchism' (Benjamin 1978: 11).

If Benjamin's early encounters with the city were occasionally with his mother, they were more commonly mediated by the presence of nurses, maids, and servants. It is with them, after all, that his text begins: they 'introduce' the city. If Benjamin remembers one nurse as the 'cold shadow' which intervened between desire and fulfilment, it was nevertheless the maids of the 'nether world', like the prostitutes in the street, who were the focus of his desire. Because of the social and spatial divisions of the bourgeois household, the courtyard below could itself become 'one of the places where the city opened itself to the child'. As he lay in bed, the noise of carpet-beating 'engraved itself more indelibly in the child's memory than the voice of the beloved in that of the man, the carpet-beating that was the language of the nether world, of servant girls' (Benjamin 1978: 44). It was the maid who, 'belonging' both to the bourgeois family and to 'the nether world', mediated between the home and the lure of the city. The 'obstinate and voluptuous hovering on the brink' (Benjamin 1978: 11) which the boy experiences in the network of streets could also be experienced in the emanations from 'below stairs' in the house.

Perhaps the very concept of 'hovering on the brink', with its implications of boundaries, abysses and scarcely imaginable transgressions, was itself the necessary encoding through which the adult (mis)recognized his childhood pleasures. For the 'language of the

6a Hannah Cullwick kneeling, 'dressed in her dirt', *c.* 1863 (Munby Collection, Trinity College Cambridge, Class Mark 119⁴)

6b Hannah Cullwick dressed as a 'slave', *c.* 1862 (Munby Collection, Trinity College Cambridge, Class Mark 119⁷⁶)

nether world' was not only the forbidden sounds which drifted up from the courtyard to the boy's bedroom. It was also the words, the gestures, the 'gifts' which the middle-class child was permitted, however briefly, to exchange with his nurse. It is striking how Freud's patients, like Benjamin, return as obsessively to their nurses as to their parents. Thus, 'Rat Man' recalls Fräulein Peter who looked after him when he was four or five: 'I was lying beside her, and begged her to let me creep under her skirt. . . . She had very little on, and I fingered her genitals and the lower part of her body . . .' (Freud 1909: 41). When 'Rat Man' was six, Fräulein Peter was replaced by Fräulein Lina who, despite her greater modesty, allowed him 'a great many liberties': she had abscesses on her buttocks which she was in the habit of pressing out at night. 'I used to wait eagerly for that moment to appease my curiosity' (Freud 1909: 42). In Benjamin's *Berlin Chronicle*, the social topography which separates the respectable house from the slum is remapped in the separation of the child's bedroom from 'the nether world' of the servants. But what is socially excluded or subordinated is symbolically central in the formation of desire. In her fine article on 'Class and Gender in Victorian England' (to which we are indebted throughout this chapter), Leonore Davidoff quotes several memoirs which reveal this social topography of desire binding the middle-class child to the maid:

> In the maid's room I read romances . . . bound volumes which lay concealed beneath Karoline's underclothes in the bottom drawer. Without the exchange of a word, we both knew that I would not have been allowed to read them if I had asked my mother . . . [There] was something in these romances which made one think of tainted water that had been forgotten in a carafe; of all the foul and unwholesome smells whereby the town became familiar to my senses.

> The servants of the house made windows for us into the outside world.
>
> (Quoted in Davidoff 1979: 96, 98)

And a schoolmaster's daughter wrote of Deptford, where one of her family's maids lived:

> This name meant for me unimaginable squalor. I was never taken there; somehow I was brought up to think of it as dark, dirty,

common, low. Yet I hugged a secret fascination with the very idea of it.

(Quoted in Davidoff 1979: 98)

In the narrative of Freud's 'Rat Man', the topography of desire, dependent upon the socially and physically 'low', is traced out on the body of a paid servant.

The connection of the bourgeois boy's desire to a woman of low social status and to dirt is particularly prominent in the case of 'Wolf Man'. Under analysis, 'Wolf Man' recalls his nursery maid, Grusha: she 'was kneeling on the floor, and beside her a pail and a short broom made of a bundle of twigs' (Freud 1918c: 330). Later, as an adult, 'Wolf Man' had been attracted to a 'young peasant girl' but he had not approached her until he was 'overwhelmed by his love' one day when he found her 'kneeling on the floor and engaged in scrubbing it' (Freud 1918c: 333). A few years later, 'he saw a peasant girl kneeling by the pond and employed in washing clothes in it. He fell in love with the girl instantly and with irresistible violence, although he had not yet been able to get even a glimpse of her face. By her posture and occupation she had taken the place of Grusha for him' (Freud 1918c: 332–3). In the analysis, Freud came to the conclusion that 'all ["Wolf Man's"] later love-objects were surrogates for [Grusha]', the nursery maid (Freud 1918c: 333). And Freud carefully notes that his patient fixates upon a specific *posture* of the maid, in which she is '*physically* debased' (Freud 1918c: 333, Freud's italics). But Freud is so intent upon demonstrating that 'Wolf Man's' obsession with Grusha is the signifier of a primal scene in which 'Wolf Man' observed his father making love to his mother *a tergo* that he is forced to minimize the figure of the maid. Grusha (the 'dirty' object) will only be considered as long as she leads back to the family romance.

Freud, in other words, brilliantly imagines the splitting of the subject, but then he proceeds to suppress the social terrain through which that splitting is articulated. The drama is played out in an imagined household where servants bear a symbolic part mainly as displacements of the biological parents. The significance of Grusha's kneeling can thus be recuperated for the family narrative on the condition that she figures forth the 'bestial' coupling of the 'real' parents. Hence, the physical debasement of the maid is displaced by the *exceptional* scene of bourgeois 'animality'. (Later Freud came to believe that the scene was fantasized.)

But a woman kneeling on all fours was no exceptional scene in the nineteenth or early twentieth century. On the contrary, kneeling was one of the habitual postures of the maid of all work. The following are typical entries from the diary of Hannah Cullwick, a Victorian maidservant:

> Clean'd the steps and flags on my knees. Blackleaded the scraper in front of the house; clean'd the street flags too on my knees. Wash'd up in the scullery. Clean'd the pantry on my knees and scour'd the tables.

> Clean'd the hall and steps and flags on my knees. Swept and dusted the rooms. Got breakfast up. Made the beds and emptied the slops. Clean'd and wash'd up and clean'd the plate. Clean'd the stairs and the pantry on my knees . . . Left the kitchen dirty and went to bed very tired and dirty.
>
> (Cullwick 1854–73: 106, 109)

The spotless homes of the bourgeoisie depended upon hired servants who became 'tired and dirty', cleaning on their hands and knees. At the same time, the bourgeois child was made to learn a repertoire of bodily postures which was the antithesis of the maid's: 'little ladies and gentlemen did not sit on steps; they stood absolutely straight; they did not whistle, scuff, or slouch' (Davidoff 1979: 97). The opposition between the erect bourgeois and the kneeling maid recurs again and again in Cullwick's diary:

> carrying luggage up and down, laying carpets as the lady wanted 'em and one proud one stood over me as I knelt and was crawling on the floor once. Instead of her showing me how with her hands she kick'd me with her foot and pointed.

> As I was cleaning the hall on my hands and knees one morning a gentleman came down to go out, and I let him step over me as he was in a hurry. Of course, he never thought anything of it, neither did I, only of the difference 'twixt him and me.

> I clean'd the steps in the wet this morning. I look'd a thorough drudge, and some men pass'd by and star'd at me as I was on my knees. One said, 'What a dirty creature!' The other laugh'd.
>
> (Cullwick 1854–73: 46, 57, 189–90)

And yet the opposition between maid and middle-class adult suppressed the intimate connections between maid and middle-class child. Maids 'fed, nappied, washed, dressed, potted, put to bed', whilst the upper-middle-class parent rarely took 'any active part in the physical care of toddlers or infants' (Davidoff 1979: 94). And if, as the child grew, the intimacy of maid and child was dissolved, it was not only Walter Benjamin who recalled how the noise of servants 'engraved itself more indelibly in the child's memory than the voice of the beloved in that of the man' (1978: 44). Munby provides us with the most detailed examples of a bourgeois male's fixation upon the maid at her 'lowest' and dirtiest. Through his diaries and photographs, he recorded women who were miners, dust-women, robbers, 'niggers' (sic), and chimney-sweeps. But above all he records his relationship to Hannah Cullwick, the maid of all work whom he secretly married. His diaries and photographs fixate upon the image of Hannah, scrubbing the floor or grate, with sleeves rolled up and blackened arms and face. Frequently Munby could spy upon her whilst she worked (Hudson 1972: 89). Cullwick herself records such an occasion in 1870:

> I got up early, for Massa [i.e. Munby] was coming at 1/2 past eight to see me clean the steps and do the sign of my 'lowness' like I did a while ago . . . and i wanted to be black from doing the grate as well. . . . i did the dining room fire – got my arms blackened and wiped my mouth and nose across with my black hand. . . . I washed the doorsteps and flags and when I saw Massa coming I got the door mat out and shook it in the road and then i laid it on the causeway and knelt on all fours and swept it well o' both side wi the hand brush and last of all i knelt an wiped my face on the dirty mat in front of all the folks what pass'd by and Massa was looking on from a few doors up . . . and then i rubbed my face on it and put my lips again it and i thought now i was one o' the lowest drudges as could be.
>
> (Quoted in Davidoff 1979: 116)

What we may note here is the conjunction of the maid kneeling in the dirt and the standing voyeur who looks on with fascination. Munby also recorded in his diaries the marriage of Lord Robert Montagu to a housemaid, Catherine Wade, in 1862: Montagu had first seen the maid when he walked past her 'as she was on her knees in the street cleaning steps' (Hudson 1972: 168).

The opposition of working-class maid and upper-class male, then, depended upon a physical and social separation which was constitutive of desire. But it was a desire which was traversed by contradictions. On the one hand, the 'lowness' of the maid reinforced antithetically the status of the gentleman. Thus, Munby loved not only a blackened Hannah, but also a Hannah who was ignorant, and although it was he who insisted that she keep a diary, he felt threatened when she began to read philosophy. He thought novels would be more suitable reading (Cullwick 1854–73: 288). But on the other hand, Munby worshipped Cullwick's physical strength and contrasted it to his own puniness and whiteness: 'you could never scrub like me', she tells him (Hudson 1972: 386). And whilst she washes his feet and even licks his boots, he sits upon her knee as, when he was a child, he must have sat upon the knee of his own 'faithful and Respected Nurse', who was also called Hannah (Hudson 1972: 8) Hannah Cullwick notes in her diary:

> I am not fit to be seen by ladies, and I told Massa about it when he was sitting on my lap o' Sunday.

> i nurs'd him on my lap ever so long and we talk'd.
>   (Cullwick 1854–73: 170, 183)

The maid, then, was not only a figure of 'lowness'; she was also a figure of comfort and power.

Why, then, is the maid written out of Freud's analyses, dissolved into the symbolic dyad of the mother and the father? (The following account is indebted to Jim Swan's fine essay, '*Mater* and nannie: Freud's two mothers and the discovery of the Oedipus complex' (Swan 1974).) The question is the more pressing because Freud wrote remarkably little about his own mother. Even more striking is the fact that, in the weeks that led up to the concept-formation of the Oedipus complex in the summer and autumn of 1897, he dreamed not of his mother but of the Czech, Roman Catholic maid who looked after him in the first two-and-a-half years of his life. On 15 October, 1897, Freud wrote to Fliess: 'I have found in my own case, too, falling in love with the mother and jealousy of the father, and I now regard it as a universal event of early childhood' (Freud 1897: I, 265). And he goes on in the same letter to ascribe the appeal of Oedipus Rex and of Hamlet to their representation of this 'universal event'. But twelve days before, Freud had written to Fliess that the 'prime originator' of his problems was his 'ugly but clever' nurse (Freud 1897: I, 262). In the same letter, he wrote that he had dreamed about her:

> She was my teacher in sexual matters and scolded me for being clumsy and not being able to do anything. (This is always how neurotic impotence comes about; it is thus that fear of incapacity at school obtains its sexual substratum.) At the same time I saw the skull of a small animal and in the dream I thought 'Pig!' . . . So I was a little fool. The whole dream was full of the most mortifying allusions to my present powerlessness as a therapist. Perhaps this is where an inclination to believe that hysteria is incurable has its start.
>
> (Freud 1897: I, 262–3)

There are several aspects of this letter which require elucidation, particularly in the light of Freud's later work. Firstly, it is the *nurse* who initiates the young Freud in sexual matters. But when Freud came to write on 'Femininity' in 'New introductory lectures on psychoanalysis', the nurse has been displaced by the mother:

> the seducer is regularly the mother. Here, however, the phantasy touches the ground of reality, for it was really the mother who by her activities over the child's bodily hygiene inevitably stimulated, and perhaps even aroused for the first time, pleasurable sensations in her genitals
>
> (Freud 1933: 154)

Yet in the letter of 3 October, 1897, the mother is constructed in terms of her physical distance and propriety. There, Freud hypothesizes that his libido was aroused by seeing his '*matrem*' when she was '*nudam*' on a journey. But the curious transition into Latin suggests Freud's horror at the abnormality of this encounter, an encounter which cannot be thought in his 'natural' language. The following account by a middle-class English woman of her childhood in the 1890s suggests the potential distance of the child from his or her mother:

> To me she was the perfect mother. I would not have liked her to dose me, bathe me, comfort me or hold my head when I was sick. These intimate functions were performed by Nanny or by Annie our nurserymaid . . . I did not like Mother even to see me in the bath.
>
> (Quoted in Davidoff 1979: 95)

In the nineteenth-century bourgeois family, it was commonly the maid, not the mother, who performed the 'intimate functions'.

Secondly, the maid who performs the 'intimate functions', despite her class subordination, has power over the child. Not only does the nurse arouse the child, but she can also shame him, calling him 'pig' or 'little fool'. Despite the woman's low status, the child is in crucial ways even lower, because of his size, his dependency, his fumbling attempts at language, his inability to control his bodily functions. And yet this woman who nurses, touches, talks to him is only a paid servant, liable to be dismissed at a moment's notice. In the dream which Freud recorded in the letter of 3 October, he writes that his nurse made him 'carry off "*Zehners*" (ten-kreuzer pieces) and give them to her' (Freud 1897: I, 263).

Freud was puzzled by the importance of the nurse in his dream, and he asked his mother about her. His mother replied that '"it was discovered that she was a thief, and all the shiny Kreuzers and Zehners and all the toys that had been given to you were found in her possession. Your brother Philipp himself went for the policeman and she was given ten months in prison' (Freud 1897: I, 264). In other words, not only was the nurse who looked after Freud for the first two-and-a-half years dismissed, but she was disgraced and imprisoned.

With this new information, Freud wrote again to Fliess on 15 October but now he tried to *correct* his earlier analysis which he claimed was 'a wrong interpretation' (Freud 1897: I, 264):

> I wrote you that [the nurse] led me into stealing Zehners and giving them to her. The dream really meant that she stole them herself. For the dream-picture was a memory of my taking money from the mother of a doctor – that is, wrongfully. The correct interpretation is: I = she, and the mother of a doctor equals my mother.
>
> (Freud 1897: I, 264)

What is striking about this reinterpretation is that the nurse disappears, absorbed into the figure of Freud, and the transaction in which Freud gave money to the nurse is displaced by a transaction in which he steals money from his mother (who had not figured at all in his previous account). In fact, Freud's reinterpretation depends upon a curious double manoeuvre, as Jim Swan has pointed out (Swan 1974: 41). On the one hand, the nurse can now take all the blame:

'the dream *really* meant that she stole them herself' (our italics). On the other hand, the maid can be forgotten, since she only stands in for Freud.

The next paragraph of Freud's letter, though, suggests the inadequacy of this reinterpretation. For Freud returns again to the figure of the nurse, trying to understand the impression which her disappearance made upon him:

> A scene then occurred to me which, for the last 29 years, has occasionally emerged in my conscious memory, without my understanding it. My mother was nowhere to be found. I was screaming my head off. My brother Philipp, twenty years older than me, was holding open a cupboard for me, and, when I found that my mother was not inside it either, I began crying still more, till, looking slim and beautiful, she came in by the door.
>
> (Freud 1897: I, 264)

Freud explains his grief at the empty cupboard as follows: 'when I missed my mother, I had been afraid she had vanished from me just as the old woman had a short time before. Now I must have heard that the old woman had been locked up . . .' (Freud 1897: I, 264–5). To explain his grief at the imagined loss of his mother, he thus returns to his grief at the loss of his nurse who, as he had previously remarked, 'provided me at such an early age with the means of living and going on living' (Freud 1897: I, 262). And whereas he had previously elided the nurse with himself, he now identifies her with his mother.

Yet if Freud himself associated 'crying his heart out' with the loss of his nurse, this association is 'rectified' at the end of the same letter where Freud affirms that 'falling in love with the mother' is the 'universal event'. At one level, the disappearance of the nurse seems to correspond to an attempt by Freud to rewrite unconscious desires in closer conformity to the endogamous rules of the bourgeoisie. Paradoxically, to desire one's mother, despite the incestuous implications, is more acceptable than to desire a hired help. And Freud seems to validate his emphasis upon his mother by the conscious adult reconstruction which opposes the 'slim and beautiful' mother to the 'ugly, elderly' nurse. Thus, Freud's grief (he cried 'his heart out' for nurse and mother alike) is split between an acceptable and an unacceptable mother: 'his actual mother – whose nakedness he can mention only in Latin – and his Nannie whom he remembers in association with numerous disturbing sexual experiences' (Swan 1974: 34). And in the concept-formation of the Oedipus complex, Freud effaces the 'unacceptable' mother.

The process by which Freud wrote the maid out of the family romance is illuminated by his treatment of a dream which he reported to Fliess on 31 May, 1897, some four-and-a-half months before his 'discovery' of the Oedipus complex. In the dream, he was going up a staircase 'with very few clothes on' when he saw a woman following him and he was 'glued to the spot': 'the accompanying feeling was not anxiety but an erotic excitation' (Freud 1897: I, 254). He records this dream again in 'The interpretation of dreams':

> I was very incompletely dressed and was going upstairs from a flat on the ground floor to a higher storey. I was going up three steps at a time and was delighted at my agility. Suddenly I saw a maid-servant coming down the stairs – coming towards me, that is. I felt ashamed and tried to hurry, and at this point the feeling of being inhibited set in: I was glued to the steps and unable to budge from the spot.
>
> (Freud 1900b: 335–6)

There are three significant changes in the second account: the woman is now named as 'a maid-servant'; she is coming down the stairs, not following him up; and he feels 'ashamed', not erotically excited. The naming of the woman as a maid-servant does not, of course, contradict his previous account of the dream: it just gives it greater precision. But the second two changes radically alter both the content and the interpretation of the dream. Now, as he leaps agilely up the stairs, the descending maid fills him with anxiety. And Freud generalizes that 'feelings of being inhibited, of being glued to the spot' are closely akin to feelings of anxiety' (Freud 1900b: 335). He thus directly contradicts his earlier interpretation in which the feeling which accompanied his paralysis was '*not* anxiety by an erotic excitation' (our italics).

What can account for the way in which Freud rewrites this dream? We would suggest that the reinterpretation is consequent upon the naming of the woman as a maid-servant. Coming down the stairs, she now psychologically impedes his upward ascent, making him aware that he is 'very incompletely dressed' and thus symbolically degrading him. He is humiliatingly at the mercy of a 'mere' maid. In 'The interpretation of dreams', Freud bolsters this account by noting that shortly before the dream he had been visiting an old lady twice a day. Freud had been in the habit of spitting on the staircase on the way up to her room, much to the disgust of the concierge, an 'elderly and surly woman' (Freud 1900b: 337). The day before the dream, a maid-servant had also accused him of not wiping his boots and of dirtying the carpet. And even in his own house, Freud admits, his 'reputation for tidiness was not of the highest.' (Freud 1900b: 337).

In analysing the dream, Freud is led back to the nurse 'in whose charge I had been from some date during my earliest infancy till I was two and a half' (Freud 1900b: 347). And the nurse, he recalls, was particularly harsh if he 'failed to reach the required standard of cleanliness' (Freud 1900b: 347). The maid coming down the stairs, then, was 'a reincarnation of the prehistoric old nurse' who had shamed him by attacking his dirtiness. Yet here Freud produces an extraordinary conjuring trick. Describing the nurse as 'old and ugly', associating her with his lack of cleanliness, he can now construct her in terms of the rational bourgeois subject's sense of shame and anxiety. And as a result he totally erases what is central to his first account of the dream: that he felt 'not anxiety but erotic excitation'. Freud completes this process of erasure by appealing to the manifest content of the dream: 'the maid-servant whom I dreamt about was older than I am, surly and far from attractive' (336). Thus, Freud implies, the dream could not have been primarily erotic. Through this 'correction' of both the dream and its interpretation, Freud separates desire from dirt, the maid, the ugly, the socially 'low'. Rewriting the unconscious in terms of the explicit norms of bourgeois society, he can pursue his agile ascent to his 'slim and beautiful' mother whilst the maid moves past him, downwards, in her descent to 'the nether world'.

Yet the maid could never be entirely left behind. On the one hand, she was the potent reminder of the child's helplessness, a helplessness to which the adult doctor was still prone. As we noted above, in his letter to Fliess of 3 October, 1897, his recollections of being scolded and called a 'little fool' precede his sense of his failure as a doctor: 'the whole dream was full of the most mortifying allusions to my present powerlessness as a therapist' (Freud 1897: I, 262–3). But on the other hand, Freud read the nurse as a displacement of himself:

> The dream can be summed up as 'bad treatment'. Just as the old woman [the nurse] got money from me for her bad treatment of me, so today I get money from my bad treatment of my patients.
>
> (Freud 1897: I, 263)

Psychoanalyst and maid are alike in that, in opposition to parents, both accept money in exchange for their care. So whilst analyst and maid deal with the most intimate psychic and physical details of their 'patients'' lives, their relation to their charges is determined economically. The economic transaction is, indeed, central to the psychoanalytic theory of transference. For within analysis, the patient comes to understand that his or her emotions are a repetition of those which were formed by the mother/child dyad, and to acknowledge this repetition it is necessary to accept that the analyst is 'only a stand-in'. 'What facilitates the recognition of the [patient's] feeling as transference, as an inappropriate repetition, is the fact that the analyst is paid' (Gallop 1982: 143).

But the economic transaction troubles Freud, and not only because he fears that he gives 'bad treatment' in exchange for the patient's money. In the letter of 3 October, his identification of himself with the nurse is immediately followed by this sentence: '[a] special part was played by Frau Qu., whose remark you reported to me: I ought not to take anything from her as she was the wife of a colleague' (Freud 1897: I, 263). In the case of Frau Qu., the symbolic inscription of the analyst *in loco parentis* is overdetermined by the 'family-arity' which binds Freud to his colleagues. Should not his relation to his patients/'children'/friends be one of affection, untainted by the cash nexus?

But if the money which the analyst receives is symbolically related to the abuse of power, money also testifies to the analyst's powerlessness. Like the maid, the analyst is hired; like the maid, he or she can be dismissed. And like the maid, the analyst is a source of sexual knowledge. Freud wrote of Dora's governess that she

> used to read every sort of book on sexual life and similar subjects, and talked to [Dora] about them, at the same time asking her quite frankly not to mention their conversations to her parents, as one could never tell what line they would take about them. For some time I looked upon this woman as the source of all Dora's

secret knowledge, and perhaps I was not entirely wrong in this.

(Freud 1905b: 68)

And yet Dora had demanded the dismissal of her governess, and she dismissed Freud, paying him off and leaving him with only a 'fragment', as he calls it, of an analysis. If in analysing his dream of his nurse, Freud equates himself with her ('I = she'), his own identity is as unstable as that of a woman who provided 'the means of living and going on living' and who was nevertheless dismissed.

What is at stake in the effacement of the nurse, then, is not primarily an empirical question of the relation between Freud, his nurse and his mother. Rather, it is the symbolic terms of psychoanalysis itself. In his letter to Fliess of 31 May, 1897, as we have noted, Freud described a dream in which a woman (later identified as a maid) caused 'an erotic excitation' in him. In the same letter, he included some rough drafts in which incest, although 'impious', is conceptualized as a mechanism through which 'the members of a family hold together permanently and become incapable of contact with strangers' (Freud 1897: I, 257). In his writings of 1897, Freud unconsciously repeats this mechanism, divorcing himself from the dismissed nurse and aligning himself with a family that would 'hold together permanently': as he later put it in 'The psychopathology of everyday life', 'I would make the problem of interpretation easier for myself and would ask my mother . . .' (Freud 1900: 91). As a result, the family romance could be freed from the exogamous factors symbolically inscribed in the nurse and in money (the stolen Zehners). Freud thus repeated the symbolic order (with its loving and incestuous triad of mother/father/child) which he attempted to analyse.

In the case history of 'Wolf Man', Freud returned to the process by which 'a nurse comes to play the mother's part or where the two become fused together' (Freud 1918: 363). There, he constructed a theoretical model which would indeed hold 'the members of a family . . . together permanently'. The symbolic order of the family romance was, he now claimed, inscribed *biologically*: it was an 'hereditary scheme', 'phylogenetically inherited' (Freud 1918: 363). In other words, the family circle was closed off not only from the maid but from the possibility of cultural transformation: the symbolic order was placed in the immutable world of nature, not in the historical work of social struggle. And yet, as Jane Gallop observes,

> The family never was, in any of Freud's texts, completely closed off from questions of economic class. And the most insistent locus of that intrusion into the family circle (intrusion of the symbolic into the imaginary) is the maid/governess/nurse. As Cixous says 'she is the hole in the social cell'.
>
> (Gallop 1982: 144)

The 'hole' opens up again and again in Freud's texts, but equally insistently a one-directional process of displacement is invoked. The nurse is a displacement of the mother, the socially 'debased' are displacements of the parents, never vice versa.

Thus, 'Wolf Man's' obsessions with beggars, cripples, a footman, a dumb water-carrier (Freud 1918: 244–5, 326–7, 338) are reinscribed within the family romance, with the result that problems of *class* are deliberately turned aside:

> [The dumb water-carrier] served the patient as a father-surrogate just as Grusha served him as a mother-surrogate. I do not think there is any justification for regarding this as an example of the intention to debase, even though it is true that both parents have come to be servants. A child pays no regard to social distinctions, which have little meaning for him as yet.
>
> (Freud 1918: 338)

Here, surely, Freud is evasive. Children may have no *elaborated* concept of class, but the formation of 'Wolf Man's' psyche depends, as Freud so clearly demonstrates, on the transformation of the bodily 'high' and 'low' into social distinctions. Indeed, such a transformation structures two of 'Wolf Man's' obsessional neuroses in childhood: 'whenever he saw three heaps of horse-dung lying in the road', he could not help thinking of the Holy Trinity; and whilst devoutly kissing the religious pictures in his room before going to bed, he was obliged to think 'God-swine' or 'God-shit' (Freud 1918: 244 –5). The notion of God as uncontaminated and transcendent is, of course, one of the most potent symbolic forms of social purity. And the child, in his or her initiation into the 'transcendence' of the bourgeoisie, must learn to distinguish him/herself from the swinish, the piggish, the hog-like. S/he must not 'eat like a pig'; s/he must not slouch at table; s/he must not get food on her/himself. Nowhere is this process of initiation more clearly illuminated than in Kafka's 'Letter to his father':

> for me as a child everything you shouted at me was positively a heavenly commandment, I never forgot it, it remained for me the most important means of forming a judgement of the world . . . Since as a child I was together with you chiefly at meals, your teaching was to a large extent teaching about proper behaviour at table . . . Bones mustn't be cracked with the teeth . . . Vinegar must not be sipped noisily . . . The main thing was that the bread should be cut straight. . . . One had to take care that no scraps fell on the floor.[1]
>
> (Kafka 1954: 167)

To become socially 'high', as Norbert Elias has argued, it is necessary for the child to be at a controlling distance from food and dirt alike (Elias 1978).

Is it surprising, then, that the young 'Wolf Man', without any theological training, rediscovered Manicheeism? How could Christ be perfect if he 'had a behind too' (Freud 1918: 298). 'Wolf Man' consoled himself with the thought that the bottom is just a continuation of the legs, 'but hardly had he pacified his dread of having to humiliate the sacred figure, when it flared up again as the further question arose whether Christ used to shit too' (Freud 1918: 298). But 'Wolf Man' had an ingenious solution to this problem: 'Since Christ had made wine *out* of nothing, he could also have made food *into* nothing and in this way have avoided defaecating' (Freud 1918: 299). In devoting himself to Christ, then, the child un-learned his own relation to excrement. He had to separate himself from his earlier self, as Christ had put away childish things. If, as Freud argued, small animals were for 'Wolf Man' 'representations of small children' (Freud 1918: 351), in torturing them (as in tormenting beetles and cutting caterpillars into pieces (Freud 1918: 244)), he was perhaps demonizing, even as he fixated upon, the little boy whom he must 'put away'.

But 'Wolf Man's' developmental process was a socially complex one, as he was entrusted to guardians of ever higher social status. From Grusha, the serving maid, 'Wolf Man' was passed to Nanya; from Nanya to the English governess; from the English governess to the schoolmaster Wolf (a transition of gender as well as status). And with Wolf, he learned Latin, the language of educational status, whilst he was required to 'forget' the baby-talk of the body. His process of 'forgetting' the body produced its own symptoms: anorexia (which lasted until he was told 'about one of his uncles who had refused to eat in the same way and had wasted away to death while he was still young' (Freud 1918: 338)); constipation. When he began his analysis with Freud, 'Wolf Man' had not had 'spontaneous evacuations' for months and he had become accustomed to enemas (Freud 1918: 311). It is as if he had found a partial solution to the relation between godhead and humanity: the former was attainable only if one 'avoided defaecating' (Freud 1918: 299).

But how was the 3-year-old who shamelessly defecated in his English governess's bed transformed into the anxious 4-year-old who, after making a mess in his trousers, said that 'he could not go on living like that' (Freud 1918: 313)? According to Freud, the child's transformation depended upon identification with his mother who, when she had been haemorrhaging, had used the same words ('I cannot go on living like this' (Freud 1918: 313–4)). But even if we accept this problematic interpretation, it is still necessary to emphasize that the change in the boy's attitude to defecation is, at the same time, a change in class identification. When he had defecated in the governess's bed, he had done this as an act of defiance against the woman who had called his beloved Nanya 'a witch' (Freud 1918: 242). In other words, he sided with the lower-class woman who had largely attended to his body against the new foreign employee who would henceforward attend to his mind. During the same period (the patient's elisions are, of course, revealing, whether or not they correspond to the chronology of his childhood), his sister had played with his penis and had told him that Nanya 'used to do the same thing with all kinds of people – for instance, with the gardener: she used to stand him on his head, and then take hold of his genitals' (248). The act of masturbation, explicitly forbidden by Nanya, is nevertheless associated with her. It is as if the forbidden act could be projected only as a part of the inverted world of the subordinated classes. It was also during this period, according to 'Wolf Man', that he began to scream 'like a savage' (Freud 1918: 242), so that it was doubtful whether he would be able to attend school. The statement, then, that 'he could not go on living like that' (defecating, masturbating, behaving 'like a savage') had an all-too-literal social application. To become his parents' child, he must forgo those pleasures which he associated with serving maids (Grusha and Nanya) and with what would henceforth be named 'dirt'. He must, in other words, distance himself from the subordinated classes even as he distanced himself from the physical processes and products of his own body.

We can now suggest an analysis of 'Wolf Man's' ceremonial breathing, through which he atoned for his blasphemies by exhaling the evil spirits and inhaling the Holy Spirit (in his native language, Russian, 'breath' and 'spirit' were the same word). According to Freud, 'Wolf Man' only started this ceremonial breathing after seeing his father ill in hospital, but from then on he exhaled whenever he saw cripples, beggars, or poor people (Freud 1918: 303). But why should the child associate his father's illness with beggars and the poor? Does not this association depend upon the *prior* association of illness with poverty? He 'could not go on like this' because within the symbolic discourse of the bourgeoisie, illness, disease, poverty, sexuality, blasphemy and the lower classes were inextricably connected. The control of the boundaries of the body (in breathing, eating, defecating) secured an identity which was constantly played out in terms of class difference. The pure child would grow up into the healthy parent only if he *exhaled* those 'evil spirits' which had already 'contaminated' him in the form of household servants. (In even more paranoid vein, Parent-Duchatelet had warned that maids were often clandestine prostitutes, infiltrating the bourgeois household. Such a 'sly' prostitute then 'corrupts and seduces innocence and . . . [by] assuming appearances the most honourable paralyzes authority . . . and spreads with impunity the most frightful contagion and immorality the most flagrant' (quoted in Walkowitz 1980: 34).

But, of course, the child could never exhale the 'evil spirits'. The socially excluded returned in the form of psychic desire. The adult 'Wolf Man' fixated upon peasant women, kneeling and scrubbing floors, an act which in his fantasy was irrevocably connected to *his* childhood delight in dirt rather than to the economic bonds which linked the *maid* to the cleaning up of the bourgeois home. Freud interpreted his patient's obsession with 'large and conspicuous buttocks' and his inability to derive any pleasure from copulating 'except from behind' as referring back to a primal scene in which 'Wolf Man's' father made love to his mother from behind. Yet Freud himself had doubts as to the reality of the primal scene: such scenes, as he noted, are not 'recollections' but 'the products of construction' during the patient's analysis (Freud 1918: 284). If Freud returns 'Wolf Man's' fixation to the script of the family romance, it is because he has decided already that that script is ontologically prior, an 'hereditary schema'. What Freud fails to consider is the pleasure which 'Wolf Man' might derive from an *inverted world*, where the desired object must always be of lower status, where dirt triumphs over the family hierarchy, where 'the bottom' is the source of all delight.

And at the level of fantasy, the inverted world could not be sealed off from the domain of bourgeois respectability. It was, perhaps, fear of the mutual contamination of the two domains rather than fear of the return of a primal scene which led 'Wolf Man' to resist telling Freud that the name of the peasant woman to whom he was compulsively attracted and from whom he had contracted gonorrhoea was Matrona (Freud 1918: 331). But the elision of maid and mother depended upon their prior splitting, a splitting which fissured motherhood itself.

This fissure produces the dream which Walter Benjamin records in *A Berlin Chronicle*. As a child, Benjamin had dreamed about a ghost, but the ghost itself had been displaced by 'the site of its operations', a site

> known, tantalizing, and inaccessible to me, namely the corner of my parents' bedroom that was separated from the rest of the chamber by an arch with a heavy, faded-violet curtain, and in which my mother's dressing gowns, house dresses and shawls were suspended. The darkness behind the curtain was impenetrable, and this corner was the sinister, nocturnal counterpart of that bright, beatific realm that opened occasionally with my mother's linen cupboard, in which, piled up on the shelves, edged with white trimming and bearing a blue-embroidered text from Schiller's 'The Bell', lay the sheets, table-cloths, napkins, and pillowcases . . . These were the hell and paradise into which the ancient magic of hearth and home had been sundered.
>
> (Benjamin 1978: 54)

His mother is split metonymically between the two sites: the nocturnal, inaccessible domain of dressing gowns and dresses, and the 'bright beatific realm' of clean linen. And from the former realm, the ghost steals his mother's silken fabrics.

The following day, Benjamin had kept the dream to himself but he recalls, with the vividness of a memory 'isolated by shock', that evening, when '[one] of our maids stands a long while at the wrought-iron gate . . . It is time to go to bed' (Benjamin 1978: 53). During the night, a band of burglars, led by a deaf-mute, broke into the house and by the morning '[the] house had been stripped of everything' (Benjamin 1978: 54). The young Benjamin was later questioned by the police about the suspected complicity between the maid and the burglars.

In retrospect, his dream seemed prophetic, but his own position in relation to the dream remained perplexing. For not only had he kept silent about it, but he was *proud* of his silence. Yet his silence positioned him with the maid, as the burglars' accomplice. His silence, then, implied his ambivalence about the robbery: on the one hand, it was a terrifying contamination of the bourgeois household; on the other, it was the 'logical' acting out of the 'hell and paradise' into which his mother had been 'sundered' in his dream. In the boy's fantasy, the mother was also the maid whose hand unlocked the gate to the murderous deaf-mute. She must be split, as he was, between the pieties of the household and the 'blasphemous indifference' of the teeming streets of Berlin. She must be party to his own yearning for 'the flight into sabotage and anarchism' (Benjamin 1978: 11), to his own delight in 'the language of the nether world' which ascended to him from the courtyard where 'the city opened itself to the child' (Benjamin 1978: 44). Like the ghost, the mother mediates between the linen cupboard and the sinister and forbidden corner of the parental bedroom. But, 'standing between', the mother symbolically repeats the maid who 'introduced [Benjamin] to the city' (Benjamin 1978: 3), the maid who, standing at the gate, mediated between the inside and the outside of the house. The figure of the maid inscribed 'the hole in the social cell', the site of transgressive desire. And 'the language of the "nether world", as Walter Benjamin wrote, 'engraved itself more indelibly in the child's memory than the voice of the beloved in that of the man' (Benjamin 1978: 44).

NOTE

1 For Kafka, however, the crucial point was that his father did not obey the injunctions which he enforced upon his children: 'At table one wasn't allowed to do anything but eat, but you cleaned and cut your fingernails, sharpened pencils, cleaned your ears with the toothpick'.

5

Bourgeois Hysteria
and the Carnivalesque

While she was being massaged she told me only that the children's governess had brought her an ethnological atlas and that some of the pictures in it of American Indians dressed up as animals had given her a great shock. 'Only think, if they came to life' (she shuddered). I instructed her not to be frightened of the pictures of the Red Indians but to laugh heartily at them. And this did in fact happen after she had woken up: she looked at the book, asked whether I had seen it, opened it at the page and laughed at the grotesque figures, without a trace of fear and without any strain in her features.

'Studies on hysteria', Frau Emmy von N. (Freud 1893: 109–110)

Carnival debris spills out of the mouths of those terrified Viennese women in Freud's 'Studies on hysteria'. 'Don't you hear the horses stamping in the circus?' Frau Emmy von N. implores Freud at a moment of particularly abject horror. It is striking how the broken fragments of carnival, terrifying and disconnected, glide through the discourse of the hysteric. Occasionally, as in the extract quoted above, it appears that Freud's therapeutic project was simply the reinflexion of this grotesque material into comic form. When Frau Emmy can at last look at the 'grotesque figures' and 'laugh without a trace of fear', it is as if Freud had managed a singular restitution, salvaging torn shreds of carnival from their phobic alienation in the bourgeois unconscious by making them once more the object of cathartic laughter.

It is of course significant that the carnivalesque practice which produced the phobic symptom in Frau Emmy is that of an alien, non-European culture. Not the least significant element in the middle-class rejection of the indigenous carnival tradition in the late nineteenth century in Europe was a compensatory plundering of ethnographic material – masks, rituals, symbols – from colonized cultures. In this respect Joseph Conrad was doing no more than Frau Emmy in placing 'savage rites' at the heart of European darkness in the 1890s.

As we know, within a very few years Freud was to abandon the cathartic approach which he used with his early hysterical patients and to lose interest in the attempt to precipitate the abreactive rituals which might reinflect the grotesque and the disgusting into a *comic* form. There is some contention that this was not necessarily a positive move (Scheff: 1979), but in any event it is a notable feature of the early case histories that it is *the patients themselves* who, in their pastiche appropriations of festive, carnival, religious and pantomimic gestures, suggest kinds of alleviation to their own suffering. Anna O. is credited by Ernest Jones as being the real discoverer of the cathartic method and Breuer developed and formalized her practical notions in his own method (Scheff 1979: 28). Freud's gradual move away from abreactive ritual of a cathartic kind towards associative methods of self-consciousness is entirely consonant with his desire to produce a professional, *scientific* psychology. This is because science, particularly in the late nineteenth century, was deeply hostile to ritual. It even saw itself, on occasion, as self-consciously improving upon those areas of social life which, once governed by 'irrational' rituals, could now be brought under scientific control. Havelock Ellis provides a telling example in his essay on 'Eugenics and love' in a book entitled *The Task of Social Hygiene* (1912) (a title not unconnected to our present concerns):

> It is scarcely necessary to show how the ancient customs associated with St Valentine's Day are taken up again and placed on a higher plane by the great movement which is now beginning to shape itself among us. The old Valentine unions were made by a process of caprice tempered more or less by sound instincts and good sense. In the sexual selection of the future the same results will be attained by more or less deliberate and conscious recognition of the great laws and tendencies which investigation [i.e., eugenics] is

DER NASWEISE.

Obn vnd vndtn, wirdt Beisamen gefundtn,
Nasn vnd gsicht Bringt dem nasweisn bericht.
Ich wolt sein auch der gscheidist allein;
Wegens hasn, Bekamb ich dise nasn;
Ders wil sein, dem fleußt balt alles ein,
Drauf gilts gauch Jungks, der bißn begert ain trunck.

H. Vlrich sc.

7 'Nose-Wise' (untranslatable pun, 'clever dick'), copper-plate engraving
by Heinrich Ulrich, Nuremberg, *c.* 1600

slowly bringing to light. The new St Valentine will be a saint of science rather than of folk-lore.

(Ellis 1912: 205)

Indeed science only emerged as an autonomous set of discursive values after a prolonged struggle against ritual and it marked out its own identity by the distance which it established from 'mere superstition' — science's label for, among other things, a large body of social practices of a therapeutic kind. Scheff has suggested that there is a strongly cognitive bias against ritual and catharsis in much recent work in psychology and anthropology. A re-reading of hysteria case studies (not only Freud's) in relation to the ritualistic and symbolic material of carnival suggests new ways of interpreting the hostility, the felt incompatibility, of rational knowledge to ritual behaviour.

In the *Studies on Hysteria* many of the images and symbols which were once the focus of various pleasures in European carnival have become transformed into the morbid symptoms of private terror. Again and again these patients suffer acute attacks of disgust, literally vomiting out horrors and obsessions which look surprisingly like the rotted residue of traditional carnival practices. At the same time the patients seem to be reaching out, in their highly stylized gestures and discourses, towards a repertoire of carnival material as both expression and support. They attempt to mediate their terrors by enacting private, made-up carnivals. In the absence of social forms they attempt to produce their own by pastiche and parody in an effort to embody semiotically their distress. Once noticed, it becomes apparent that there is a second narrative fragmented and marginalized, lodged within the emergent psychoanalytic discourse. It witnesses a complex interconnection between hints and scraps of parodic festive form and the body of the hysteric. In his general remarks on hysterical attacks (Freud 1909b), Freud himself even makes this 'other narrative' part of his definition of hysteria, without, however, making anything of it:

> When one psychoanalyses a patient subject to hysterical attacks one soon gains the conviction that these attacks are nothing but phantasies projected and translated into motor activity and *represented in pantomime*.

(Freud 1909b: 153, our italics)

Freud goes on to talk about the distortion which 'the pantomimic representation of phantasy' undergoes as a result of censorship. Yet the semiotic encoding of the hysterical symptom in pantomime mimicry is given as the very form of representation of fantasy: Freud's definition of hysteria makes pantomime the *symptomatic* locus of the Imaginary, that second-order signifying system which 'translates' and 'represents' the anterior language of the unconscious. Thus when Julia Kristeva attempted to synthesize the Bakhtinian opposition between the classical and grotesque with the Lacanian terms of the symbolic and the Imaginary, there was warrant for the connection not only at the theoretical level but in this 'other narrative' of the hysteric (Kristeva 1974). Yet such is the low status of popular ritual and dramatic representation that Freud never 'sees' his own reference to pantomime as anything other than metaphorical. Towards the end of a letter to Fliess written in 1896, Freud remarks on what Charcot had dubbed the 'clownism' phase of hysterical attacks. He writes of:

> the 'clownism' in boys' hysteria, the imitation of animals and circus scenes . . . a compulsion to repeat dating from their youth [in which they] seek their satisfaction to the accompaniment of the craziest capers, somersaults and grimaces.
>
> (Freud 1954: 182)

Even though Charcot's typology of hysterical styles is unreliable and contrived (Didi-Huberman: 1982), especially for the photographic representations, the 'clownism' was frequently attested to as a symptomatic aspect of hysteria. Freud, in the explanation which he offers to Fliess in the letter, refers to the 'perversion of the seducers' (the patients themselves) who, he says, 'connect up nursery games and sexual scenes'. This is something we explored in the preceding chapter in relation to the nurse-maid: here, offered as an explanation of the clownism, it does not take sufficient account of the whole range of festive material scattered through various studies on hysteria and which together create a subtext irreducible to nursery games. There are indeed deep connections between childhood rituals, games and carnivalesque practices (White: 1983), but here Freud's insistence upon a purely sexual aetiology obscures a fundamental socio-historical matrix of the symptom.

The carnival material of the case studies witnesses an historical repression and return. The repression includes the gradual, relentless attack on the 'grotesque body' of carnival by the emergent middle and professional classes from the Renaissance onwards. Interestingly, scholars of European popular culture have occasionally wanted to connect up, backwards as it were, Renaissance festive form to Freud's ideas. Thus C. L. Barber claims that 'A saturnalian attitude, assumed by a clear-cut gesture toward liberty, brings mirth, an accession of wanton vitality. In terms of Freud's analysis of wit, the energy normally occupied in maintaining inhibition is freed for celebration' (Barber 1959: 7). But Barber's reference to Freud seems like a reaching after validation which confuses the historically complex relation of the discourse of psychoanalysis to festive practices. The demonization and the exclusion of the carnivalesque has to be related to the victorious emergence of specifically bourgeois practices and languages which reinflected and incorporated this material within a negative, individualist framework. In one way or another Freud's patients can be seen as enacting desperate ritual fragments salvaged from a festive tradition, *the self-exclusion from which* had been one of the identifying features of their social class. The language of bourgeois neurosis both disavows and appropriates the domain of calendrical festive practices. Thus the 'highly gifted lady' of the case studies celebrated a whole series of what she called 'festivals of remembrance', annually re-enacting the various scenes of her affliction.

It might at first seem plausible to view the discourses of neurosis as the *psychic* irruption of *social* practices which had been suppressed. Certainly, in the long-term history from the seventeenth to the twentieth century, as we have seen above, there were literally thousands of acts of legislation introduced which attempted to eliminate carnival and popular festivity from European life. In different areas of Europe the pace varied, depending upon religious, class and economic factors. But everywhere, against the periodic revival of local festivity and occasional reversals, a fundamental ritual order of western culture came under attack – its feasting, violence, drinking, processions, fairs, wakes, rowdy spectacle and outrageous clamour were subject to surveillance and repressive control. Throughout the course of this book we have remarked on many particulars of this general process. In 1855 the Great Donnybrook Fair of Dublin was abolished in the very same year that

Bartholomew Fair in London finally succumbed to the determined attack of the London City Missions Society. In the decade following the Fairs Act of 1871 over 700 fairs, mops and wakes were abolished in England. By the 1880s the Paris carnival was rapidly being transformed into a trade show cum civic/military parade (Faure: 1978), and although the 'cortège du boeuf gras' processed round the streets until 1914, 'little by little it was suppressed and restricted because it was said to cause a traffic problem' (Pillement 1972: 383). In 1873 the famous Nice carnival was taken over by a 'comité des Fêtes', brought under bureaucratic bourgeois control and reorganized quite self-consciously as a tourist attraction for the increasing numbers who spent time on the Riviera and who were finding neighbouring San Remo's new casino a bigger draw (Sidro 1979: 57–62). As Wolfgang Hartmann has shown (1976), in Germany in the aftermath of the Franco-Prussian war, traditional processions and festivities were rapidly militarized and incorporated into the symbolism and 'classical body' of the State. This dramatic transformation of the ritual calendar had implications not only for each stratum of the social formation, particularly for those which were disengaging *themselves* from ongoing practices, but for the basic structures of symbolic activity in Europe: carnival was now everywhere and nowhere.

We have illustrated in the introduction and in Chapter 1 how many social historians treat the attack on carnival as a victory over popular culture, first by the Absolutist state and then by the middle classes, a process which is viewed as the more or less complete destruction of popular festivity: the end of carnival. In this vision of the complete elimination of the ritual calendar there is the implicit assumption that, in so far as it was the culture of a rural population which was disappearing, the modernization of Europe led inevitably to the supersession of traditional festivity – it was simply one of the many casualties in the movement towards an urban, industrial society. On the other hand recent literary criticism, following Bakhtin, has found elements of the carnivalesque everywhere it has looked in *modern* as well as traditional literature. Critics now discover the forms, symbols, rituals and structures of carnival to be among the fundamental elements in the aesthetics of modernism (White: 1982).

By and large literary critics have not connected with the work of social historians to ask how or why this carnivalesque material should persistently inform modern art because, busy with the task of textual analysis, they move too easily from social practice to textual composition. Yet the social historians who have charted the trans-formations of carnival as a social practice have not registered its *displacements* into bourgeois discourses like art and psychoanalysis: adopting a naively empirical view they have outlined a simple disappearance, the elimination of the carnivalesque.

But, as we have shown, carnival did not simply disappear. At least four different processes were involved in its ostensible break-up: fragmentation; marginalization; sublimation; repression.

Carnival had always been a loose amalgam of procession, feasting, competition, games and spectacle, combining diverse elements from a large repertoire and varying from place to place. Even the great carnivals of Venice, Naples, Nice, Paris and Nuremberg were fluid and changeable in their combination of practices. During the long and uneven process of suppression (we often find that a carnival is banned over and over again, only to re-emerge each time in a slightly altered fashion), there was a tendency for the basic mixture to break down, certain elements becoming separated from others. Feasting became separated from performance, spectacle from procession: the grotesque body was fragmented. At the same time it began to be marginalized both in terms of social class and geographical location. It is important to note that even as late as the nineteenth century, in some places, carnival remained a ritual involving most classes and sections of a community – the disengaging of the middle class from it was a slow and uneven matter. Part of that process was, as we have seen, the 'disowning' of carnival and its symbolic resources, a gradual reconstruction of the idea of carnival as the culture of the Other. This act of disavowal on the part of the emergent bourgeoisie, with its sentimentalism and its disgust, *made* carnival into the festival of the Other. It encoded all that which the proper bourgeois must strive *not to be* in order to preserve a stable and 'correct' sense of self.

William Addison (1953) charts many of these geographical mar-ginalizations in the English context in the seventeenth and eighteenth centuries. Within a town the fair, mop, wake or carnival, which had once taken over the whole of the town and permitted neither outside nor outsider to its rule, was confined to certain areas and gradually driven out from the well-to-do neighbourhoods. In the last years of the Bury St Edmunds Fair it was 'banished from the aristocratic quarter of Angel Hill and confined to St Mary's and St James's squares' (Addison 1953: 163). In and around London:

> Both regular and irregular fairs were being steadily pushed from the centre outwards as London grew and the open spaces were built over. Greenwich and Stepney were the most popular at one time. Others – Croydon's for example – came to the fore later when railways extended the range of pleasure as well as the range of boredom, until towards the end of the nineteenth century London was encircled by these country fairs, some of which were, in fact, ancient charter fairs made popular by easier transport. . . . Most of them were regarded by the magistrates as nuisances, and sooner or later most of those without charters were suppressed. Yet such was the popularity of these country fairs round London that to suppress them in one place led inevitably to an outbreak elsewhere, and often where control was more difficult. As the legal adviser to the City Corporation had said in the 1730's, 'It is at all times difficult by law to put down the ancient customs and practices of the multitude.'
>
> (Addison 1953: 100)

In England the sites of 'carnival' moved more and more to the coastal periphery, to the seaside (Manning-Sanders 1951; Hern 1967; and see especially Walton 1982). The development of Scarborough, Brighton, Blackpool, Clacton, Margate and other seaside resorts reflects a process of liminality which, in different ways, was taking place across Europe as a whole. The seaside was partially legitimated as a carnivalesque site of pleasure on the grounds of health, since it combined the (largely mythical) medicinal virtues of the spa resorts with tourism and the fairground. It can be argued that this marginalization is a *result* of other, anterior processes of bourgeois displacement and even repression. But even so, this historical process of marginalization must be seen as an historical tendency distinct from the actual elimination of carnival.

There is a remarkable case of hysteria documented by a Dr Schnyder from Berne (Schnyder 1912) which brings together this process of marginalization in England and the symptoms of hysteria in a strange and telling way. Schnyder was influenced by Freud early in the latter's career and wrote 'Le cas de Renata', his case study, as a contribution to the study of hysteria along broadly Freudian lines. 'Renata' was 25 years old when she came to Schnyder suffering from hysterical symptoms together with her brother, a priest, also diagnosed as an hysteric, and Schnyder treated them both at the same time.

'Renata' (the 'reborn', a name which she gave herself after the successful termination of her treatment), describes how her hysteria began on a visit from her home town of Berne to the seaside resort of Brighton in England. She recounts how the onset of her vomiting, headaches and anorexia was precipitated by her seeing the holiday-makers on Brighton beach. Coming from a very strict upper-middle-class Catholic family background in Switzerland, she was unable to cope with what Schnyder paraphrases as 'le spectacle de la promiscuité des sexes offerte par une plage mondaine'. Renata sought help from a local Catholic priest to try to contain the deep fears triggered by the 'promiscuity of sexes on the crowded beach'. The incident is doubly significant in that it reveals both the special phobic power of the carnivalesque or festive scene for the hysteric and at the same time nicely illustrates the way in which even the marginalized forms of popular festivity could suddenly re-emerge in the heart of bourgeois life as the very site of potential neurosis.

Bakhtin is right to suggest that post-romantic culture is, to a considerable extent, subjectivized and interiorized and on this account frequently related to private terrors, isolation and insanity rather than to robust kinds of social celebration and critique. Bakhtin however does not give us a convincing explanation of this *sublimation* of carnival. The social historians, on the other hand, tend not to consider processes of sublimation at all: for them carnival came to an end and that was that. They tend not to believe in the return of the repressed.

But a convincing map of the transformation of carnival involves tracing migrations, concealment, metamorphoses, fragmentations, internalization and neurotic sublimations. The *disjecta membra* of the grotesque body of carnival found curious lodgement throughout the whole social order of late nineteenth- and early twentieth-century Europe. These dispersed carnivalesque elements represent more than the insignificant nomadic residues of the ritual tradition. We have argued elsewhere how much modern 'transgressive literature', from Sade to Thomas Pynchon, transforms popular festive material into a

'Carnival of the Night' (White 1982). In the long process of disowning carnival and rejecting its periodical inversions of the body and the social hierarchy, bourgeois society problematized its own relation to the power of the 'low', enclosing itself, indeed often defining itself, by its suppression of the 'base' languages of carnival.

As important as this was the fact that carnival was being marginalized *temporally* as well as spatially. The carnival calendar of oscillation between production and consumption which had once structured the whole year was displaced by the imposition of the working week under the pressure of capitalist industrial work regimes. The semiotic polarities, the symbolic clusters of classical and grotesque, were no longer *temporally* pinned into a calendrical or seasonal cycle, and this involved a degree of unpredictability in moment and surface of emergence. The 'carnivalesque' might erupt from the literary text, as in so much surrealist art, or from the advertisement hoarding, or from a pop festival or a jazz concert.

Marie Cardinal in her autobiographical novel *Les Mots pour le Dire* (1975), which won the Prix Littre in 1976 (translated into English as *The Words To Say It*) (Cardinal 1984), gives a remarkable, harrowing account of her hysterical breakdown and the seven years' psychoanalysis which she underwent in the process of her treatment. We shall return in some detail to Cardinal's account below, but here it is worth remarking how, like 'Renata', her first attack was precipitated by a form of the modern carnivalesque scene, in this case a jazz concert given by Louis Armstrong:

> My first anxiety attack occurred during a Louis Armstrong concert. I was nineteen or twenty . . . the atmosphere warmed up fast . . . it tore at the nerves of those who followed it . . . my heart began to accelerate, becoming more important than the music, shaking the bars of my rib cage, compressing my lungs so the air could no longer enter them. Gripped by panic at the idea of dying there in the middle of spasms, stomping feet, and the crowd howling, I ran into the street like someone possessed . . . 'I'm going to die, I'm going to die, I'm going to die.'
>
> (Cardinal 1984: 35–6)

The occasional and irregular nature of the event compounds the phobic isolation and unexpected eruption of panic in the subject, whose status here is that of a visitor, a stranger even, at the festival.

The relation of the individual body-subject to the communal event and the intense rhythmic motility of the crowd has become complex, unpredictably free-floating and thereby largely beyond the controlling horizon of expectation in the individual life-history.

The result is a fantasy *bricolage* which may often merge into the sensational and the shocking once the culture has set it adrift from its previous location in the repetitious and familiar cycles of calendar time. In flux, dispersed across new artistic and psychic domains, these carnivalesque fragments formed unstable discursive compounds, sometimes disruptive, sometimes therapeutic, within the very constitution of bourgeois subjectivity. Hysteria in the late nineteenth century was doubtless compounded in part by this material and that which had been excluded at the level of social identity (the 'symbolic') returned at the level of subjective articulation, as both phobia and fascination, in the individual patient. Yet of course this did not make it an 'individual' matter. The commonness of the carnivalesque material in the hysterical discourse witnesses a cultural and an historical phenomenon, something which entraps and 'speaks' the patients in a way which cannot be accounted for purely within the terms of familial structure. It is striking how the thematics of carnival pleasure – eating, inversion, mess, dirt, sex and stylized body movements – find their neurasthenic, unstable and mimicked counterparts in the discourse of hysteria.

In her unfinished autobiography Jean Rhys gives a cameo of the phobic fascination afflicting bourgeois women in their exclusion from the carnivalesque as they were educated to be nice, clean, well-behaved little girls. Rhys writes of her childhood around 1900:

> The three days before Lent were carnival in Roseau. We couldn't dress up or join in but we could watch from the open window and not through the jalousies. There were gaily masked crowds with a band. Listening, I would give anything, anything to be able to dance like that, the life surged up to us sitting stiff and well-behaved, looking on. As usual my feelings were mixed, because I was afraid of the masks.

> (Rhys 1979: 42)

Rhys perfectly captures the three elements which are so tangibly connected in the case history of Frau Emmy von N. when she too looked upon the alien masks with fear. Placed on the outside of a grotesque carnival body which is articulated as social pleasure and celebration, the female bourgeois subject introjects the spectacle as both the pathos of exclusion ('why can't that be me?') and as a negative representation which becomes phobic precisely through the law of her exclusion, the interdiction which defines her difference ('You must not be *that*'). In this case the link is made all the more clearly by the regulation of the little girl's body which Rhys describes as 'stiff and well-behaved'.

Carnival was too disgusting for bourgeois life to endure except as sentimental spectacle. Even then its specular identifications could only be momentary, fleeting and partial – voyeuristic glimpses of a promiscuous loss of status and decorum which the bourgeoisie had had to deny as abhorrent in order to emerge as a distinct and 'proper' class.

INVERSION AND DIRT

One of the essential ways of describing carnival focuses upon the *ritual inversions* which it habitually involves. In the Introduction we looked at some of the literature describing this 'reversible world' and world upside down (WUD) which encodes ways that carnival inverts the everyday hierarchies, structures, rules and customs of its social formation. Status degradation through exposure of the grotesque aspects of the body and exorbitant exaggeration of its features is an essential aspect of this. We showed on p. 17 its linking up of the inversion of hierarchy (kings become servants, officers serve the ranks, boys become bishops, men dress as women and so on) with a comic privileging of the bottom part of the body (feet, knees, legs, buttocks, genitals, anus) over the rational and spiritual control of the head.

Carnival gives symbolic and ritual play, and active display, to the inmixing of the subject, to the heterodox, messy, excessive and unfinished informalities of the body and social life. It attacks the authority of the ego (by rituals of degradation and by the use of masks and costume) and flaunts the material body as a pleasurable grotesquerie – protuberant, fat, disproportionate, open at its orifices. The carnivalesque inversion mounts a co-ordinated *double* attack upon the 'Ideal-Ich', calling the bluff on foreclosure: it denies with a laugh the ludicrous pose of autonomy adopted by the subject within the hierarchical arrangements of the symbolic at the same moment as it re-opens the body-boundary, the closed orifices of which normally guarantee the repressive mechanism itself.

One of the grimmest sources of nausea for Frau Emmy is meat-fat, the principal symbol of Mardi Gras ('Greasy Tuesday') and Carne Levare (the roasting and taking up of meat which probably gave carnival its name). Fat, dripping and suet were essential to carnival celebration, clearly visible in the French opposition between Carnival and Lent, *jours gras* and *jours maigres*, which were usually personified between a fat man and a lean woman. Hysterics privately enact the battle between Carnival and Lent, a battle in which the anorexic figure of Lent – a figure represented as emaciated, old and female, a figure of humourless fasting and sexual abstinence – is invariably the victor. It is as if the hysteric has no mechanism for coping with the *mediation* of the grotesque body in everyday life except by violent acts of exclusion. In these violent struggles it is not surprising that fragmented elements of the carnival repertoire should be seized upon as weapons.

In Freud's early studies it is above all the woman's body which becomes the battle-ground in the hysterical repression of the grotesque form. The women hysterics, horrified by fat, associate their own developing bodies with both dirt and fat. It is an association which may or may not be clinically identical to anorexia (Bruch 1965). 'Renata', for instance, in Schnyder's case study, like Anna O., changes her native language into English when struggling to both express and deny certain unbearable fears. 'Renata' has a catechism of terms which she recites in English (her native tongue is French): among these catechistic terms 'Woman-Shame-Fat' is a particularly telling and poignant set which she repeats over and over to Schnyder. She remarks:

When I looked at the shape of my body I was ashamed of being a woman. I wondered what men really thought about women – I was humiliated being a woman and annoyed to feel anyone looking at me. Being fat seemed to me particularly humiliating because the shape of my body seemed even more to blame. I really didn't want anyone to be able to distinguish the female outline of my body beneath my clothes.

(Schnyder 1912: 218)

'Renata' is so appalled by the thought of her own body becoming fat that she gets up in the night and tightly straps herself into her corset to prevent her body swelling up in the night. This nocturnal rite, often repeated, reveals how the hysteric enacts compulsive Lenten acts of mortification in the struggle ('Renata' calls it 'la guerre à tout sentiment, à toute sensation') against her own body.

A common mechanism, which the hysteric employs in order to cope with the imminent sense of the body surging up against itself in a way experienced as 'sensation', is a top/bottom displacement, reversing, in an uncanny manner, the *ritual inversion* of the body found in carnival. In carnival the exaggeratedly bulging and dirty lower stratum is given priority and turned into the source of comic display. In the hysteric, terrors associated with the lower bodily stratum are converted into symptoms of the top half of the body. 'Renata's' vomiting is eventually traced to the feeling of pleasure which she has in her womb when she eats. She vomits, she says, to 'repousser ces sensations'. In a footnote to the Dora case Freud discusses the displacement upwards of 'catarrh' in a 12 year-old girl, transforming her vaginal discharge, about which she was deeply anxious, into a nervous cough (Freud 1909b: 101n.15). In the case of Dora herself, she transfers the 'pressure of Herr K.'s embrace' from the lower to the higher part of her body.

Furthermore, there is a curious passage in the *Dora* analysis where Freud discovers another and more serious displacement in Dora's body. She, too, suffers from a leucorrhoeal discharge, and any intensification of this leads to her vomiting and refusing to eat. Terrors and pleasures associated with the lower half of the body are registered as displaced symptoms in the top half.

Freud's bland ascription of Dora's symptom to woman's 'vanity', as well as being one of the notorious moments in the text where the full force of Freud's sexism is all too apparent, is also inadequate to the problem of purity and disgust with respect to the woman's body (see Rose 1978; Gallop 1982 et al. for the readings of *Dora* which have fully explored the mysogyny of this text). Freud writes:

> The pride taken by women in the appearance of their genitals is quite a special feature of their vanity; and disorders of the genitals which they think calculated to inspire feelings of repugnance or even disgust have an incredible power of humiliating them, of lowering their self-esteem, and of making them irritable, sensitive

and distrustful. An abnormal secretion of the mucous membrane of the vagina is looked upon as a source of disgust.

(Freud 1909b: 103)

We can put this in a quite contrary way: deprived of the language and the means to accurately map and explore the lower regions of their own bodies, women were frequently only able to designate the genitals and the anus through non-specific images of repugnance. The words to say it, in Marie Cardinal's account of her hysteria, were simply not there. Only alienated medical terms or 'rude' words and these were of little avail against the relentless message that, whatever it was, it was dirty, unmentionable, *unacceptable*. 'Disgust' is the operative term in hysteria and contrary to Freud's express attempt to discredit the importance of the question of purity beyond a single sexual aetiology, the question of disgust and purity is culturally irreducible.

It is also intimately connected to the fate of the carnivalesque. In the following passage from *The Words to Say It* Cardinal describes a moment late in her analysis when, with extraordinary joy, she comes to accept those parts of her body that since early childhood she had disowned as 'filthy'. The chain of signification which leads from the acceptance of her own 'lower bodily stratum', through her images of a circus and clowns and on to the realization of why she had never liked Rabelais, is a quite fascinating confirmation of the powerful associative connection which the subject makes between hysteria and the carnivalesque:

> Then I understood there was an entire area of the body which I had never accepted and which somehow never belonged to me. The zone between my legs could be only expressed in shameful words, and had never been the object of my conscious thought. No word contained my anus (since this term was only acceptable in a scientific or medical context, it constituted a sickness in itself). Any word that I pronounced that contained my anus would immediately have brought down upon me scandal and filth, and, above all, the confusion in my own mind. As for what passed through there, I could only bring myself to say the 'number two' [which she says in English, not French] of my childhood.
>
> I was an invalid and it was while I was laughing that I made the discovery. I was made to think of circus clowns who slap their

great shoes in the sawdust, seemingly unaware of a little red bulb which lights up their rear ends as they say with an exaggerated and pretentious mimicry: 'I'm sooooo smart,' making the children laugh. They are grotesque because they appear to ignore what is happening at the base of their spines.

I rediscovered laughter. Poking fun at myself was delicious. I'd lived until the age of thirty-six with an opening in my body with the horrible name 'anus'. I had no ass. What a farce. I understood better why I had never liked Rabelais.

(Cardinal 1984: 174–5)

Cardinal reverses the Bakhtinian order: she begins by reading her own body's repression and ends by rediscovering Rabelais. Deprived not only of an appropriate discourse about her body but of cultural modes of humour which enable her to own it comfortably (laughter is here the acceptance of the anus), she turns – like so many other hysteria patients – to the carnivalesque and the circus for the images through which she may recognize *herself* without disgust.

Disgust is a key category in the case histories just as it is in relation to the bourgeois rejection of carnival. Carnivalesque practices were 'filthy' when measured by the emergent hegemonic standards of bourgeois life. How often we find the post-Romantic writer separating out his or her central character at the moment of carnival or popular festivity, endowing that character with a special sensitivity and isolated self-consciousness over against the crude conviviality of the revellers. There is no more easily recognizable scene of bourgeois pathos than the lonely crowd in which individual identity is achieved *over against* all the others, through the sad realization of not-belonging. That moment, in which the subject is made the outsider to the crowd, an onlooker, compensating for exclusion through the deployment of the discriminating gaze, is at the very root of bourgeois sensibility. Who would not exchange vulgar participation in the jostle of the crowd for the gift of discriminating judgement? At the carnival the truly fine spirit will only find disillusionment:

The ball was almost over, the candles were burning low; the players, drunk or fast asleep, had abandoned their instruments; the crowd had thinned and everyone had let fall their masks; huge streams of red and white paint flowed down these faces, revealing livid flesh, blotched and flabby – a disgusting spectacle of decayed coquetry.

(Starobinski 1964: 86)

In *The Civilizing Process* Norbert Elias charts a gradual raising of what he calls 'the threshold of shame and embarrassment' until the nineteenth century. He shows how aspects of the body, its secretions and fluids, which had formerly been acceptable even to court élites and afforded no particular social or psychological difficulties in manners or conduct, were first projected as characteristic of the 'bestial' lower orders and then gradually expelled from the culture altogether. Stephen Greenblatt adds in his brilliant article 'Filthy rites':

> In this separation, the 'lower bodily stratum' steadily loses any connection with anything other than the increasingly disreputable dreams of alchemists and cranks. Eventually, all the body's products, except tears, become simply unmentionable in decent society.
>
> (Greenblatt 1982)

In the 'Studies on hysteria' Freud uses the resonant term 'the agencies of disgust' to describe the forces arrayed against him in the struggle to cure hysterics. Those 'agencies of disgust' are the same agencies which, in their public form, mobilized civic and religious authorities against carnival. The connection is a charged and difficult one, but if it can be clarified we might have the outline of a thoroughly historicized, social understanding of mechanisms which Freud tended to interpret in universal terms. It would certainly appear that the carnivalesque practices from which the bourgeoisie distanced themselves emerged in the late nineteenth century as pathological contents in the discursive material of the analysand.

Hysteria, which as a social pathology seems to have 'peaked' around the end of the nineteenth century and declined quite rapidly thereafter (Veith 1965), marks a significant moment in this long process. In this same period bourgeois culture produced a compensatory range of peripheral 'bohemias' which afforded 'liminoid' symbolic repertoires of a kind approximating to those of earlier carnival forms. Since 'respectable women' were defined precisely by their self-distancing from such indecent domains they were the social group most remote from any access to available symbolic articulations of the lower body. Certainly, the bourgeois bohemias, like surrealism and expressionism, took over in displaced form much of the inversion, grotesque body symbolism, festive ambivalence and transgression which had once been the provenance of carnival.

We are now in a position to try and account for the kinship of certain hysterical manifestations and carnival. They correspond, privately and publicly respectively, to the 'staging' of the normally *repressed poles* of certain binary structures through which a culture thinks itself. 'Staging' is indeed the word and recent research has revealed how far Charcot and others were prepared to exploit the theatricality of hysteria in such a way as to *reproduce* the iconographic sensationalism of freakshows at the fair (Didi-Huberman 1982). Carnival was the repeated, periodic celebration of the grotesque body – fattening food, intoxicating drink, sexual promiscuity, altered ego-identity, the inverse and the heteroglot. All these are the opposite poles to the terms governing everyday work and are usually repressed. Carnival allowed the society involved to mediate into periodic ritual the culturally structured 'otherness' of its governing categories. We might call this process of periodic mediation *active reinforcement*. Categories *opposite* to the ones normally enforced are given an actual and active staging during the festival. This contrasts strongly with the mechanism of hysteria which Freud called *reactive reinforcement* and which he felt was fundamental to the pathology of hysteria:

> Contrary thoughts are always closely connected with each other and are often paired off in such a way that the *one thought is exaggeratedly conscious while its counterpart is repressed and unconscious*. This relation between the two thoughts is an effect of the process of repression. For repression is often achieved by means of excessive reinforcement of the thought contrary to the one which is to be repressed. This process I shall call *reactive reinforcement*, and the thought which asserts itself exaggeratedly in consciousness and ... cannot be removed I call a *reactive thought*.
>
> (Freud 1909b: 72)

This passage is consonant with what anthropology and linguistics have posited as the binaryism of symbolic functioning. Carnival could be seen as a cultural and collective mechanism for the staging of the dyadic, opposite terms to those in operation in the sphere of daily production. In its rejection of these rituals, bourgeois life elevated its status but simultaneously became increasingly vulnerable to the unexpected, destabilized emergence of these 'othernesses': social mediation and active reinforcement were transformed by a class reliant upon pure repression into the mechanism of *reactive reinforcement*.

Deleuze and Guattari are thus wrong when, in *Anti-Oedipus* they remark that 'the psychoanalyst parks his circus in the dumbfounded unconscious, a real P. T. Barnum in the fields and factories' (Deleuze and Guattari 1983: 298–9). It is not the analyst but the patient who reaches out to the showman and the circus. Freud, for one, was quite typical in preferring to look above such things when his patients presented them to him, frankly sharing the general propensity of his class to define itself by sublimation: by precisely *overlooking* the carnivalesque scene.

Thus in one of his early letters to his fiancée Martha Bernays he discusses a visit which she had made to the Wandsbeck Fair. He agrees with her that the self-indulgence of the common people is 'neither pleasant nor edifying'. He goes on to add that their own pleasures such as 'an hour's chat nestling close to one's love' or 'the reading of a book' have disabled them from participating in such common festivities.

For the rising middle classes it seemed as though all that messy, disruptive, violent nonsense of carnival was at last being done away with. In fact, even if the carnival was over, a strange carnivalesque diaspora was already taking place.

Conclusion

It has been argued that 'the demarcating imperative' divides up human and non-human, society and nature, 'on the basis of the simple logic of excluding filth' (Chase 1984: 194; Kristeva 1982: 68). Differentiation, in other words, is dependent upon disgust. The division of the social into high and low, the polite and the vulgar, simultaneously maps out divisions between the civilized and the grotesque body, between author and hack, between social purity and social hybridization. These divisions, as we have argued, cut across the social formation, topography and the body, in such a way that subject identity cannot be considered independently of these domains. The bourgeois subject continuously defined and re-defined itself through the exclusion of what it marked out as 'low' – as dirty, repulsive, noisy, contaminating. Yet that very act of exclusion was constitutive of its identity. The low was internalized under the sign of negation and disgust.

But disgust always bears the imprint of desire. These low domains, apparently expelled as 'Other', return as the object of nostalgia, longing and fascination. The forest, the fair, the theatre, the slum, the circus, the seaside-resort, the 'savage': all these, placed at the outer limit of civil life, become symbolic contents of bourgeois desire. These contents, or domains, are subject to misrecognition and distortion precisely because idealization and phobic avoidance have *systematically* informed their discursive history. Thus on the one hand, these sites have been singled out by some social historians in a nostalgic and privileged way as the ever-vanishing trace of 'real community'. But this precisely duplicates, at the level of academic discourse, the object of analysis. On the other hand, 'rigorous theory' has tended to look down upon 'mere content' as obvious, crude and vulgar, redeemable only through a process of abstraction and refinement. Here we find the opposite but equally characteristic gesture of 'the civilizing process'. In other words contemporary analysis has tended either to fetishize or repress the *contents* of these domains. In so doing, academic work clearly reveals its discursive mirroring of the subject-formation of the middle classes.

This fetishism or repression is equally likely to occur in attempts to 'think' the body. We have argued that the body cannot be thought separately from the social formation, symbolic topography and the constitution of the subject. The body is neither a purely natural given nor is it merely a text al metaphor, it is a privileged operator for the transcoding of these c her areas. Thinking the body is thinking social topography and v rsa. The dissociation of the two is a distinctive ideological m apparent in contemporary analysis as in the history which we ha en tracing. If Ben Jonson, for instance, attempts to transcend the 'grossly physical', the 'return to the body' of so much recent theory is but the mirror-image of this prior repudiation. Both processes partake of the same mystification. Even Foucault, who has most brilliantly demonstrated the construction of desire through the regulation of the body, retains a residual, but active nostalgia for 'the' body which he invokes as a self-substantiating value. It is not that, as Culler has tried to assert, any appeal to the body is a kind of mystification: it is rather that the body is actively produced by the junction and disjunction of symbolic domains and can never be legitimately evaluated 'in itself'.

To this extent the critique of carnival, as an ideal and as an analytic concept, which we gave in the introduction to the present volume, is valid for the body as well. Naturally enough, since it has been a major aspect of our project to reveal how intimately these two realms are interconnected in the definition of status and subject identity. Celebratory invocations of the body, like celebratory invocations of carnival, emerge out of similar mechanisms of symbolic re-territorialization, processes of rejection which attempted to guarantee the dignified self-sufficiency of bourgeois professional life. Their *apparent* disjunction, indeed their falling into separate disciplinary areas (social history/anthropology on the one hand and psychology on the other), was a decisive historical separation and symptomatic of the process of differentiation which we have been examining.

That overall process, the formation of the cultural Imaginary of the middle class in post-Renaissance Europe, involved an internal distancing from the popular which was complex and often contradictory in its effects. We have had cause throughout this book to reflect on an unnoticed slide between two quite distinct kinds of 'grotesque', the grotesque as the 'Other' of the defining group or self, and the grotesque as a boundary phenomenon of hybridization or inmixing, in which self and other become enmeshed in an inclusive, heterogeneous, dangerously unstable zone. What starts as a *simple* repulsion or rejection of symbolic matter foreign to the self inaugurates a process of introjection and negation which is always *complex* in its effects. In order to fathom this complexity, this inner dynamic of the boundary constructions necessary to collective identity, we have to avoid conflating the two different forms of the grotesque. If the two are confused, it becomes impossible to see that a fundamental mechanism of identity formation *produces* the second, hybrid grotesque at the level of the political unconscious *by the very struggle to exclude the first grotesque.* That is to say, when the bourgeoisie consolidated itself as a respectable and conventional body by withdrawing itself from the popular, it constructed the popular as grotesque otherness: but by this act of withdrawal and consolidation it produced *another grotesque*, an identity-in-difference which was nothing other than its fantasy relation, its negative symbiosis, with that which it had rejected in its social practices. We can represent the process schematically:

1 OFFICIAL IDENTITY $A = \text{not-}B$ (i.e. the SYMBOLIC/MONOLOGIC)

2 POLITICAL UNCONSCIOUS $A = A/B$ (i.e. the IMAGINARY/DIALOGIC)

The point is that the *exclusion* necessary to the formation of social identity at level one is simultaneously a *production* at the level of the Imaginary, and a production, what is more, of a complex hybrid fantasy emerging out of the very attempt to demarcate boundaries, to unite and purify the social collectivity. It was not by accident therefore that an anthropology which began by exploring the ordering mechanisms of social classification was led onto the question of pollution rites and filth. As Mary Douglas writes:

In short, our pollution behaviour is the reaction which condemns any object or idea likely to confuse or contradict cherished classifications.

(Douglas 1966: 48)

The general processes of classification which bear most closely upon the identity of the collectivity are indissociable from the heterodox symbolic material of the Imaginary. Indeed, the latter is actively produced by the suppression of extraterritoriality and is never exhausted by the a priori family configuration. The unconscious is to this extent *necessarily* a political unconscious as Jameson avers, for the exclusion of other social groups and classes in the struggle to achieve categorical self-identity appears as a special dialogism, an agon of voices – sometimes even as *argument* – within the shared Imaginary of the class in question. The very drive to achieve a singularity of collective identity is simultaneously productive of unconscious heterogeneity, with its variety of hybrid figures, competing sovereignties and exorbitant demands.

'Domain', as we have insisted throughout, is crucial to this process. The kind of cultural semantics which we have explored in this book has returned, again and again, to the question of displacements between *sites* of discourse – the fairground, the marketplace, the coffee-house, the theatre, the slum, the domestic interior of the bourgeois household. The grouping together of sites of discourse, the acceptance and the rejection of place, with its laws and protocols of language, is at once a coding of social identity. In thus sketching out the conflict of terrains in the geography of the bourgeois Imaginary we have interrogated the boundaries and hierarchies which connect, by separation, classes and discourses. Each place within the social ensemble is a particular site of production of discourse, a specific semantic field, but each domain in turn can easily be reconstructed within the terms of other domains and according to the hierarchies and ranks governing the social formation as a whole. No discourse whatsoever escapes this process. If the 'fair', for example, situates and produces a wide range of linguistic forms, it can easily be re-formed outside of its own purlieu (e.g. in the church or in the university). This reintroduces the question of domination back into the field of discourse.

The complexity of this 'double-articulation' arises from the fact that these domains and their discursive practices are at once interconnected and dissociated, both at the level of class identities and in the grotesque hybridizations of the unconscious. Indeed a valuable way of thinking about ideology is to conceive of it as the way discursive traffic and exchange between different domains are structured and controlled. The bourgeoisie inherited, not just the symbolic terms of the old hierarchies, in the midst of which they had to carve out their own particular semantic sphere, but also the hierarchy of the *places of production* of those symbols, the court, the country house, the church on the one hand and the marketplace, the tavern and the fair on the other, each with its own rules governing interaction, the body and language. We have a model then, in which equal weight must be given to both words in the term 'discursive domain': if every location is a specific discursive practice, location itself is in turn 'placed' and ranked according to the topographical priorities of the discourse in question.

Our emphasis upon elements of 'content' within semantic fields has been one way of understanding this complexity. Contents are important because they are always already inscribed within discursive hierarchies and therefore identifiably in or out of place. They not only carry meaning according to their historical and contextual embedding within the stratification of discourse, they also 'locate' meaning; they orient and delimit signification in specific ways. By attending to content elements such as the pig, the rat and the maid in their differential relation to sites of discourse we have been able to show *both* how the 'low' and the 'high' are constructed through these elements *and* how these elements take on meaning according to the shifting historical nature of class relations.

We have tried to move away from any simple before/after model in doing this, for we have been acutely aware that most attempts to map out historically shifting conceptions of the carnival and the body have succumbed, at some point, to an idealist or idealizing moment of apocalypse or nostalgia around the 'disappearance' of carnival and the 'loss' of the body. This is not to say, following the opposite error, that there is no change. What we have analysed is a structural rearrangement and reconfiguration of domain and hierarchy within a cultural semantics for which *all* the terms change, sometimes drastically. There are, of course, certain appearances and disappearances (hippodromes, spas, coffee-houses) but we have underscored that the significance of these is *relational*. The 'coffee-house', for example, had greater signifying power as a site of meaning-making because of the relation in which it stood to other sites of discourse (on the basis of changing class authority) in the eighteenth century. In deliberate opposition to talk of the 'disappearance' of carnival culture and the loss or privatization of the body, we have traced out the contradictory movement of (and between) semantic territories within a structural model of uneven development. Over-simplification and sentimentality for 'lost' realms can be avoided by mapping the *inner articulation* of semantic domains/sites of discourse within the historical formation of class subjects.

From this perspective, in which 'place' is not merely a name but something like a mode of discursive production and also a psychic content – and for which exclusion may be more crucial than presence – the whole question of *displacement* has to be re-thought. The question arises of *the gradient and direction of flow of metaphor and symbolic substitution from one domain to another.* Precisely because semantic domains are hierarchically arranged, metaphorical displacements from one domain to another can never be purely arbitrary. Each domain is discursively saturated with its own social history and unequally placed with respect to other domains: substitutions and exchanges of semantic matter between them are always sensitive to this hierarchy of provenance. In consequence, displacements may occur in one direction and not in another, or alternatively they may encounter kinds of social resistance which they would not if flowing in the contrary direction.

Thus when Freud, as we noted in Chapter 4, proposed that the maid was a metaphorical substitute for the biological mother, the opposite notion – that the mother might be a displacement of the maid – did not occur to him because of the *social* gradient up which such a displacement had to move. But even when the gradient of displacement is downwards, as in the hysterical phobia, the specific forms of representation are never arbitrary. 'Rat Man' and 'Wolf Man', for instance, find their metaphorical proper names not in an unmotivated raid upon the taxonomic categories of rodents and mammals, but in the terrors conjured up by semantic material from cultural domains (the slum, the forest) extraterritorial to their own constructed identities as socio-historical subjects.

Displacement, according to this view, can be seen as a particular kind or subset of the transcoding mechanisms of which we spoke at the outset. This does not entail an appropriation of the psychoanalytic process by and for culturalism or 'vulgar sociologism', since we eschew that bankrupt opposition between social and psychic process which emerged from an ideological division of subject from society in nineteenth-century bourgeois thought. If displacement, following its own literalness, is conceived of as a process of shifting or slipping between different places or domains of discourse, then it must be constituted in and by the gaps and oppositions of these domains. It will be always subject to the ruptures, dislocations, blockages and gradients which exist in the hierarchy of speaking–subject–positions which make up the social formation.

If displacement in general can be considered as a strong transcoding of semiotic material and its corresponding position of utterance across unequal semantic territories, then it follows that 'sublimation' may be treated in the same way. That is to say, sublimation is a process of upward displacement through the social stratification of discourse. It is both a semiosis and a class variable, detectable only in a perceived *difference* from 'unsublimated' practices. It is in fact the main mechanism whereby a group or class or individual bids for symbolic superiority over others: sublimation is inseparable from strategies of cultural domination. 'Civilization and its discontents' (Freud 1930) tends to reproduce this manoeuvre without analysing it. The act of sublimation which for Freud is the founding gesture of 'civilization' is of course only perceptible against a generalized backcloth of uncivilized or savage behaviour. What is in question is not some abstract 'repression of instinct' but the validating of one set of social practices over against others. As a matter of fact one can never repress, or sublimate, an *instinct*: one can however repress an already-existing social or class *practice* by an act of censorship and discursive transcendence. This is the basic process examined in Norbert Elias's remarkable study of the hegemonic strategies of court society.

Sublimation may be detected not only in the rejection of social practices stigmatized as 'vulgar', it may be seen subtly at work in the upward transcoding of such practices. Consider the following delightful quotation from Sir Thomas Browne:

> For even that vulgar and Taverne musicke, which makes one man merry, another mad, strikes me into a deepe fit of devotion, and a

profound contemplation of the first Composer; there is something in it of Divinity more than the ear discovers.

(Sir Thomas Browne 1964: 84)

Here, between the merry and the mad, the sensitive soul marks out its own spiritual superiority, not by despising the tavern and the popular festive scene, but by discovering a special transcendental quality to the rough music and through it an intuition of the divine where others find but coarse pleasure. Of course, it is a divinity *more than the ear discovers*, and thereby confers the double blessing that those of a finely attuned spiritual sensitivity do not even have to listen to the music. The whole passage is an exercise in the accumulation of symbolic capital (and therefore of social elevation) which accrues to the sensitive soul when she or he can differentiate her/himself from the commonality by a sublime translation of popular culture into 'higher' discursive terms.

Another way of approaching the question of displacement and sublimation is to underscore the insufficiency of a phrase, much in vogue and emerging from Saussurian linguistics, which is frequently evoked in connection with these terms: the 'chain of signifiers'. Whilst it is true that meaning does indeed slip away down a chain of substitutions because of the relational and differential nature of linguistic signs, the smooth metaphor of 'chain' wrongly suggests a certain regularity and equality of the 'links' which make up each different term. On the contrary, the most significant kinds of displacement are *across* diverse territories of semantic material and always appear to involve steep gradients, even precipitous leaps, between socially unequal discursive domains. Indeed, as we have seen throughout the preceding chapters the predilection for vertiginous transcodings between extremely 'high' and extremely 'low' sites of discourse cannot be understood in any other way, and certainly not through the socio-historically inert 'signifying chain'.

By refusing the abstract concept of 'difference' in our understanding of displacement, hybridization and the grotesque, we have tried to show that the mechanisms of identity-formation never operate in a neutral semantic field. On the contrary, they operate a special dialogism with its own implicit principles of domination and subordination. This special dialogism is both 'psychological' and 'ideological' to the extent that its vertical transcodings regulate the body and discursive laws through the formation of manners, habits and attitudes *appropriate* (and it is this 'appropriateness' which is the crucial regulative factor) to each social domain.

What was so peculiar to the development of the middle class over the long period which we have been looking at was its contradictory, one might almost say 'eccentric', relationship to such hierarchies and vertical rankings of place and language. The bourgeoisie mystified the interconnection of domains and explicitly refused their hierarchies in the name of democracy and equality. Indeed the radical democratic project was nothing more nor less than this process, in which a 'neutral', 'middling', 'democratic', 'rational' subject was laboriously constructed by a rejection of all specific and particular domains. Surveying all the motley and partial languages of the Court, the aristocracy, the Church and the low populace from the privileged perspective of the public sphere, the rational democratic subject of bourgeois reason was constitutively unable to see that it was *this* process which made 'him' what 'he' was. Thus whilst the 'free' democratic individual appeared to be contentless, a point of judgement and rational evaluation which was purely formal and perspectival, in fact it was constituted through and through by the clamour of particular voices to which it tried to be universally superior. It is on this account that the very blandness and transparency of bourgeois reason is in fact nothing other than the critical negation of a social 'colourfulness', of a heterogeneous diversity of specific contents, upon which it is, nonetheless, completely dependent.

This dependency which re-emerges at the heart of the critical endeavour to produce an independent middle subject; this heterogeneity which re-emerges from the very attempt to achieve a formal, balanced and empty neutrality; this vertiginous and disorienting calling of voices from above and below; all this *clutter* and *mess* of the bourgeois Imaginary inevitably forestalled its radical democratic project. It led not only to the *ressentiment* structure so often remarked upon in accounts of bourgeois desire, it led to a self-critical restlessness, which, as Nietzsche saw, was unparalleled outside of ascetic religious orders. Its attempts to still the low and distracting voices within (its attempts to 'come clean' about its identity) only exacerbated its duality, the sense, sometimes appalling, sometimes exhilarating, of being an outsider to itself. To point out that in the realm of authorship the bourgeoisie is by definition self-critical, its own other to itself, is not for a moment to suggest that it is therefore always progressive. On the contrary, we have argued that it *uses* the whole world as its theatre in a particularly instrumental fashion, the very subjects which it politically excludes becoming exotic costumes which it assumes in order to play out the disorders of its own identity. It is in fact doubtful whether the bourgeoisie has ever returned from that *Voyage de Bougainville* where, in imaginary mimicry of a natural and critical native voice, colonized and on the edge of annihilation, it could at last speak to itself of all that it desired and denied.

In recent critical thought this speaking to itself in the delirium of its repressed others has taken on considerable political significance. Particularly in the writing of Foucault and Kristeva, transgression, whereby bourgeois writing smashes the rigidities of its own identity by projecting itself into the forbidden territories of precisely those excluded in its own political formation, has come to seem a positive and desirable kind of romantic politics. In his 'Preface to Transgression' Foucault wrote:

> Transgression. Perhaps one day it will seem as decisive for our culture, as much a part of its soil, as the experience of contradiction was at an earlier time for dialectical thought. But in spite of so many scattered signs, the language in which transgression will find its space and the illumination of its being lies almost entirely in the future.
>
> (Foucault 1977: 33)

What is clear is that, far from being a project of the future, Foucault is identifying and indemnifying what is perhaps the most characteristic manoeuvre of bourgeois identity. For Foucault transgression is the interrogation of boundaries, 'a realm, no doubt, where what is in question is the limit rather than the identity of a culture'. But cultural identity is inseparable from limits, it is always a boundary phenomenon and its order is always constructed around the figures of its territorial edge. By forcing the threshold and interrogating the liminal position, bourgeois romanticism and its modernist inheritors stage a festival of the political unconscious and reveal the repressions and social rejections which formed it. Transgression becomes a kind of reverse or counter-sublimation, undoing the discursive hierarchies and stratifications of bodies and cultures which bourgeois society has produced as the mechanism of its symbolic dominance.

It would be wrong to associate the exhilarating sense of freedom which transgression affords with any necessary or automatic political progressiveness (Dollimore 1985). Often it is a powerful ritual or symbolic practice whereby the dominant squanders its symbolic capital so as to get in touch with the fields of desire which it denied itself as the price paid for its political power. Not a repressive desublimation (for just as transgression is not intrinsically progressive, nor is it intrinsically conservative), it is a counter-sublimation, a delirious expenditure of the symbolic capital accrued (through the regulation of the body and the decathexis of habitus) in the successful struggle of bourgeois hegemony.

Thus when Julia Kristeva returns to the carnivalesque scene as the potential site of political subversion she confuses the projection of bourgeois desire with the destruction of its class identity. The bourgeoisie, as we have seen throughout this book, is perpetually rediscovering the carnivalesque as a radical source of transcendence. Indeed that act of rediscovery itself, in which the middle classes excitedly discover their own pleasures and desires under the sign of the Other, in the realm of the Other, is constitutive of the very formation of middleclass identity. In *Desire in Language* Kristeva writes:

> Carnivalesque discourse breaks through the laws of a language censored by grammar and semantics and, at the same time, is a social and political protest. There is no equivalence, but rather identity between challenging official linguistic codes and challenging official law.
>
> (Kristeva 1980: 65)

Kristeva here proposes the extreme position that the infraction of *formal* literary codes of language is identical to challenging official law. Not only is this very rarely the case, but unless one addresses the question of the *domain of discourse* and the degree to which carnivalesque practice has actually shifted or realigned domains, then the equation is politically meaningless. Only a challenge to the hierarchy of *sites* of discourse, which usually comes from groups and classes 'situated' by the dominant in low or marginal positions, carries the promise of politically transformative power.

The Politics and Poetics of Transgression

Control of the major sites of discourse is fundamental to political change: the endless 'rediscovery' of the carnivalesque within modern literature is but a common trope *within* that particular site of discourse. In saying this we do not intend to minimize the enormous importance such a figure has within the Imaginary and hence within the political unconscious. As we have seen, the carnivalesque was marked out as an intensely powerful semiotic realm precisely because bourgeois culture constructed its self-identity by rejecting it. The 'poetics' of transgression reveals the disgust, fear and desire which inform the dramatic self-representation of that culture through the 'scene of its low Other'. This poetics reveals quite clearly the contradictory *political* construction of bourgeois democracy. For bourgeois democracy emerged with a class which, whilst indeed progressive in its best political aspirations, had encoded in its manners, morals and imaginative writings, in its body, bearing and taste, a subliminal élitism which was constitutive of its historical being. Whatever the radical nature of its 'universal' democratic demand, it had engraved in its subjective identity all the marks by which it felt itself to be a different, distinctive and superior class.

Bibliography

MMB = *Mikhail Mikhailovich Bakhtin: His Circle, His Influence*. Papers presented at the International Colloquium, Queen's University, Kingston, Ontario, 7–9 October 1983.

Achard, P. (1980) 'History and the politics of language in France: a review essay', *History Workshop Journal*, 10, 175–83.

Adams, J. N. (1982) *The Latin Sexual Vocabulary*, London, Duckworth.

Adams, R. M. (1977) *Badmouth: Fugitive Papers on the Dark Side*, Berkeley, University of California Press.

Addison, W. (1953) *English Fairs and Markets*, London, Batsford.

Agulhon, M. (1982) *The Republic in the Village* (tr. J. Lloyd), Cambridge, Cambridge University Press.

Althusser, L. (1971) *Lenin and Philosophy and Other Essays* (tr. B. Brewster), London, New Left Books.

Anderson, B. (1983) *Imagined Communities*, London, Verso.

Anderson, P. (1979) *Lineages of the Absolutist State*, London, Verso.

Andrews, W. (1887) *Famous Frosts and Frost Fairs in Great Britain. Chronicled from the earliest to the present time*, London, G. Redway.

Anon. (1641) *Bartholomew Fair*, London, Richard Harper.

Anon. (1647) *The Dagonizing of Bartholomew Fayre*, London.

Anon. (1649) *A Bartholomew Fairing*, London.

Anon. (1728) 'The female Dunciad', in Guerinot, J. V. (ed.) *Pamphlet Attacks on Alexander Pope*, London, Methuen, 1969.

Anon. (1735) 'The poet finish'd in prose', in Guerinot, J. V. (ed.) *Pamphlet Attacks on Alexander Pope*, London, Methuen, 1969.

Anstruther, I. (1963) *The Knight and the Umbrella: An Account of the Eglinton Tournament*, London, Geoffrey Bles.

Apter, M. J. (1982) 'Metaphor as synergy', in Miall, D. S. (ed.) *Metaphor: Problems and Perspectives*, Brighton, Harvester, 55–70.

Armitage, J. (1977) *Man at Play*, London, Warne.

Armstrong, N. (1982) 'The rise of feminine authority in the novel', *Novel*, 15, 2, 127–45.

Arthur, K. (1982) 'Bakhtin, Kristeva and carnival', unpublished dissertation, Melbourne.

Atherton, H. M. (1974) *Political Prints in the Age of Hogarth*, Oxford, Clarendon Press.

Babcock, B. (1978) *The Reversible World: Symbolic Inversion in Art and Society*, Ithaca, Cornell University Press.

Bakhtin, M. M. (1968) *Rabelais and his World* (tr. H. Iswolsky), Cambridge, Mass., MIT Press.

Bakhtin, M. M. (1981) *The Dialogic Imagination: Four Essays* (ed. M. Holquist, tr. C. Emerson and M. Holquist), Austin, Texas University Press.

Bakhtin, M. M. (1985) *The Formal Method in Literary Scholarship* (tr. A. J. Wehrle), Cambridge, Mass., Harvard University Press.

Bakhtin, M. M., Medvedev, P. N. and Voloshinov, V. N. (1983) 'Bakhtin school papers' in Shukman, A. (ed.) *Russian Poetics in Translation*, vol. 10.

Balandier, G. (1970) *Political Anthropology*, London, Allen Lane.

Balzac, H. (1977) *Selected Short Stories* (tr. S. Raphael), Harmondsworth, Penguin.

Barasch, F. K. (1971) *The Grotesque: A Study in Meanings*, The Hague, Mouton.

Barber, C. L. (1959) *Shakespeare's Festive Comedies: A Study of Dramatic Form and its Relation to Social Custom*, Princeton, New Jersey, Princeton University Press.

Barclay, A. (1509) *The Ship of Fools* (ed. T. H. Jamieson) Edinburgh, Paterson, 1874, 2 vols.

Barish, J. A. (1972) 'Feasting and judging in Jonsonian comedy', *Renaissance Drama*, 5, 3–35.

Barker, F. (1984) *The Tremulous Private Body: Essays on Subjection*, London, Methuen.

Baroja, J. C. (1965) *El Carnaval: Analisis historico-cultural*, Madrid, Taurus.

Barrell, J. (1980) *The Dark Side of the Landscape: The Rural Poor in English Painting*, Cambridge, Cambridge University Press.

Barrell, J. (1983) *English Literature in History 1730–1780: An Equal, Wide Survey*, London, Hutchinson.

Barton, A. (1984) *Ben Jonson, Dramatist*, Cambridge, Cambridge University Press.

Bateson, F. W. (1971) 'Addison, Steele and the periodical essay', in Lonsdale, R. (ed.) *The Sphere History of Literature in the English Language*, 4, London, Sphere, 144–63.

Bibliography

Baudelaire, C. (1983) *Intimate Journals* (tr. C. Isherwood), San Francisco, City Lights Books.

Belmont, N. (1982) 'The symbolic function of the wedding procession in the popular ritual of marriage', in Foster, R. and Ranum, O. (eds.) *Ritual, Religion and the Sacred*, Baltimore, Johns Hopkins University Press.

Benedetta, M. (1936) *The Street Markets of London*, London, Miles.

Benjamin, W. (1978) *Reflections: Essays, Aphorisms, Autobiographical Writings* (tr. E. Jephcott), New York, Harcourt Brace Jovanovich.

Bennett, T. (1979) *Formalism and Marxism*, London, Methuen.

Bercé, Y-M. (1976) *Fête et Révolte*, Paris, Hachette.

Bessaignet, P. (1982) *La Jeunesse, la Fête et l'École*, Plan de la Tour (Var), Université de Nice (Ethnologie), Editions d'Aujourd'hui.

Bhabha, H. (1984) 'Of mimicry and man: the ambivalence of colonial discourse', *October*, 28, 125–34.

Billington, S. (1984) *A Social History of the Fool*, Brighton, Harvester.

Blacking, J. (ed.) (1977) *The Anthropology of the Body*, London, New York, San Francisco, Academic Press, ASA Monograph 15.

Blok, A. (1980) 'Rams and billy-goats: breaking the Mediterranean code of honour', unpublished manuscript, Nijmegen, Catholic University.

Böhmer, K. (1985) *Die Verkehrte Welt: Moral und Nonsens in der Bildsatire*, Munich, Lipp.

Boiteux, M. (1977) 'Carnaval annexé: essai de lecture d'une fête romaine', *Annales*, 32, 2, 356–77.

Bonnain-Moerdyk, R. and Moerdyk, D. (1977) 'À propos du charivari: discours bourgeois et coûtumes populaires', *Annales*, 32, 2, 381–98.

Booth, Wayne C. (1983) 'Freedom of interpretation: Bakhtin and the challenge of feminist criticism', in Mitchell, W. J. T. (ed.) *The Politics of Interpretation*, Chicago, University of Chicago Press, 51–82.

Boswell, J. (1950) *Boswell's London Journal 1762–1763* (ed. F. A. Pottle), New York, McGraw-Hill.

Bouissac, P. (1976) *Circus and Culture: a Semiotic Approach*, Bloomington, Indiana University Press.

Bouissac, P. (1981) 'Persiflage de l'institution amoureuse', *Anthropologie et Société*, 5, 3, 35–45.

Bouissac, P. (1982) 'The profanation of the sacred in circus clown performances', in 'Symposium on Theatre and Ritual', unpublished manuscript, Toronto, Werner-Gren Foundation.

Boulton, W. (1901) *Amusements of Old London*, London, The Tabard Press, 1970, 2 vols.

Bourdieu, P. (1977) *Outline of a Theory of Practice* (tr. R. Nice), Cambridge, Cambridge University Press.

Bourdieu, P. (1977b) 'The economics of linguistic exchanges' (tr. R. Nice), *Social Science Information*, 16, 6, 645–68.

Bourdieu, P. (1977c) 'On symbolic power', *Annales*, 32, 1, 405–11.

Bourdieu, P. (1984) *Distinction: A Social Critique of the Judgement of Taste* (tr. R. Nice), London, Routledge & Kegan Paul.

Bové, C. M. (1983) 'The Text as Dialogue in Bakhtin and Kristeva', *University of Ottawa Quarterly* [special Bakhtin issue], 53, 1, 117–24.

Bowen, B. (1981) 'Lenten eels and carnival sausages', *L'Esprit Créateur*, 21, 1, 12–25.

Bowman, S. and Vardley, L. (1981) *Pigs*, New York, Macmillan.

Braudel, F. (1982) *Civilization and Capitalism: 15th–18th Century*, vol. II (*The Wheels of Commerce*) (tr. S. Reynolds), New York, Harper & Row.

Brewer, J. (1979) 'Theatre and counter-theatre in Georgian politics: the mock elections at Garrat', *Radical History Review*, 22, 7–40.

Brewer, J., McKendrick, N. and Plumb, J. H. (1983) *The Birth of a Consumer Society: The Commercialization of Eighteenth-century England*, London, Hutchinson.

Briggs, A. (1961) 'Cholera and society in the nineteenth century', *Past and Present*, 19, 76–96.

Bristol, M. (1973) 'Acting out Utopia: the politics of carnival', *Performance*, 1, 6, 13–28.

Bristol, M. (1983) 'Carnival and the institutions of theater in Elizabethan England', *English Literary History*, 50, 637–54.

Britton, C. (1974) 'The dialogic text and the "texte pluriel"', *University of Essex Occasional Papers, Poetics 14*, Colchester, University of Essex.

Brooke-Rose, C. (1981) *A Rhetoric of the Unreal*, Cambridge, Cambridge University Press.

Browne, Sir T. (1964) 'Religio medici' in Keynes, Sir G. (ed.) *Works*, London, Faber, vol. 1.

Bruch, H. (1965) 'The psychiatric differential diagnosis of "anorexia nervosa"', in Meyer, J. E. and Feldmann, H. (eds.) *Anorexia Nervosa*, Stuttgart, George Thieme Verlag.

Burford, E. J. (1976) *Bawds and Lodgings: A History of the London Bankside Brothels*, London, Peter Owen.

Burke, P. (1978) *Popular Culture in Early Modern Europe*, London, Temple Smith.

Burke, P. (1981) 'Languages and anti-languages in early modern Italy', *History Workshop Journal*, 11, 24–32.

Burke, T. (1946) *The English Townsman*, London, Batsford.

Burke, T. (1946b) *English Night Life*, London, Batsford.

Bushaway, B. (1982) *By Rite: Custom, Ceremony and Community in England 1700–1880*, Studies in Popular Culture, London, Junction Books.

Butler, S. (1967) *Hudibras* (ed. J. Wilders), Oxford, Oxford University Press.

Cannon, J. (1985) *Aristocratic Century: The Peerage in Eighteenth-century England*, Cambridge, Cambridge University Press.

Caputi, A. (1978) *Buffo: the Genius of Vulgar Comedy*, Detroit, Wayne State University Press.

Bibliography

Cardinal, M. (1984) *The Words to Say It* (tr. P. Goodhart), London, Picador/Pan Books.

Carmean Jr., E. A. (1980) *Picasso: The Saltimbanques*, Washington DC, National Gallery of Art.

Carroll, D. (1975) 'Freud and the myth of origin', *New Literary History*, VI, 3, 513–28.

Carroll, L. (1937) *The Complete Work of Lewis Carroll*, New York, Random House.

Carter, A. (1984) *Nights at the Circus*, New York, Viking.

Carver, T. (1982) *Marx's Social Theory*, Oxford, Oxford University Press.

Castle, T. (1984) 'The carnivalization of eighteenth-century English narrative', *Publications of the Modern Language Association*, 99, 5, 903–16.

Chadwick, E. (1842) *Report . . . on an Inquiry into the Sanitary Conditions of the Labouring Population of Great Britain*, London, W. Clowes.

Chadwick, E. (1874) *Transactions of the Sanitary Institute of Great Britain*, London.

Chadwick, E. (1880) 'On the norms of sanitation in the school stages of life' in *Report of the Third Congress of the Sanitary Institute of Great Britain*, London, C. L. Marsh.

Chambers, R. (1863–4) *The Book of Days*, London, W. and R. Chambers, 2 vols.

Chase, C. (1984) 'Review of "Powers of horror" and "Desire in language"', J. Kristeva', *Criticism*, XXVI, 2, 193–201.

Chevalier, B. (1982) 'L'alimentation carnée à la fin du XVe siècle: réalité et symboles' in Margolin, J.-C. and Sauzet, R. (eds.) *Pratiques et Discours Alimentaires à la Renaissance*, Paris, Maisonneuve et Larose.

Chevalier, L. (1973) *Laboring Classes and Dangerous Classes* (tr. F. Jellinek), Princeton, Princeton University Press.

Clark, K. and Holquist, M. (1984) *Mikhail Bakhtin*, Cambridge, Mass., Harvard University Press.

Clark, P. (1983) *The English Alehouse: A Social History 1200–1830*, London, Longman.

Clifford, J. (1981) 'On ethnographic surrealism', *Comparative Studies in Society and History*, 23, 4, 539–64.

Cooper, G. (1961) *Festivals of Europe*, London, Percival Marshall.

Corredor, E. (1983) 'Lukács and Bakhtin: A dialogue on fiction', *University of Ottawa Quarterly* [special Bakhtin issue], 53, 1, 97–107.

Cullwick, H. (1854–73) *The Diaries of Hannah Cullwick*, ed. L. Stanley, London, Virago, 1984.

Cunningham, H. (1980) *Leisure in the Industrial Revolution*, London, Croom Helm.

Curll, E. (1728) 'Codrus' in Guerinot, J. V. (ed.) *Pamphlet Attacks on Alexander Pope*, London, Methuen, 1969.

Curtis, T. C. and Speck, W. A. (1976) 'The societies for the reformation of manners: a case study in the theory and practice of moral reform', *Literature and History*, 3, 45–64.

Curtius, E. R. (1953) *European Literature and the Latin Middle Ages*, London, Routledge & Kegan Paul, 1979.

Davidoff, L. (1979) 'Class and gender in Victorian England: the diaries of Arthur J. Munby and Hannah Cullwick', *Feminist Studies*, 5, 1, 89–141.

Davies, Sir J. (1612) *Discovery of the True Causes why Ireland was Never Entirely Subdued*, London.

Davis, N. Z. (1975) *Society and Culture in Early Modern France*, Stanford, Stanford University Press.

Davis, N. Z. (1981) 'The sacred and the body social', *Past and Present*, 90.

Dawes, F. V. (1984) *Not in Front of the Servants: A True Portrait of Upstairs/Downstairs Life*, London, Hutchinson.

Defoe, D. (1962) *A Tour Through The Whole Island of Great Britain*, London, Everyman, 2 vols.

Defoe, D. (1975) *Selected Writings* (ed. J. T. Boulton), Cambridge, Cambridge University Press.

Dekker, T. (1967) 'The Gull's Hornbook', in Pendray, E. D. (ed.) *Thomas Dekker*, Stratford-upon-Avon Library, 4, London, Edward Arnold.

Deleuze, G. and Guattari, F. (1983) *Anti-Oedipus: Capitalism and Schizophrenia* (tr. R. Hurley, M. Seem, and H. Lane), Minneapolis, University of Minnesota Press.

Desplatt, C. (1982) *Charivaris en Gascogne: La 'Morale des Peuples' du XVI au XX Siècle*, Paris, Bibliothèque Berger-Levrault.

Détienne, M. (1979) *Dionysos Slain* (tr. M. Mueller and L. Mueller), Baltimore, Johns Hopkins University Press.

Dewhirst, S. (1985) 'The provoked prince, or: virtue tested. politics and festivities in the Duchy of Brunswick-Wolfenbüttel', *Modern Language Review*, 80, 1, 80–9.

Dickens, C. (1857) *Little Dorrit* (ed. H. P. Sucksmith), Oxford, Clarendon Press, 1979.

Dickens, C. (1861) *Great Expectations* (ed. A. Calder), Harmondsworth, Penguin, 1965.

Dickens, C. (1865) *Our Mutual Friend* (ed. Stephen Gill), Harmondsworth, Penguin, 1971.

Didi-Huberman, G. (1982) *Invention de l'Hystérie: Charcot et l'Iconographie Photographique*, Paris, Macula.

Disher, M. W. (1950) *Pleasures of London*, London, Hale.

Dollimore, J. (1984) *Radical Tragedy: Religion, Ideology and Power in the Drama of Shakespeare and his Contemporaries*, Brighton, Harvester.

Dollimore, J. (1985) 'Transgression and surveillance in *Measure for Measure*', in Dollimore, J. and Sinfield, A. (eds.) *Political Shakespeare: New Essays in Cultural Materialism*, Manchester, Manchester University Press.

Dollimore, J. and Sinfield, A. (1985) *Political Shakespeare: New Essays in Cultural Materialism*, Manchester, Manchester University Press.

Donaldson, I. (1970) *The World Upside-Down: Comedy from Jonson to Fielding*, Oxford, Oxford University Press.

Doody, M. A. (1985) *The Daring Muse: Augustan Poetry Reconsidered*, Cambridge, Cambridge University Press.

Douglas, M. (1966) *Purity and Danger: An Analysis of Concepts of Pollution and Taboo*, London, Routledge & Kegan Paul.

Douglas, M. (1973) *Natural Symbols: Explorations in Cosmology*, Harmondsworth, Penguin.

Dryden, J. (1926) *Essays of John Dryden* (ed. W. P. Ker), Oxford, Clarendon Press.

Dryden, J. (1958) *Poems and Fables* (ed. J. Kinsley), Oxford, Oxford University Press.

Dryden, J. (1966) *Literary Criticism of John Dryden* (ed. A. C. Kirsch), Lincoln, Neb., University of Nebraska Press.

DuBruck, E. (1981) 'Homo ludens–homo cogitans: images of fifteenth-century man in German carnival plays' *Fifteenth Century Studies*, 4, 61–78.

Dunford, T. (1984) 'Consumption of the world: reading, eating and imitation in "Every Man out of His Humour"', *English Literary Renaissance*, 14, 2, 131–47.

Dutton, R. (1983) *Ben Jonson: To the First Folio*, Cambridge, Cambridge University Press.

Dyos, H. J. and Reeder, D. A. (1973) 'Slums and suburbs', in Dyos, H. J. and Wolff, M. (eds.) *The Victorian City*, London, Routledge & Kegan Paul, vol. I, 359–86.

Dyos, H. J. and Wolff, M. (1973) *The Victorian City*, London, Routledge & Kegan Paul, 2 vols.

Eagleton, T. (1976) *Criticism and Ideology: A Study in Marxist Literary Theory*, London, New Left Books.

Eagleton, T. (1981) *Walter Benjamin: Towards a Revolutionary Criticism*, London, Verso.

Eagleton, T. (1984) *The Function of Criticism*, London, Verso.

Eco, U., Ivanov, V. V. and Rector, M. (1984) *Carnival*, Berlin, New York, Amsterdam, Mouton.

Edwards, G. (1970) *Hogmanay and Tiffany*, London, Geoffrey Bles.

Ehrman, J. (1968) 'Homo ludens revisited', *Yale French Studies*, 41 (Game-Play-Literature), 31–57.

Elias, N. (1978) *The Civilizing Process*, vol. 1 (*The History of Manners*) (tr. E. Jephcott), New York, Pantheon.

Elias, N. (1982) *The Civilizing Process*, vol. 2 (*Power and Civility*) (tr. E. Jephcott), New York, Pantheon.

Elias, N. (1983) *The Court Society* (tr. E. Jephcott), New York, Pantheon.

Ellis, A. (1956) *The Penny Universities: A History of the Coffee-Houses*, London, Secker & Warburg.

Ellis, H. (1912) 'Eugenics and love', in *The Task of Social Hygiene*, Boston and New York, Houghton Mifflin, 193–216.

Emerson, C. (1983) 'Translating Bakhtin: . . .', *University of Ottawa Quarterly* [special issue on Bakhtin], 53, 1, 23–33.

Engels, F. (1971) *The Condition of the Working Class in England* (tr. W. O. Henderson and W. H. Chaloner), Oxford, Blackwell.

Fairholt, F. W. (1843) *History of the Lord Mayors' Pageants*, London, privately printed by the Percy Society.

Farrell, K. (1984) 'Heroism, culture, and dread in "The Sign of the Four" ', *Studies in the Novel*, 16, 1, 32–51.

Faure, A. (1978) *Paris Carême-prenant*, Paris, Hachette

Fiedler, L. (1978) *Freaks: Myths and Images of the Secret Self*, New York, Simon & Schuster.

Fielding, H. (1742) *The History and Adventures of Joseph Andrews* (ed. D. Brooks), Oxford, Oxford University Press, 1971.

Findlater, R. (1955) *Grimaldi: King of Clowns*, London, Macgibbon & Kee.

Finer, S. E. (1952) *The Life and Times of Sir Edwin Chadwick*, London, Methuen.

Fish, S. (1984) 'Authors-readers: Jonson's community of the same', *Representations*, 7, 26–58.

Fisher, S. (1972) 'Body image', in *International Encyclopedia of the Social Sciences* (ed. D. Sills), Collier-Macmillan, vol. 2, 2nd edn, 113–16.

Fisher, S. and Cleveland, S. E., (1958) *Body Image and Personality*, Princeton, Van Nostrand.

Forgacs, D. (1984) 'National-popular: genealogy of a concept', *Formations: Of Nations and People*, London, Routledge & Kegan Paul.

Foucault, M. (1977) *Language/Counter-memory/Practice* (ed. D. F. Bouchard, tr. D. F. Bouchard and S. Simon), Ithaca, Cornell University Press.

Foucault, M. (1978) *The History of Sexuality, I: An Introduction* (tr. R. Hurley), New York, Pantheon.

Foucault, M. (1979) *Discipline and Punish: the Birth of the Prison* (tr. Alan Sheridan), New York, Random House.

Foucault, M. (1980) *Power/Knowledge: Selected Interviews and Other Writings 1972–1977* (ed. Colin Gordon), New York, Pantheon.

Fraser, R. (1984) *In Search of a Past: The Manor House, Amnersfield, 1933–1945*, London, Verso.

Freud, S. (1893) 'Studies on hysteria', in Richards, A. (ed.) *Pelican Freud Library* 3 (tr. J. Strachey and A. Strachey), Harmondsworth, Penguin, 1974.

Freud, S. (1897) 'Extracts from the Fliess Papers', in Strachey, J. with Freud, A. (eds. and trs.) *The Complete Psychological Works*, London, Hogarth Press, vol. 1, 1966.

Freud, S. (1900) 'The psychopathology of everyday life', in Strachey, J. (ed.) *Pelican Freud Library* 5 (tr. A. Tyson), Harmondsworth, Penguin, 1975.

Freud, S. (1900b) 'The interpretation of dreams', in Richards, A. and Strachey, J. (eds.) *Pelican Freud Library* 4 (tr. J. Strachey), Harmondsworth, Penguin, 1976.

Freud, S. (1905) 'Three essays on the theory of sexuality', in Richards, A. (ed.) *Penguin Freud Library* 7 (tr. A. Strachey and J. Strachey), Harmondsworth, Penguin, 1977.

Bibliography

Freud, S. (1905b) 'Fragment of an analysis of a case of hysteria ("Dora")', in Richards, A. (ed.) *Pelican Freud Library* 8 (tr. J. Strachey and A. Strachey), Harmondsworth, Penguin, 1977.

Freud, S. (1907) 'The sexual enlightenment of children', in Richards, A. (ed.) *Pelican Freud Library* 7 (tr. J. Strachey), Harmondsworth, Penguin, 1977.

Freud, S. (1908) 'On the sexual theories of children', in Richards, A. (ed.) *Pelican Freud Library* 7 (tr. J. Strachey), Harmondsworth, Penguin, 1977.

Freud, S. (1908b) 'Character and anal eroticism', in Richards, A. (ed.) *Pelican Freud Library* 7 (tr. J. Strachey), Harmondsworth, Penguin, 1977.

Freud, S. (1909) 'Notes upon a case of obsessional neurosis (the "Rat Man")', in Richards, A. (ed.) *Pelican Freud Library* 9 (tr. J. Strachey), Harmondsworth, Penguin, 1979.

Freud, S. (1909b) 'General remarks on hysterical attacks', in *Dora: An Analysis of a Case of Hysteria* (tr. D. Bryan), New York, Macmillan, 153–7, 1963.

Freud, S. (1911) 'Psychoanalytic notes on an autobiographical account of a case of paranoia (Schreber)', in Richards, A. (ed.) *Pelican Freud Library* 9, (tr. J. Strachey), Harmondsworth, Penguin, 1979.

Freud, S. (1912) 'On the universal tendency to debasement in the sphere of love', in Richards, A. (ed.) *Pelican Freud Library* 7 (tr. J. Strachey), Harmondsworth, Penguin, 1977.

Freud, S. (1917) 'On transformations of instinct, exemplified by anal eroticism', in Richards, A. (ed.) *Pelican Freud Library* 7 (tr. J. Strachey), Harmondsworth, Penguin, 1979.

Freud, S. (1918) 'From the history of an infantile neurosis (the "Wolf Man")', in Richards, A. (ed.) *Pelican Freud Library* 9 (tr. J. Strachey), Harmondsworth, Penguin, 1979.

Freud, S. (1925) 'Negation', in Richards, A. (ed.) *Pelican Freud Library* 11 (tr. J. Strachey), Harmondsworth, Penguin, 1984.

Freud, S. (1930) 'Civilization and its discontents', in Dickson, A. (ed.) *Pelican Freud Library* 12 (tr. J. Strachey), Harmondsworth, Penguin 1985.

Freud, S. (1933) 'New introductory lectures on psychoanalysis', in Richards, A. and Strachey, J. (eds.) *Pelican Freud Library* 2 (tr. J. Strachey), Harmondsworth, Penguin, 1973.

Freud, S. (1954) *Sigmund Freud's Letters to Wilhelm Fliess, Drafts and Notes* (ed. M. Bonaparte, A. Freud and E. Kris, tr. E. Masbacher and J. Strachey) New York, Basic Books.

Gaignebet, C. (1974) *Le Carnaval*, Paris, Payot.

Gallop, J. (1982) *The Daughter's Seduction: Feminism and Psychoanalysis*, Ithaca, Cornell University Press.

Geertz, C. (1973) *The Interpretation of Cultures*, New York, Basic Books.

Geisberg, M. (1974) *The German Single-leaf Woodcut: 1500–1550* (ed. and rev. W. L. Strauss), New York, Hacker, 4 vols.

Gildon, C. (1718) 'Memoirs', in Geurinot, J. V. (ed.) *Pamphlet Attacks on Alexander Pope*, London, Methuen, 1969.

Gilman, S. L. (1974) 'The parodic sermon in European perspective', in *Beitrage zur Literatur des XV bis XVIII Jahrhunderts*, Bd.VI, Wiesbaden, Franz Steiner Verlag.

Ginzburg, C. (1980) *The Cheese and the Worms* (tr. J. Tedeschi and A. Tedeschi), Baltimore, Johns Hopkins University Press.

Girard, R. (1977) *Violence and the Sacred* (tr. P. Gregory), Baltimore, Johns Hopkins University Press.

Gluckman, M. (1963) *Order and Rebellion in Tribal Africa: Collected Essays with an Autobiographical Introduction*, London, Cohen.

Gluckman, M. (1965) *Custom and Conflict in Africa*, Oxford, Blackwell.

Godard, B. (1983) 'World of wonders', MMB, 51–9.

Goethe Institute. (1985) *The Topsy-Turvy World: Exhibition Catalogue: Selections from the Günther Böhmer Collection of Popular Prints*, Amsterdam, Paris, London, New York.

Golby, J. M. and Purdue, A. W. (1984) *The Civilisation of the Crowd: Popular Culture in England 1750–1900*, London, Batsford Academic.

Goldberg, J. (1983) *James I and the Politics of Literature: Jonson, Shakespeare, Donne and their Contemporaries*, Baltimore, Johns Hopkins University Press.

Goody, J. (1982) *Cooking, Cuisine and Class: A Study in Comparative Sociology*, Cambridge, Cambridge University Press.

Gramsci, A. (1985) *Selections from Cultural Writings* (ed. D. Forgacs and G. Nowell-Smith, tr. W. Boelhower), London, Lawrence and Wishart.

Greenblatt, S. (1976) 'Learning to curse: aspects of linguistic colonialism in the sixteenth century', in Chiappelli, F. (ed.) *First Images of America*, Berkeley, University of California Press.

Greenblatt, S. (1980) *Renaissance Self-fashioning: From More to Shakespeare*, Chicago, University of Chicago Press.

Greenblatt, S. (1981) 'Invisible bullets: Renaissance authority and its subversion', *Glyph*, 8, 40–61.

Greenblatt, S. (1982) 'Filthy rites', *Daedalus*, iii, 3, 1–16.

Greenblatt, S. (1983) 'Murdering peasants: status, genre and the representation of rebellion', *Representations*, I, 1–29.

Grigg, K. A. (1973) ' "All roads lead to Rome": the role of the nursemaid in Freud's dreams', *Journal of the American Psychoanalytical Association*, 27, 1, 108–26.

Guerinot, J. V. (1969) *Pamphlet Attacks on Alexander Pope 1711–1744*, London, Methuen.

Habermas, J. (1962) *Strukturwändel der Öffentlichkeit*, Berlin, Neuwied, Luchterhand.

Hall, S. (ed.) (1976) *Resistance Through Rituals: Youth Subculture in Post-war Britain* (ed. S. Hall and T. Jefferson), London, Hutchinson.

Hall, S. et al. (1978) *Policing the Crisis: Mugging, the State and Law and Order*, London, Macmillan.

Handleman, D. (1982) 'Reflexivity in festival and other cultural events', in Douglas, M. (ed.) *Essays in the Sociology of Perception*, London, Routledge & Kegan Paul, 162–90.

Bibliography

Hanson, F. A. (1981) 'The semiotics of ritual', *Semiotica*, 33, 1/2, 169–78.

Harrington, Sir J. (1596) *The Metamorphosis of Ajax* (ed. Elizabeth Story Donno), London, Routledge & Kegan Paul, 1962.

Harris, M. (1978) *Cows, Pigs, Wars and Witches: The Riddles of Culture*, New York, Random House.

Harrison, F. (1982) *Strange Land: The Countryside: Myth and Reality*, London, Sidgwick & Jackson.

Hartmann, W. (1976) *Der Historische Festzug: Seine Entstehung und Entwicklung im 19. und 20. Jahrhunderts*, Studien zur Kunst des 19 Jahrhunderts, 35, Munich, Prestel.

Hayman, D. (1983) 'Towards a mechanics of mode: beyond Bakhtin', *Novel*, 16, 2, 101–20.

Haynes, J. (1984) 'Festivity and the dramatic economy of Jonson's "Bartholomew Fair"', *English Literary History*, 51, 4, 645–68.

Hechter, M. (1975) *Internal Colonialism*, London, Routledge & Kegan Paul.

Helgerson, R. (1983) *Self-crowned Laureates: Spenser, Jonson, Milton and the Literary System*, Berkeley, University of California Press.

Henderson, J. (1975) *The Maculate Muse: Obscene Language in Attic Comedy*, New Haven, Yale University Press.

Henley, J. (1723) 'Tom O'Bedlam's Dunciad; Or Pope Alexander the pig', in Guerinot, J. V. (ed.) *Pamphlet Attacks on Alexander Pope*, London, Methuen, 1969.

Henley, J. (1743) 'Why how now, Gossip Pope?' in Guerinot, J. V. (ed.) *Pamphlet Attacks on Alexander Pope*, London, Methuen, 1969.

Hennock, E. P. (1957) 'Urban sanitary reform a generation before Chadwick?', *Economic History Review*, 2nd series, X, 1, 113–20.

Henry, P. (1981) 'On language and the body', in McCabe, C. (ed.) *The Talking Cure: Essays in Psychoanalysis and Language*, London, Macmillan.

Hern, A. (1967) *The Seaside Holiday: The History of the English Seaside Resort*, London, Cresset Press.

Hertz, N. (1983) 'Medusa's head: male hysteria under political pressure', *Representations*, 4, 27–54.

Herzfeld, M. (1980) 'Disemia', in Herzfeld, M. and Lenhart, M. D. (eds.) *Semiotics 1980*, New York and London, Plenum Press, 205–15.

Herzfeld, M. (1980) 'The Dowry in Greece: terminological usage and historical reconstruction', *Ethnohistory*, 27, 3, 225–41.

Herzfeld, M. (1981) 'An indigenous theory of meaning and its elicitation in performative context', *Semiotica*, 34, 1/2, 113–41.

Hill, C. (1969) *Society and Puritanism in Pre-Revolutionary England*, London, Panther.

Hill, C. (1975) *The World Turned Upside Down: Radical Ideas during the English Revolution*, Harmondsworth, Penguin.

Hill, E. (1972) *The Trinidad Carnival*, Austin, University of Texas Press.

Himmelfarb, G. (1973) 'The Culture of poverty', in Dyos, H. J. and Wolff, M. (eds.) *The Victorian City*, London, Routledge & Kegan Paul, vol. 2, 707–36.

Hobsbawm, E. (1981) *Bandits*, New York, Pantheon.

Hohendahl, P. U. (1982) *The Institution of Criticism*, Ithaca, Cornell University Press.

Hole, C. (1947) *English Home Life 1500 to 1800*, London, Batsford.

Hole, C. (1949) *English Sports and Pastimes*, London, Batsford.

Holland, P. (1979) *The Ornament of Action: Text and Performance in Restoration Comedy*, Cambridge, Cambridge University Press.

Hollstein, F. W. H. (1954) *Dutch and Flemish Engravings and Woodcuts c. 1450–1700*, Amsterdam, Hertzberger, 29 vols.

Howard, A. (1964) *Endless Cavalcade: A Diary of British Festivals and Customs*, London, Arthur Barker.

Howkins, A. (1981) 'The taming of Whitsun: the changing face of a nineteenth-century rural holiday', in Yeo, E. and Yeo, S. (eds.) *Popular Culture and Class Conflict*, Brighton, Harvester, 187–208.

Hudson, D. (1972) *Munby, Man of Two Worlds: The Life and Diaries of Arthur J. Munby*, London, John Murray.

Hugo, V. (1980) *Les Misérables* (tr. N. Denny), Harmondsworth, Penguin, 2 vols.

Hunt, L. (1984) *Politics, Culture and Class in the French Revolution*, Berkeley, University of California Press.

Hutcheon, L. (1983) 'The carnivalesque and contemporary narrative: popular culture and the erotic', *University of Ottawa Quarterly* [special Bakhtin issue], 53, 1, 83–94.

Hyers, M. C. (ed.) (1969) *Holy Laughter: Essays on Religion in the Comic Perspective*, New York, Seabury Press.

Ijsewijn, J. (1976) 'Neo-Latin satire: "Sermo" and "Satyra Menippea"', in Bolgar, R. R. (ed.) *Classical Influences on European Culture 1500–1700*, Cambridge, Cambridge University Press, 41–55.

Ingram, M. (1981) (1977) 'Le charivari dans l'Angleterre du XVIe et du XVIIe siècle', in Le Goff, J. and Schmitt, J.-C. (eds.) *Le Charivari*, Paris, The Hague and New York, Mouton.

Ivanov, V. V. (1976) 'The significance of Bakhtin's ideas on sign, utterance and dialogue for modern semiotics', in *Papers on Poetics and Semiotics 4*, Tel Aviv, The Israeli Institute for Poetics and Semiotics, Tel-Aviv University.

Jack, I. (1942) *Augustan Satire: Intention and Idiom in English Poetry 1660–1750*, Oxford, Clarendon Press.

Jacquot, J. (1975) *Fêtes de la Renaissance*, Brussels, CNRS, 3 vols.

James, A. (1982) 'Confections, concoctions and conceptions', in Waites, B. et al. (eds.) *Popular Culture Past and Present*, London, Croom Helm, 294–307.

Jameson, F. (1981) *The Political Unconscious: Narrative as a Socially Symbolic Act*, Ithaca, Cornell University Press.

John, A. V. (1984) *By the Sweat of their Brow: Women Workers at Victorian Coalmines*, London, Routledge & Kegan Paul.

Jones, A. R. (1983) 'Inside the outsider: Nashe's "Unfortunate traveller" and Bakhtin's polyphonic novel', *English Literary History*, 50, 1, 61–82.

Bibliography

Jonson, B. (1925–52) *Ben Jonson: Works* (ed. C. H. Herford and P. Simpson), Oxford, Clarendon Press, 11 vols.

Jonson, B. (1977) *Bartholomew Fair* (ed. G. R. Hibbard), New Mermaid Series, New York, Norton.

Judge, R. (1979) *The Jack-in-the-Green: A Mayday Custom*, Cambridge, D. S. Brewer.

Kafka, F. (1949) *In the Penal Settlement: Tales and Short Prose Works*, London, Secker & Warburg.

Kafka, F. (1954) 'Letter to his father', in *Wedding Preparations in the Country* (tr. K. Wilkins and E. Wilkins), London, Secker & Warburg.

Kaplan, C. (1983) 'Wild nights: pleasure/sexuality/feminism', in *Formations of Pleasure*, London, Routledge & Kegan Paul.

Kayser, W. (1981) *The Grotesque in Art and Literature* (tr. Ulrich Weisstein), New York, Columbia University Press.

Keating, P. J. (1973) 'Fact and Fiction in the East End', in Dyos, H. J. and Wolff, M. (eds.) *The Victorian City*, London, Routledge & Kegan Paul, II, 585–602.

Keith-Lucas, B. (1954) 'Some influences affecting the development of sanitary legislation in England', *Economic History Review*, 2nd series, VI (3), 290–6.

Kesten, H. (1959) *Dichter im Café*, Vienna, K. Desch.

Krapp, R. M. (1946) 'Class analysis of a literary controversy: Wit and Sense in seventeenth-century English literature', *Science and Society*, 10, 80–92.

Kristeva, J. (1974) *La Révolution du Langage Poètique*, Paris, Seuil.

Kristeva, J. (1980) *Desire in Language* (ed. L. S. Roudiez, tr. T. Gora, A. Jardine and L. S. Roudiez), New York, Columbia University Press.

Kristeva, J. (1982) *Powers of Horror: An Essay on Abjection* (tr. L. S. Roudiez), New York, Columbia University Press.

Kunzle, D. (1973) *The Early Comic Strip: Narrative Strips and Picture Stories in the European Broadsheet c. 1450–1825*, Berkeley, University of California Press.

Kunzle, D. (1978) 'World upside down: iconography of a European broadsheet type', in Babcock, B. (ed.) *The Reversible World*, Ithaca, Cornell University Press, 39–94.

LaCapra, D. (1983) *Rethinking Intellectual History: Texts, Contexts, Language*, Ithaca, Cornell University Press.

Lacan, J. (1982) *Feminine Sexuality* (ed. J. Mitchell and J. Rose, tr. J. Rose), London, Macmillan.

Laclau, E. (1979) *Politics and Ideology in Marxist Theory*, London, Verso.

Lambert, M. and Marx, E. (1951) *English Popular Art*, London, Batsford.

Laplanche, J. and Pontalis, J.-B. (1968) 'Fantasy and the origins of sexuality', *International Journal of Psychoanalysis*, 49, 1, 1–18.

Larson, M. S. (1977) *The Rise of Professionalism*, Berkeley, University of California Press.

Lavenda, R. H. (1980) 'The festival of progress: the globalizing world-system and the transformation of the Caracas carnival', *Journal of Popular Culture*, 14, 3, 465–75.

Laver, J. (1972) *The Age of Illusion: Manners and Morals 1750–1848*, Worcester and London, Ebenezer Bayliss & Sons.

Le Goff, J. (1980) *Time, Work and Culture in the Middle Ages* (tr. A. Goldhammer), Chicago, University of Chicago Press.

Le Goff, J. and Schmitt, J.-C. (eds.) (1981) *Le Charivari*, Paris, The Hague and New York, Mouton.

Le Roy Ladurie, E. (1981) *Carnival in Romans* (tr. M. Feeney), Harmondsworth, Penguin.

Leach, E. (1961) 'Time and false noses', in Leach, E. (ed.) *Rethinking Anthropology*, Monograph/Social Anthropology 22, London, Athlone Press, 132–6.

Leach, E. (1964) 'Anthropological aspects of language: animal categories and verbal abuse', in Lenneberg, E. H. (ed.) *New Directions in the Study of Language*, Cambridge, Mass., MIT Press, 23–63.

Leduc-Park, R. (1983) 'Du carnivalesque au dionysiaque et du dialogisme au grégarisme', MMB (Coll.), Kingston, Ontario, Queen's University, 92.

Leith, D. (1983) *A Social History of English*, London, Routledge & Kegan Paul.

Lévi-Strauss, C. (1978) *The Origin of Table Manners: Mythologies*, 3 (tr. J. Weightman and D. Weightman), New York, Harper & Row.

Locke, J. (1902) *Some Thoughts Concerning Education* (ed. R. H. Quick), Cambridge, Cambridge University Press.

Lodge, D. (1982) 'Double discourses; Joyce and Bakhtin', *James Joyce Broadsheet*, 11.

Lord, G. de F. (1977) *Heroic Mockery: Variations on Epic Themes from Homer to Joyce*, Newark, University of Delaware Press.

Makarius, L. (1970) 'Ritual clowns and symbolic behaviour', *Diogenes*, 69, 44–73.

Malcolmson, R. W. (1973) *Popular Recreations in English Society 1700–1850*, Cambridge University Press.

Malcuzynski, M.-P. (1981) 'Mikhail Bakhtin and postmodernism', unpublished paper/Special Session on Bakhtin, MLA New York, Dec. 1981.

Malcuzynski, M.-P. (1983) 'Mikhail Bakhtin and contemporary narrative theory', *University of Ottawa Quarterly* [special issue on Bakhtin], 53, 1, 51–65.

Manning-Sanders, R. (1951) *Seaside England*, London, Batsford.

Marcus, S. (1973) 'Reading the illegible', in Dyos, H. J. and Wolff, M. (eds.) *The Victorian City*, London, Routledge & Kegan Paul, vol. 1, 257–76.

Markham, G. (1614) *Cheape and Good Husbandry*, London.

Marx, K. (1951) *Marx-Engels Selected Works*, London, Lawrence and Wishart.

Marx, K. (1965) *Pre-Capitalist Economic Formations* (tr. J. Cohen), New York, International Publishers.

Marx, K. and Engels, F. (1970) *The German Ideology* (ed. C. J. Arthur), London, Lawrence and Wishart.

Massingham, H. and Massingham, P. (1950) *The London Anthology*, London, Phoenix House.

Bibliography

Matta, R. da (1974) 'Constraint and license: two Brazilian national rituals', *Burg Wartenstein Symposium, No. 64: Secular Rituals*, Washington.

Mauss, M. (1934) 'Techniques of the body', *Economy and Society*, 2, 1, 70–88, 1973.

Mayhew, H. (1861–2) *London Labour and the London Poor*, London, Frank Cass, 4 vols, 1967.

McCanles, M. (1977) 'Festival in Jonsonian comedy', *Renaissance Drama*, 8, 203–19.

McKendrick, N. et al. (1982) *The Birth of a Consumer Society: Commercialization of Eighteenth-century England*, London, Hutchinson.

McKenna, A. J. (1983) 'After Bakhtin: on the future of laughter and its history in France', *University of Ottawa Quarterly* [special issue on Bakhtin], 53, 1, 67–82.

Meillassoux, C. (1981) *Maidens, Meals and Money: Capitalism and the Domestic Community*, Cambridge, Cambridge University Press.

Merrell, H. (1984) 'Writing riots: representations of the riotous body', unpublished MA dissertation, University of Sussex.

Monas, S. (1983) 'Finnegans Wake: carnival, polyphony and chronotope', MMB (Coll.), Kingston, Ontario, Queen's University.

Montrose, L. A. (1979) 'The purpose of playing: reflections on a Shakespearean anthropology', *Helios*, 7, 2, 51–74.

Morley, H. (1859) *Memoirs of Bartholomew Fair*, London, Chapman and Hall.

Muir, E. (1981) *Civic Ritual in Renaissance Venice*, Princeton, Princeton University Press.

Mullaney, S. (1983) '"Strange things, gross terms, curious customs": the Rehearsal of Cultures in the Late Renaissance', *Representations*, 3, 40–67.

Needham, R. (ed.) (1973) *Right and Left: Essays in Dual Symbolic Classification*, Chicago, University of Chicago Press.

Negt, O. and Kluge, A. (1972) *Öffentlichkeit und Erfahrung*, Frankfurt/Main, Suhrkamp.

Neville Havins, P. J. (1976) *The Spas of England*, London, Hale Press.

Olson, N. (ed.) (1979) *Gavarni: The Carnival Lithographs*, New Haven, Yale University Art Gallery.

Orgel, S. (1981) 'What is a text?' *Research Opportunities in Renaissance Drama*, 2, 4, 3–6.

Ortner, S. B. (ed.) (1981) *Sexual Meanings: The Cultural Construction of Gender and Sexuality*, Cambridge, Cambridge University Press.

Parrinder, P. (1984) *James Joyce*, Cambridge, Cambridge University Press.

Parrinder, P. (1985) 'Pamphleteer's progress', *London Review of Books*, 7 February, 16–17.

Paulson, R. (1979) *Popular and Polite Art in the Age of Hogarth and Fielding*, Notre Dame, Ind., University of Notre Dame Press.

Pearlman, E. (1979) 'Ben Jonson: an anatomy', *English Literary Renaissance*, 9, 3, 364–94.

Pearson, G. (1983) *Hooligan: A History of Respectable Fears*, London, Macmillan.

Pechey, G. (1976) 'The London motif in some eighteenth-century contexts: a semiotic study', *Literature and History*, 4, 2–29.

Pepys, S. (1660–9) *The Diary of Samuel Pepys* (ed. R. Latham and W. Matthews), London, G. Bell & Sons, 11 vols, (1970–83).

Perlina, N. (1983) 'Bakhtin–Medvedev–Volosinov: an apple of discourse', *University of Ottawa Quarterly* [special issue on Bakhtin], 53, 1, 35–47.

Peterson, M. J. (1970) 'The Victorian governess: status incongruence in family and society', *Victorian Studies*, XIV, 1, 7–26.

Phythian-Adams, C. (1983) 'Milk and soot: the changing vocabulary of a popular ritual in Stuart and Hanoverian London', in Fraser, D. and Sutcliffe, A. *Pursuit of Urban History*, London, Edward Arnold, 83–104.

Pillement, G. (1972) *Paris en Fête* Paris, Grasset.

Platter, T. (1963) *Journal of a Younger Brother: The Life of Thomas Platter* (ed. and tr. S. Jennett), London, Muller.

Polhemus, T. (ed.) (1978) *The Body Reader: Social Aspects of the Human Body*, New York, Pantheon.

Pomorska, K. (1978) 'Mikhail Bakhtin and his verbal universe', *Poetics and Theory of Literature* (PTL), 3, 379–86.

Pope, A. (1966) *Poetical Works* (ed. H. Davis), Oxford, Oxford University Press.

Rappaport, R. A. (1968) *Pigs for Ancestors: Ritual in the Ecology of a New Guinea People*, New Haven, Yale University Press.

Rawson, C. J. (1975) 'Order and misrule: eighteenth-century English literature in the 1970s', *English Literary History*, 42, 471–505.

Rawson, C. J. (ed.) (1984) *English Satire and the Satiric Tradition*, Oxford, Blackwell.

Rebhorn, W. A. (1978) *Courtly Performances: Masking and Festivity in Castiglione's 'Book of the Courtier'*, Detroit, Wayne State University Press.

Rhodes, N. (1980) *Elizabethan Grotesque*, London, Routledge & Kegan Paul.

Rhys, J. (1979) *Smile Please: An Unfinished Autobiography*, Berkeley, Creative Arts Books.

Rimbault, E. R. (1859) 'Gleanings for the history of Bartholomew Fair', *Notes and Queries*, 2nd series, VIII, 161–3.

Robin, R. (1983) 'La littérature yiddish soviétique: minorité nationale/polyphonisme' (MMB Coll.), Kingston, Ontario, Queen's University.

Roger, J. T. (1866) *History of Agricultural Prices in England*, I, Oxford, Oxford University Press.

Rogers, P. (1972) *Grub Street: Studies in a Subculture*, London, Methuen.

Rollins, H. E. (1922) *A Pepysian Garland*, Cambridge, Mass., Harvard University Press.

Rollins, H. E. (1923) *Cavalier and Puritan: Ballads and Broadsides Illustrating the Period of the Great Rebellion 1640–1660*, New York, New York University Press.

Bibliography

Rose, J. (1978) '"Dora" – fragment of an analysis', *M/F*, 2, 5–21.

Rosenfeld, S. (1960) *The Theatre of the London Fairs in the Eighteenth Century*, Cambridge, Cambridge University Press.

Rubin, G. (1975) 'The Traffic in Women: notes on the "political economy" of sex', in Reiter, R. R. (ed.), *Towards an Anthropology of Women*, New York, Monthly Review Press, 157–210.

Ruthven, M. (1984) 'Cassandras at camp', *Times Literary Supplement*, 21 Sept., 1048a.

Said, E. (1979) *Orientalism*, New York, Vintage Books.

Said, E. (1984) *The World, the Text and the Critic*, London, Faber & Faber.

Sales, R. (1983) *English Literature in History 1780–1830: Pastoral and Politics*, London, Hutchinson.

Salgado, G. (1984) *The Elizabethan Underworld*, Gloucester, Alan Sutton.

Salingar, L. (1979) 'Crowd and public in "Bartholomew Fair"', *Renaissance Drama*, 10, 141–59.

Samuel, R. (1981) *East End Underworld: Chapters in the Life of Arthur Harding*, London, Routledge & Kegan Paul.

Schama, S. (1979) 'The unruly realm: appetite and restraint in seventeenth-century Holland', *Daedalus*, 108, 3, 103–23.

Scheff, T. J. (1979) *Catharsis in Healing, Ritual and Drama*, Berkeley, University of California Press.

Schilder, P. (1935) *Appearance of the Human Body*, New York, International Universities Press.

Schnyder, L. (1912) 'Le cas de Renata: contribution à l'étude de l'hystérie', *Archives de Psychologie*, 12, 201–62.

Schoenwald, R. L. (1973) 'Training urban man: a hypothesis about the sanitary movement', in Dyos, H. J. and Wolff, M. (eds.) *The Victorian City*, London, Routledge & Kegan Paul, vol 2, 669–92.

Screech, M. A. (1979) *Rabelais*, London, Duckworth.

Screech, M. A. (1984) 'Homage to Rabelais', *London Review of Books*, 6, 17.

Scribner, R. (1978) 'Reformation, carnival and the world turned upside-down', *Social History*, III, 3, 303–29.

Scribner, R. (1981) *For the Sake of the Simple Folk: Popular Propaganda for the German Reformation*, Cambridge, Cambridge University Press.

Shakespeare, W. (1974) *The Riverside Shakespeare* (ed. G. Blakemore Evans), Boston, Houghton Mifflin.

Sharratt, B. (1985) 'John Skelton: finding a voice: notes after Bakhtin', unpublished manuscript, University of Kent.

Short, J. (1983) 'Le carnivalesque dans le théâtre de Jean-Claude Germain', MMB (Coll.), Kingston, Ontario, Queen's University.

Sidney, Sir P. (1907) *Sidney's Apologie for Poetrie* (ed. J. C. Collins), Oxford, Clarendon Press.

Sidro, A. (1979) *Le Carnaval de Nice et ses Fous*, Nice, Éditions Serre.

Slinn, W. (1975) 'Experience as pageant: subjectivism in "Fifine at the Fair"', *English Literary History*, 42, 651–68.

Smedley, J. (1728) 'The metamorphosis', in Guerinot, J. V. (ed.) *Pamphlet Attacks on Alexander Pope*, London, Methuen, 1969.

Spenser, E. (1970) *A View of the Present State of Ireland* (ed. W. L. Renwick), Oxford, Clarendon Press.

Spufford, M. (1981) *Small Books and Pleasant Histories: Popular Fiction and its Readership in the Seventeenth Century*, London, Methuen.

Stallybrass, P. (1985) ' "Drunk with the cup of liberty": Robin Hood, the carnivalesque, and the rhetoric of violence in early modern England', *Semiotica*, 54, 1/2, 113–45.

Stallybrass, P. (1986) 'The body enclosed', in Ferguson, M., Quilligan, M. and Vickers, N. (eds.) *Rewriting the Renaissance: The Discourses of Sexual Difference in Early Modern Europe*, Chicago, University of Chicago Press.

Stamm, R. (1982) 'On the carnivalesque', *Wedge*, 1, 47–55.

Stamm, R. and Johnson, R. (eds.) (1982) *Brazilian Cinema*, East Brunswick, East Brunswick Associated University Presses.

Starkey, D. (1977) 'Representation through intimacy: symbolism of monarchy and court office in early-modern England', in Ioan Lewis (ed.) *Symbol and Sentiment*, London, Academic Press, 186–224.

Starobinski, J. (1964) *The Invention of Liberty* (tr. B. C. Swift), Geneva, Skira.

Starobinski, J. (1970) *Portrait de l'Artiste en Saltimbanque*, Geneva, Skira.

Stedman Jones, G. (1971) *Outcast London*, Oxford, Clarendon Press.

Stedman Jones, G. (1983) *Languages of Class*, Cambridge, Cambridge University Press.

Steele, P. (1978) *Jonathan Swift: Preacher and Jester*, Oxford, Clarendon Press.

Steinberg, L. (1983) 'The sexuality of Christ in Renaissance art and in modern oblivion', *October*, 25, 1–222.

Stevenson, J. (1979) *Popular Disturbances in England 1700–1870*, London, Longman.

Stoeltje, B. J. (1983) 'The performance of the exotic: rodeo made strange', *Semiotica*, 44, 1/2, 137–47.

Stridbeck, C. G. (1956) ' "Combat between Carnival and Lent" by Pieter Bruegel the Elder', *Journal of the Warburg and Courtauld Institute*, 19, 96–109.

Strong, S. A. (1903) *A Catalogue of Letters . . . at Welbeck*, London, John Murray.

Swan, J. (1974) 'Mater and nannie: Freud's two mothers and the discovery of the Oedipus complex', *American Imago*, 31, 1, 1–64.

Swift, J. (1704) *A Tale of a Tub*, London and New York, Dent & Dutton, 1968.

Swift, J. (1983) *The Complete Poems* (ed. P. Rogers), Harmondsworth, Penguin.

Tait, J. (1917) 'The declaration of sports for Lancashire (1617)', *English Historical Review*, XXXII, 561–8.

Bibliography

Tanner, T. (1979) *Adultery in the Novel: Contract and Transgression*, Baltimore, Johns Hopkins University Press.

Taylor, A. M. (1957) 'Sights and Monsters and Gulliver's "Voyage to Brobdingnag"', *Tulane Studies in English*, 28–82.

Tennenhouse, L. (1982) 'Representing power: "Measure for Measure" in its time', *Genre*, 15(2–3), 139–56.

Tennenhouse, L. (1985) 'Strategies of State and political plays: A Midsummer Night's Dream, Henry IV, Henry V, Henry VIII', in Dollimore, J. and Sinfield, A. (eds.) *Political Shakespeare: New Essays in Cultural Materialism*, Manchester, Manchester University Press, 109–28.

Terdiman, R. (1985) *Discourse/Counter-discourse: Theory and Practice of Symbolic Resistance in Nineteenth-Century France*, Ithaca, Cornell University Press.

Tetel, M. (1981) 'Carnival and beyond', *L'Esprit Créateur*, 21, 1, 88–104.

Thirsk, J. (1967) 'Farming techniques', in Thirsk, J. (ed.) *The Agrarian History of England and Wales, IV*, Cambridge, Cambridge University Press.

Thomas, K. (1983) *Man and the Natural World: A History of the Modern Sensibility*, New York, Pantheon.

Thomas, K. V. (1977) 'The place of laughter in Tudor and Stuart England', *Times Literary Supplement*, 21 Jan., 3906, 77.

Thompson, C. (1983) 'The semiotics of M. M. Bakhtin', *University of Ottawa Quarterly* [special issue on Bakhtin], 53, 1, 11–21.

Thompson, E. P. (1972) '"Rough music": le charivari anglais', *Annales ESC*, 27.2, 285–312.

Thomson, P. (1972) *The Grotesque*, London, Methuen.

Thurston, J. (1983) 'The carnival comes to/from Vancouver Island', MM8, 256–68.

Tilly, C. (1980) 'Charivaris, repertoires and politics', *CRSO Work Paper No. 214*, Ann Arbor, University of Michigan.

Todorov, T. (1984) 'Mikhail Bakhtin: the dialogic principle', in *Theory and History of Literature 13* (tr. W. Godzich), Minneapolis, University of Minnesota Press.

Todorov, T. (1985) *The Conquest of America* (tr. R. Howard), New York, Harper Colophon.

Toole-Stott, R. (1971) *Circus and Allied Arts: A World Bibliography*, Derby, Harper & Sons, 4 vols.

Trexler, R. C. (1984) 'Follow the flag: the Ciompi Revolt seen from the street', *Bibliothèque d'Humanisme et Renaissance*, XLVI, 2, 357–92.

Trow-Smith, R. (1957) *A History of British Livestock Husbandry*, London, Routledge & Kegan Paul.

Trudgill, E. (1973) 'Prostitution and paterfamilias', in Dyos, H. J. and Wolff, M. (eds.) *The Victorian City*, London, Routledge & Kegan Paul, vol 2, 693–705.

Turner, B. (1984) *The Body and Society*, Oxford, Blackwell.

Turner, E. (1981) 'Festivals in the work of Shakespeare: the liminal domain', unpublished conference paper, Tokyo, Symposium: Anthropology of Spectacle and Entertainment.

Turner, V. (1977) *The Ritual Process: Structure and Anti-structure*, Ithaca, Cornell University Press.

Turner, V. (1982) *From Ritual to Theatre: The Human Seriousness of Play*, New York, Performing Arts Journal Publications.

Twohig, S. O'Brien (1984) *Beckmann: Carnival*, London, Tate Gallery.

Van Buuren, M. (1983) 'Carnival in the theatre of Samuel Beckett' [abstract], in MMB (Coll.), Kingston, Ontario, Queen's University, 28.

Van Gennep, A. (1960) *The Rites of Passage* (tr. M. B. Vizedom and G. L. Caffee), Chicago, University of Chicago Press.

Van Lennep, W. (1965) *The London Stage 1660–1800*, part I, Carbondale, Southern Illinois Press.

Veith, I. (1965) *Hysteria: the history of a disease*, Chicago, University of Chicago Press.

Veyne, P. (1976) *Le Pain et le Cirque*, Paris, Seuil.

Vicinus, M. (ed.) (1972) *Suffer and Be Still: Women in the Victorian Age*, Bloomington, Indiana University Press.

Vicinus, M. (ed.) (1977) *A Widening Sphere: Changing Roles of Victorian Women*, Bloomington, Indiana University Press.

Vilar de Kerkhoff, A. M. (1983) 'Echoes of Bakhtin's dialogic principle in Puerto Rican prose fiction', MMB (Coll.), Kingston, Ontario, Queen's University.

Volosinov, V. N. (1973) *Marxism and the Philosophy of Language* (tr. M. Matejka and I. R. Titunik), New York and London, Seminar Press.

Waites, B. (ed.) (1982) *Popular Culture Past and Present* (ed. B. Waites, T. Bennett and G. Martin), London, Croom Helm.

Walford, C. (1883) *Fairs Past and Present*, London, Elliott Stock.

Walkowitz, J. (1980) *Prostitution and Victorian Society: Women, Class and the State*, Cambridge, Cambridge University Press.

Walkowitz, J. (1982) 'Jack the Ripper and the myth of male violence', *Feminist Studies*, 8, 3, 543–74.

Walton, J. (1982) 'Residential amenity, respectable morality and the rise of the entertainment industry: Blackpool, 1860–1914', in Waites, B. *et al* (eds.) *Popular Culture Past and Present*, London, Croom Helm, 133–45.

Walvin, J. (1978) *Leisure and Society 1830–1950*, London, Longman.

Wardroper, J. (1973) *Kings, Lords and Wicked Libellers: Satire and Protest 1760–1837*, London, John Murray.

Wayne, D. E. (1982) 'Drama and society in the age of Jonson: an alternative view', *Renaissance Drama*, 13, 103–29.

Weaver, J. (1728) *The History of Mimes and Pantomimes*, London.

Weber, E. (1979) *Peasants into Frenchmen: The Modernization of Rural France 1870–1914*, London, Chatto and Windus.

Weeks, J. (1981) *Sex, Politics and Society: The Regulation of Sexuality since 1800*, London, Longman.

Weimann, R. (1978) *Shakespeare and the Popular Tradition in the Theatre* (tr. R. Schwartz), Baltimore, Johns Hopkins University Press.

Bibliography

Wells, S. (1981) 'Jacobean city comedy and the ideology of the city', *English Literary History*, 48, 1, 37–60.

Welsford, E. (1968) *The Fool: His Social and Literary History*, London, Faber & Faber.

Whistler, L. (1947) *The English Festivals*, London, Heinemann.

White, A. (1982) 'Pigs and pierrots: politics of transgression in modern fiction', *Raritan*, II, 2 (Fall), 51–70. New Brunswick, New Jersey.

White, A. (1983) 'The dismal sacred word: academic language and the social reproduction of seriousness', *Literature/Teaching/Politics*, 2, 4–15.

Whitfield, C. (ed.) (1962) *Robert Dover and the Cotswold Games: Annalia Dubrensia*, Evesham, The Journal Press.

Wickham, G. (1963) *Early English Stages 1300–1660*, London, Routledge & Kegan Paul, vol. 2, part 1.

Wickham, G. (1972) *Early English Stages 1300–1660*, London, Routledge & Kegan Paul, vol. 2, part 2.

Wickham, G. (1981) *Early English Stages 1300–1660*, London, Routledge & Kegan Paul, vol. 3.

Williams, A. (1955) *Pope's Dunciad*, London, Methuen.

Williams, R. (1977) *Marxism and Literature*, Oxford, Oxford University Press.

Wilson, E. (1948) *The Triple Thinkers: Twelve Essays on Literary Subjects*, New York, Oxford University Press.

Wilson, F. P. (1970) *The Oxford Dictionary of English Proverbs*, Oxford, Oxford University Press.

Wilson, R. (1983) 'Carnival and play', MMB (Coll.), Kingston, Ontario, Queen's University, 318–21.

Wohl, A. S. (1973) 'Unfit for human habitation', in Dyos, H. J. and Wolff, M. (eds.) *The Victorian City*, London, Routledge & Kegan Paul, vol. 2, 603–24.

Wohl, A. S. (1983) *Endangered Lives: Public Health in Victorian Britain*, London, Methuen.

Wolf, E. R. (1982) *Europe and the People without History*, Berkeley, University of California Press.

Wollen, P. (1982) *Readings and Writings: Semiotic Counter-Strategies*, London, Verso.

Wordsworth, W. (1805) *The Prelude* (ed. E. de Selincourt, rev. H. Derbyshire), Oxford, Clarendon Press, 1959.

Wotton, Sir H. (1907) *The Life and Letters of Sir Henry Wotton*, (ed. L. Pearsall Smith), Oxford, Clarendon Press, vol. 1.

Wouters, C. (1979) 'Negotiating with de Swaan', unpublished manuscript, Amsterdam.

Wright, L. (1960) *Clean and Decent*, New York, The Viking Press.

Wright, T. (1865) *A History of Caricature and Grotesque in Literature and Art*, New York, Frederick Ungar, 1968.

Wrightson, K. (1981) 'Alehouse, order and reformation in rural England, 1590–1660', in Yeo, E. and Yeo, S. (eds.) *Popular Culture and Class Conflict*, Brighton, Harvester.

The Politics and Poetics of Transgression

Wuthnow, R. *et al* (1984) *Cultural Analysis*, London, Routledge & Kegan Paul.

Yamaguchi, M. (1983) 'Bakhtin and symbolic anthropology', MMB (Coll.), 323–39. Kingston, Ontario, Queen's University.

Yeo, E. and Yeo, S. (eds.) (1981) *Popular Culture and Class Conflict*, Brighton, Harvester.

Yeo, E. and Yeo, S. (1981b) 'Ways of seeing: control and leisure versus class and struggle', in Yeo, E. and Yeo, S. (eds.) *Popular Culture and Class Conflict*, Brighton, Harvester, 155–86.

Yeo, E. and Yeo, S. (1981c) 'Perceived patterns: competition and licence versus class & struggle', in Yeo, E. and Yeo, S. (eds.) *Popular Culture and Class Conflict*, Brighton, Harvester, 271–305.

Young, R. (1986 – forthcoming) 'Back to Bakhtin', in *Cultural Critique*, Minneapolis, University of Minnesota Press.

Zijderveld, A. (1982) *Reality in a Looking-glass: Rationality through an Analysis of Traditional Folly*, London, Routledge & Kegan Paul.

Zinsser, H. (1985) *Rats, Lice and History*, London, Macmillan.

Zola, E. (1954) *Germinal* (tr. L. Tancock), Harmondsworth, Penguin.

Index

Index